NE

st Frontiers

WITHDRAWN

ity

Library

5801 Wilson Avenue
St. Louis, Missouri 63110

TIMBERLINE

Mountain and Arctic Forest Frontiers

Text by Stephen F. Arno
Art by Ramona P. Hammerly

The Mountaineers • Seattle

THE MOUNTAINEERS: Organized 1906
"...to explore, study, preserve and enjoy
the natural beauty of Northwest America."

Published by The Mountaineers 800-553-4453
306 Second Ave. W., Seattle, Washington 98119

Published simultaneously in Canada by
Douglas & McIntyre Ltd., 1615 Venables Street
Vancouver, British Columbia V5L 2H1

Manufactured in the United States of America
Edited by Barbara Chasan
Book and cover design by Marge Mueller

First printing November 1984, second printing
December 1985

Cover art: Sierra juniper
on Juniper Ridge above
Tuolumne Meadows.

Frontispiece: Mountain hemlock on humps and ridges
in the Pacific Coast Mountains.

Library of Congress Cataloging in Publication Data

Arno, Stephen F.
  Timberline: mountain and arctic forest frontiers.

  Bibliography: p.
  Includes index.
  1. Timberline—North America.   2. Timberline.
I. Hammerly, Ramona P.   II. Title.
QK110.A76   1984   574.5'2642   84-14844
ISBN 0-89886-085-7

Table of Contents

Mount Rainier from Chinook Pass

Preface

Few people gazing out upon a timberline for the first time can imagine how many interacting phenomena are involved in this "forest frontier." My first awareness of timberline occurred one day in grammar school when our teacher read aloud an essay written in the early 1900s by Enos Mills (1920) called "Trees at Timberline." Mills, who is known as the "father of Rocky Mountain National Park" in Colorado, described this forest boundary in a colorful, inspiring manner; but the statement that was most astonishing to me as a 10 year old follows:

> From a stand of dead timber I cut eleven small trees and carried them in one load to my camp-fire. They were so gnarled and ancient-looking that they aroused my curiosity, and with a magnifier I counted the annual rings in each. The youngest was 146 years of age, and the oldest 258! The total age of these eleven trees was 2,191 years!

These facts seemed incredible to a youth brought up among the productive lowland forests of the Pacific Northwest.

In 1966 I completed a Master of Forestry thesis entitled "Interpreting the Timberline." This was intended to provide detailed background information to guide park naturalists in explaining timberlines to the visiting public. The U.S. National Park Service reprinted 300 copies and the Canadian Park Service also reproduced a small quantity. The reprints were soon depleted, however, and requests for the thesis continued to come from persons of varied backgrounds and interests. It became obvious that someone should produce a book on timberlines for the benefit of not only the general public but also for consultation by professional naturalists and scientists. Many years of pondering this idea finally led to the production of *Timberline: Mountain and Arctic Forest Frontiers*.

This book explains how and why timberlines develop in the mountains and polar regions of North America. This many-faceted story is based upon scientific findings that are interpreted, illustrated, and woven together in a non-technical manner. The primary sources for statements made are scientific articles; these are cited unobtrusively (by author and date) in the text and are listed alphabetically at the end of the book, so that readers can examine any topic in greater detail. Recommended reading for general audiences is included among the References and is denoted by an asterisk.

I would like to thank several reviewers who read early drafts of this book and provided suggestions and information that resulted in substantial improvements. Technical reviews were provided by Dr. Dana Bailey (Boulder, Colorado), Dr. W. Dwight Billings (Duke University), Dr. R. Alan Black (Washington State University), Dr. Jerry Franklin (Pacific Northwest Forest and Range Experiment Station), Dr. James Habeck (University of Montana), Ronald Mastrogiuseppe (Redwood National Park), and Dr. James H. Richards (Utah State University). Also, detailed editorial suggestions by Stephen Whitney (The Mountaineers • Books) and by my father, Sig Arno (Tucson, Arizona) helped make the presentation more readable for general audiences.

The writing was accomplished in five years during my "spare time," and I would like to thank my wife Bonnie and boys Matthew and Nathan for their patience.

Stephen F. Arno
Florence, Montana
April, 1984

Part One

TIMBERLINE ECOLOGY

Pattern of timberline tree growth on the south-facing slope of Saint Mary Peak in the Montana Bitterroot Range

1
The Timberline Environment

"Timberline" designates the limit of forest either high up on mountainsides, in frigid polar regions, or adjacent to grasslands. Timberlines are biological boundaries that have developed for various reasons. In different regions of North America they are composed of a number of tree species, each having distinctive adaptations which allow it to endure in a harsh environment.

As the New Zealand scientist Peter Wardle (1965) aptly put it: "Timberline is a biological boundary which doesn't escape even the most casual observer." The relatively few highways that ascend to upper timberlines in North America are popular with naturalists and outdoorspeople because they lead into scenic and fascinating realms. Many people encounter the "upper timberline" zone of patchy forest and meadows, stunted trees, and finally shrublike trees while touring U.S. or Canadian national parks, national forests, or other public recreation areas. Countless visitors have seen the "lower timberline" near the foot of mountain ranges in the semi-arid West. Those who fly over far northern Canada or Alaska can observe the expansive "arctic timberline."

Before we can explore the secrets of timberline, a few of the most basic terms must be understood. (The index can be used to relocate the first mention, and hence the definition, of each term.) "Upper" or "alpine timberline" applies to the upper elevational limits of forest and tree growth on high mountains. Rather than being an abrupt boundary, upper timberline usually forms a transition zone between the continuous forest below and the treeless alpine tundra above. As we shall soon see, upper timberline has a variety of interacting causes, mostly related to inadequate summer warmth; thus it is classed as a "cold timberline."

Another kind of timberline occurs at comparatively low elevations on mountain ranges in the semi-arid American West. This "lower timberline" forms where mountain forest gives way downslope to dry grassland, sagebrush, or tall shrubs such as chaparral or scrub oaks. Lower timberline is generally related to inadequate moisture, thus it is classed as a "dry" or "drought-caused timberline." This book deals primarily with North America's cold timberlines (alpine and arctic), but it also gives an overview of dry timberlines in the semi-arid West, since these have many interesting similarities and contrasts with cold timberlines.

Each tree species has unique upper and lower elevational limits and

*Lower and upper timberlines only 2000 feet apart on the semi-arid Lost
River Range in Idaho*

in most mountain forests the elevational ranges of species overlap considerably, like shingles on a roof. Thus, the drought-resistant tree species
that form the lower timberline give way at middle elevations to species
able to thrive and compete for growing space under more favorable conditions. These trees of the main forest zone in turn give way to cold-tolerant
species near the upper timberline.

However, in some of the driest mountain ranges of the American West
only a few species of drought-tolerant trees can survive, and then only
within narrow elevational bands. Sometimes the elevational distributions of these trees do not overlap; two separate forest belts occur, each
with its own lower and upper timberlines. This phenomenon has been
termed "double timberlines" by ecologist W. D. Billings.

The "polar" or, in the Northern Hemisphere, "arctic timberline" forms
a broad transition zone snaking its way across the northern landscape
from Labrador to northern Alaska and from northeastern Siberia to Lapland. This cold timberline, unlike the alpine timberline on mountains,
occurs at low elevations. Arctic timberline, also known as the "forest-
tundra zone," is generally a few dozen miles wide, in contrast to the
telescoped alpine timberline on mountains. Arctic timberline is broad
because going north, climate becomes colder more gradually than it does
going up a mountainside. North of the arctic timberline lies the low-
growing tundra; whereas south of this forest-tundra zone spreads the vast
taiga or boreal forest.

Let us examine the upper timberline on mountains more closely. This
transition zone is found near the top of the tallest peaks in the northeastern United States, high up on the giant volcanoes in central Mexico, and
on mountains in each of the 11 western states and throughout much of
Canada and Alaska. A person climbing upslope through the upper timberline will find that trees become increasingly stunted and are finally reduced to dwarfs. This timberline belt stretches from the "forest line" or

general upper limit of continuous forest to the "scrub" or "krummholz line" which is the general upper limit of shrublike trees or krummholz (German for "crooked wood"). European biologists call upper timberline the "kampfzone" (zone of struggle) in recognition of the severe growing conditions that trees must face. This book follows Wardle's (1974) suggestion that the terms "scrub" and "alpine scrub" be applied only to timberline plants whose shrubby forms are clearly genetic (for example, the Swiss mountain pine [*Pinus mugo*] commonly grown in rock gardens). The term "krummholz" is used for the environmentally dwarfed forms of species that become treelike in favorable sites.

Forest line is not always distinct, because in some mountain areas dense conifer growth extends up to the krummholz line. When it does, forest line could be said to occur where most high-elevation tree species are stunted and seldom develop into tall trees (greater than 50 feet). Most upper timberlines actually show a gradient of increasing tree deformity upslope; thus the positions of forest line and krummholz line are not precise.

Two other boundaries of tree growth deserve mention. Partway up through the alpine timberline zone a person will often observe "tree line"—the general upper limit of erect though stunted "trees," by definition reaching at least 13 feet in height at maturity (Little 1979). Also, scattered shrublike trees extend a short distance into the alpine zone above the krummholz line. "Krummholz limit" denotes the highest ascent of individual krummholz "cushions" on a mountainside.

Although most timberlines result from many interacting causes, the two general factors are climate and topography. At alpine timberlines the regional climate is modified by the local high-mountain topography. The air becomes colder at a "lapse rate," or rate of temperature change with increasing elevation, averaging roughly 3½°F per 1000-foot gain in elevation as one ascends the mountains. (Scales that allow quick conversion between English and metric units appear on the last page.) Both total precipitation and the amount of snowfall generally increase with increasing elevation. Thus, if the mountains are sufficiently high, a climber eventually will reach the point where the local climate is too cold, snowy, wind exposed, or otherwise severe for tree growth.

Mountain timberlines throughout most of the Northern Hemisphere are inhabited by a variety of tree species, mostly conifers, which have evolved a similarly high degree of climatic hardiness. However, each of the approximately 20 tree species that reaches alpine or arctic timberlines in North America is best adapted to a certain regional climate. Also, each species is most successful on certain kinds of sites—where topography helps create particular "microclimates," such as on dry, windswept ridges or on moist, wind-sheltered northern slopes.

GENERAL FACTORS: CLIMATE

Six general kinds of regional climates produce timberlines in North America: maritime, continental, inland-maritime, semi-desert, polar, and tropical.

Maritime

Maritime climate timberlines occur principally along the North Pacific Coast from the Klamath Mountains of northern California through the Cascades of Oregon and Washington and the Olympic Mountains of Washington. Maritime alpine timberlines continue northward through the extensive Coast Ranges of British Columbia and southern Alaska. The maritime timberlines occur at decreasing elevations northward. Thus, tree line is found near 9000 feet in the northernmost part of California, 6000 feet in northwestern Washington, 3500 feet at Juneau, Alaska, and at only 1000 feet at Seward in south-central Alaska. Farther west along the Alaskan coast, at Kodiak, timberline descends nearly to sea level. Here the Sitka spruce (*Picea sitchensis*) forest gives way to shrub thickets of

A maritime timberline above Juneau, Alaska

Sitka alder (*Alnus sinuata*), willows (*Salix* spp.), and resin birch (*Betula glandulosa*) (Viereck and Little 1972).

Maritime timberlines are deluged with extremely heavy winter snowfalls and have a cool, wet, cloudy climate year-round. Average annual precipitation ranges from 60 to 250 inches, but the southern timberline areas, especially in Oregon and northern California, experience a summer drought. This dry summer condition becomes pronounced to the east (in the Northern Rocky Mountains) and south (in the Sierra Nevada) where inland-maritime climates occur.

Average winter snowfall near timberline is 500 to 650 inches, but winter temperatures remain relatively mild. Few weather stations have been maintained at maritime alpine timberlines in North America; however, the one at Paradise Park on Mount Rainier in Washington does have a long-term record. The "climagraph" for Paradise, on page 20, shows the monthly temperatures and precipitation; this climatic pattern contrasts with those from timberline stations in other climatic regions.

A world-record winter snowfall of 90 feet was deposited at Paradise during the 1971-72 season, and maximum snow depths on the level have reached a record of 30 feet! The average annual maximum snowpack undoubtedly approaches 15 feet at many maritime timberlines. Copious blankets of snow envelop the stunted trees and insulate them from the winter cold. Moreover, south of Alaska air temperatures seldom drop below 0°F in these oceanic-influenced sites. Thus, unlike their inland and polar counterparts, trees of maritime timberlines need not adapt to extreme winter cold.

Summers are short and cool, barely adequate for melting the winter snow on northern slopes. Because of the abundant snowfall, glaciers often extend down into the timberline zone or, in Alaska, entirely through the forest zone to tidewater. In fact, late-lingering snowpack often inhibits tree regeneration and damages tree growth at maritime timberlines. The characteristic trees at these timberlines are mountain hemlock (*Tsuga mertensiana*) and Alaska-cedar (*Chamaecyparis nootkatensis*), along with the widely distributed subalpine fir (*Abies lasiocarpa*) and, in south-central Alaska, Sitka spruce.

Continental

Continental climates occur at the timberlines from central Alaska and the Yukon Territory south along the crest and eastern slope of the Rockies to northern New Mexico. In central Alaska, alpine tree line develops near the 3500-foot level, while it reaches 7500 feet in southern Alberta and nearly 12,000 feet in southern Colorado. The timberline peaks in the northeastern United States and eastern Canada have a much more humid continental climate than that of western North America. The figure on page 16 illustrates the rise in continental alpine timberlines southward in the Rockies as well as the rise in timberlines heading inland

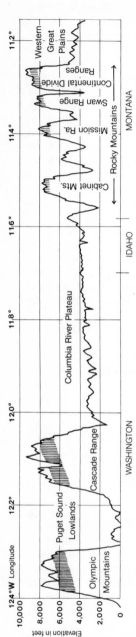

A west-to-east cross-section of the northwestern U.S. at 47½°N latitude, showing the eastward rise in the alpine timberline zone, which is shaded. This rise results from the increasingly continental climate eastward, with diminished snowfall and warmer summers at any given elevation. Total distance is about 600 miles.

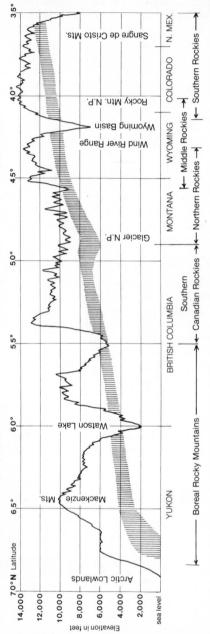

A north-to-south section along the crest of the Rocky Mountains, showing the southward rise in the alpine timberline (shaded zone). Sectioned distance is about 2300 miles.

A continental-climate timberline in Jasper National Park, Alberta

(eastward) from the Pacific Coast Mountains.

These continental mountain environments have summers that are short and cool but roughly comparable to those of the maritime timberlines. The total annual precipitation (20 to 40 inches in western North America and somewhat higher in the Northeast) is modest compared to amounts received in the maritime mountains, but summers are not especially dry. However, continental alpine timberlines have very cold winters with moderate to deep accumulations of dry, powdery snow. Snowpack does not generally linger through summer at these timberlines as it does in the maritime mountains.

In winter, continental polar air masses spread southward through these mountain ranges, bringing extremely cold, dry air and blustery winds. In the middle latitudes, from southern Alberta to Colorado, infusions of arctic air often collide with milder Pacific air masses, also accompanied by strong winds. Trees on exposed ridges are subjected to drastic temperature fluctuations as the frigid and mild air masses jostle back and forth. Temperatures change as much as 50°F in 2 hours and 80°F in 24 hours. Severe winter temperature and wind conditions prevent maritime conifers from growing here, but a different assemblage of cold-hardy species is able to survive and propagate.

Characteristic trees in western North America include white spruce (*Picea glauca*), Engelmann spruce (*P. engelmannii*), whitebark pine (*Pinus albicaulis*), and limber pine (*P. flexilis*), along with the nearly ubiquitous subalpine fir. Balsam fir (*Abies balsamea*) and black spruce (*Picea mariana*) are primary components of alpine timberlines in the northeastern United States. Lower timberlines form at the foot of the mountains south from southern Alberta, and they generally have the Rocky Mountain form of ponderosa pine (*Pinus ponderosa* var. *scopulorum*) or interior Douglas-fir (*Pseudotsuga menziesii* var. *glauca*) as the lowermost forest tree.

Weather data (climagraphs, page 20) for Climax, Colorado, Highwood Pass, Alberta, and Mount Washington, New Hampshire, are presented as examples of alpine timberlines in continental climatic areas. Climagraphs for Helena, Montana, and Yellowstone Park, Wyoming, represent lower timberlines in these climates.

Inland-maritime

Inland-maritime climates are a sort of hybrid between continental and maritime conditions. They have colder, drier winters than the coastal mountains but more cloudiness, higher humidity, and less extreme winter temperatures than the continental mountains. Average annual precipitation at upper timberlines ranges from about 30 to 65 inches, but a summer drought often occurs. Such inland-maritime environments include the western slope of the Sierra Nevada, the eastern slope of the Cascades, and the inland mountains of southern British Columbia, northern Washington, northern Idaho, northwestern Montana, and northeastern Oregon.

Alpine timberlines are inhabited by a diverse assemblage of species from both the continental and maritime timberline environments, along with species such as alpine larch (*Larix lyallii*), foxtail pine (*Pinus balfouriana*), and Sierra lodgepole pine (*P. contorta* var. *murrayana*) that are largely confined to inland-maritime areas. Lower or drought-caused timberlines at the bases of these mountains characteristically support the Pacific form of ponderosa pine (*P. ponderosa* var. *ponderosa*).

Weather records (climagraphs, page 21) from Old Glory Mountain, British Columbia, and Saint Mary Peak, Montana, are presented as examples of upper timberline conditions. The data from Stevensville, Montana, below Saint Mary Peak, represent a nearby lower timberline.

Semi-desert

Semi-desert climates in the driest regions of the American West produce fascinating mountain timberlines caused by combinations of drought, excessive heating (insolation), and cold conditions. Mountain

The semi-desert timberline below Mount Whitney on the east slope of California's Sierra Nevada

ranges as far north as southeastern Oregon, east-central Idaho, and southwestern Montana support semi-desert timberlines. Such timberlines spread southward through the Great Basin ranges of eastern California (including the eastern slope of the Sierra), Nevada, and western Utah. Still other semi-desert timberlines occupy the high mountains rising out of the Colorado, Sonoran, and Chihuahuan deserts, from southern California to west Texas and northern Mexico. Throughout these semi-desert areas, a dearth of moisture and the hot summer conditions cause lower timberlines to develop at the relatively high elevations of 6000 to 7000 feet.

The drier mountain ranges support only vestiges of a forest belt: small, scattered groves are confined to moist microsites such as draws on north-facing slopes. Some high mountains from central Nevada northward do not support any forest trees, largely because of dry conditions. Others have unique combinations of forest species (Critchfield and Allenbaugh 1969) and "relict populations"—tiny remnants of more continuous

Average monthly precipitation (shaded bars) and temperature (broken line) for timberlines in different climates. White area beneath the broken line represents a theoretical moisture deficit.

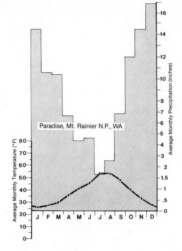

Maritime alpine timberline: Paradise, Mount Rainier, Washington (5550 feet; 46°47' N, 121°44' W) — in subalpine fir-mountain hemlock parkland.

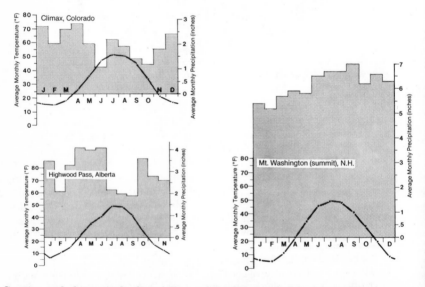

Continental alpine timberlines: (Upper left) Climax, Colorado (11,300 feet; 39°20'N, 106°13'W) — near tree line among Engelmann spruce. (Below) Highwood Pass, Alberta (7300 feet; 50°36'N, 114°59'W) — above forest line among alpine larch and subalpine fir. (Right) Mount Washington, New Hampshire (6262 feet; 44°16'N, 71°18'W) — in alpine tundra about 1200 feet above krummholz line.

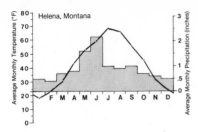

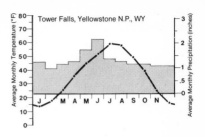

Continental lower timberlines: (Left) Helena, Montana (3828 feet; 46°36'N, 112°00'W) — Rocky Mountain ponderosa pine (limber pine on limestone). (Right) Tower Falls, Yellowstone Park, Wyoming (6266 feet; 44°55'N, 110°25'W) — inland Douglas-fir.

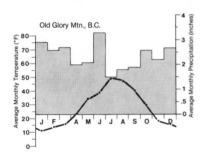

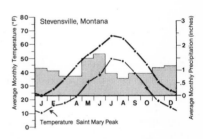

(Left) Inland-maritime alpine timberline: Old Glory Mountain, British Columbia (7700 feet; 49°09'N, 117°55'W) — krummholz line, subalpine fir. (Right) Inland-maritime lower and nearby alpine timberline: Stevensville, Montana (3370 feet; 46°31'N, 114°05'W) — near lower timberline for Pacific ponderosa pine; also shown is temperature for Saint Mary Peak (9365 feet), which is at krummholz line (precipitation on the mountain is much greater than at Stevensville).

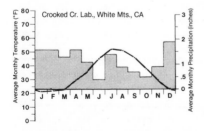

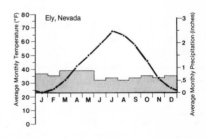

(Left) Semi-desert alpine timberline: Crooked Creek Lab, White Mountains, California (10,150 feet; 37°30'N, 118°10'W) – in subalpine bristlecone pine stands. (Right) Semi-desert lower timberline: Ely, Nevada (6253 feet; 39°17'N, 114°51'W) – in pinyon-juniper woodland belt.

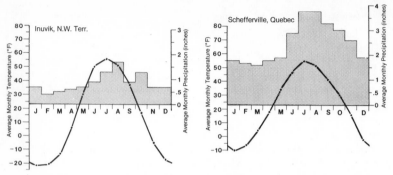

Arctic timberlines: (Left) Inuvik, Northwest Territories (223 feet; 68°18'N, 133°29'W) — in forest-tundra zone, black spruce. (Right) Schefferville, Quebec (1712 feet; 54°48'N, 66°49'W) — in forest-tundra on highlands.

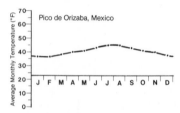

Tropical alpine timberline: Pico de Orizaba, Mexico (13,775 feet; 19°00'N, 97°15'W) — upper timberline for Mexican mountain pine (temperature data only).

stands that were widespread during the Pleistocene ice ages (12,000 or more years ago), when the climate of the interior West was much wetter.

Upper timberlines in the semi-desert areas result from cold or drought. Annual precipitation averages a scant 10 to 12 inches at some high-elevation timberlines, and there is little snow to protect low-growing trees (saplings and krummholz) from desiccation and damaging winds in winter. Often, hardly any krummholz develops at upper timberline. Instead, short, stocky trees give way upslope and on extremely windy ridges to alpine grassland or stony "fellfields"—rock and gravel "fields" with sparse, low-growing vegetation.

Timberline trees here include species characteristic of the semi-desert region, such as the Great Basin bristlecone pine (*Pinus longaeva*) at upper timberlines and pinyon pines and junipers at lower timberlines, along with the continental Rocky Mountain species.

Weather records from the White Mountains of east-central California (page 21) illustrate the climate at one of the drier upper timberlines, while those from Ely in east-central Nevada represent a lower timberline in the pinyon-juniper woodland. The dry-cold nature of these timberlines becomes evident when comparing these climagraphs with those from other climatic regions.

Polar

Polar or arctic climates produce cold timberlines at low elevations. These forest-tundra transition zones occur at high latitudes, especially in Alaska and western Canada, where the short, cool summers have nearly continuous daylight. In contrast, winters are largely dark and consistently very cold. Annual precipitation is only 6 to 20 inches at the arctic timberline in North America, and total snowfall is a modest 50 to 100 inches at most locations. However, the minimal rate of evaporation coupled with excessive ground moisture on much of the arctic lowlands prevents conditions from being too dry for trees. Soil that thaws to a depth of a few feet each summer is an important requirement for tree growth.

Much of the northernmost tree growth is a stunted forest of black spruce on boggy ground along with patchy groves of white spruce on well-drained sites.

Climates at the arctic timberline are illustrated by the weather records (page 22) from Inuvik in the Northwest Territories, and Schefferville, Quebec. Notice that despite the substantial differences between climates at polar and alpine timberlines, summer (growing season) warmth is similar. Specifically, the mean temperature of the warmest month of the year (usually July) is slightly above 50°F (10°C).

The influence of maritime and continental air masses is also important in determining the position of the arctic timberline in North America. This forest-tundra transition zone coincides with the average summer boundary between cold (arctic) air masses to the north and warmer Pacific and continental air masses to the south.

Tropical

The tropical climate of central and southern Mexico produces alpine timberlines only on the highest mountains, above 13,000 feet in elevation. At timberline it is cool and marginal for tree growth year-round, and there is no true summer or winter. Wet snow and sleet fall commonly at any time of year except in areas having a characteristically dry season. Nevertheless, above-freezing temperatures predominate all year, and a snowpack as such does not accumulate at timberline. Snowfields and glaciers do develop, however, atop peaks that rise high above the timberline zone.

Alpine timberlines in Mexico are made up of tropical pines related to trees in northern forests and develop at consistently high elevations where "growing-season" warmth seems roughly comparable to that of temperate-zone mountains farther north. In contrast, most other tropical mountain areas of the world have cold timberlines formed by tall tropical or Southern Hemisphere plants which are less comparable climatically to North American timberlines. (A worldwide comparison of cold timberlines is made in Chapter 11.)

Weather data from upper timberline on Pico de Orizaba in central Mexico are shown on page 22.

Southerly exposure (left) supports a timberline parkland, while the north slope has snow, rock, and tundra plants — above Lake Ann in the Washington Cascades.

GENERAL FACTORS: TOPOGRAPHY

North vs. South Slopes

In the Northern Hemisphere, steep south-facing slopes receive much more solar insolation and, thus, heating than north-facing slopes. This effect becomes increasingly pronounced northward from about 40°N latitude because the summer sun is confined to an increasingly low, southerly position in the sky. As a result, sites having comparable temperatures occur several hundred feet higher up on south-facing slopes than on northern slopes, and alpine timberlines generally ascend higher on southern slopes. The greatest thermal heating occurs in the afternoon, when the sun is in a southwesterly position. Therefore, southwestern aspects tend to absorb maximum warmth, and aspects ranging from southeast to west are considered warm exposures. Conversely, northwestern to eastern exposures are cool.

A marked contrast in tree and undergrowth communities often occurs between adjacent warm and cool exposures. For instance, at alpine tree line in the inland Northwest, whitebark pine forms nearly pure stands with sparse undergrowth on warm exposures; a stone's throw away across the sharp ridge crest, a stand of alpine larch and luxuriant heath covers the cool exposure.

In the mountains of western North America, prevailing winds blow from the west and southwest. These winds lift some of the snow off windward slopes and deposit it on leeward slopes. This phenomenon accentuates the warmth and dryness of southern and western slopes and makes sites on north- and east-facing slopes cooler and more moist. In some dry, windy areas, windward slopes are continually swept free of snow, and the resulting lack of snow protection prevents trees from becoming established, thus lowering the timberline.

For the lower or *drought*-caused timberlines in semi-arid mountains, the converse of the general rule applies; that is, the forest zone extends to the lowest elevations on the relatively cool-moist northern slopes.

Ridgetops vs. Basins

Similar phenomena help determine the relative position of upper timberline on ridgetops and other convex slopes versus neighboring concave topography such as draws or basins. Convex slopes are generally warmer than concave sites. In fact, cold air often settles in valley heads to the extent that frost occurs on most summer nights, whereas nearby ridges remain frost free. In many of the basins, temperatures at dawn probably average 15 to 20°F colder than temperatures on nearby ridges. Dramatic examples of cold-air ponding occur in certain high valleys or "cold-air sinks" in the eastern Alps, where basin temperatures drop as much as 54°F below those of the slopes above (Geiger 1957)!

These conditions usually enable trees to ascend to considerably higher elevations on ridges or slopes than up valley heads or in "cirques" (cup-shaped glacial basins high in the mountains). This effect is especially pronounced in the maritime mountains, where snow accumulation is excessive in the valley heads and where cold air also drains down into the valleys from glaciers above.

For example, stunted whitebark pines spread upward to the 10,000-foot level on ridges radiating from Mount Shasta in northern California, but conifers are limited to the 8000-foot level in some of the intervening glacial valleys (Cooke 1955). The effect of ridges being covered with trees while the valley heads, below, are covered with alpine tundra has been termed an "inverted timberline" (Wardle 1974). This phenomenon is especially well developed in the tropics and Southern Hemisphere, where the broadleaved trees comprising timberlines are less cold-hardy in winter than are our northern conifers.

Gentle Terrain

Mountain timberlines seldom develop fully (forest giving way to tundra) on gentle terrain. (However, within the upper timberline zone, flat areas such as mesas, small plateaus, and broad ridgetops often occur and support interesting "wind-timber" formations [e.g., ribbon-forest and snow glades, and timber atolls]. These are discussed in Chapter 2.) Lower timberlines often form at the foot of mountain ranges, where the slope breaks and gives way to gentle, treeless topography. Usually, this phenomenon is a result of a major change in soils and geology or moisture that coincides with the change of land form at the foot of the mountain. However, large fault-block mountain ranges that rise abruptly from a dry plateau may impede the passage of moisture-laden storms, so that even the gentle terrain within a mile or two of the windward side of the mountains will benefit from increased precipitation and can support a conifer woodland or forest. Comparable topography farther from the mountains does not receive as much precipitation and is thus beyond ("below") the lower timberline.

The arctic timberline in Canada does occur on essentially flat terrain, but it forms a zone often 50 to 100 miles wide, reflecting the very gradual climatic change from a forest to a tundra environment as latitude increases.

Size of the Mountain Land Mass

The "Massenerhebung effect" refers to the influence of large, mountainous plateaus in decreasing temperature lapse rates. The result of this phenomenon is that climatic and forest zones occur at the highest elevations on the largest and loftiest land masses. Consequently, timberlines on large, mountainous plateaus such as central Colorado and the Himalayas occur at higher elevations than those on isolated peaks at similar latitudes. This effect occurs because most of the body of an approaching air mass must rise to pass over a bulky upland, whereas the air mass can slide through an area containing isolated high peaks with a minimum of uplifting. However, the effect of a greater mountain mass seems inevitably coupled with that of a more continental climate, which will produce warmer summers at a given elevation and therefore result in higher timberlines. Winds are also less severe at a given elevation on a bulky land mass than on an isolated peak that barely attains the same elevation. This might also allow forests to ascend higher on more massive mountains.

SPECIFIC ENVIRONMENTAL FACTORS

Temperature

Peter Wardle (1974) suggested that "timberline is the sharpest temperature-dependent boundary in nature." Just as the term cold timberline implies, lack of heat is apparently the most important individual factor limiting the elevation or latitude to which tree species can ascend. It has long been known that winter minimum temperatures do not have much effect on formation of timberlines. Hardy conifers grow without injury in the coldest winter climates in North America and Siberia, where official minima have reached −81 and −90°F, respectively. However, even the hardiest conifers require a growing season of about two months when no more than light frosts occur.

Although many factors are involved in determining the alpine and polar limits of tree growth, such timberlines ultimately depend on the

Frost-killed new growth on Engelmann spruce

increasingly unfavorable heat balance that occurs with rising elevation or latitude (Tranquillini 1979). In subalpine and subarctic environments, increasing cold lengthens the frost period and shortens the frost-free growing season available to trees and other plants. Despite whatever adaptation to summer frosts the trees have, all require a certain amount of heat to complete their annual growth cycle. Even in high mountains of the tropics, where there is no long winter to prevent growth, tree growth is restricted by a climate whose meager daily heating is coupled with nightly frosts.

Some of the less hardy species in the subalpine forest are evidently kept from reaching tree line by an occasional hard frost in early or late summer. For instance, succulent new growth on Pacific silver fir (*Abies amabilis*) at its upper limits in Washington's North Cascades was killed by subfreezing temperatures and new snow in early July 1969; other timberline conifers had not begun shoot growth and sustained only minimal injury (Arno 1970). More dramatic was the near 0°F cold wave of mid-September 1965 that killed new growth (and some trees entirely) on Rocky Mountain lodgepole pine (*Pinus contorta* var. *latifolia*) and inland

Douglas-fir growing at their upper limits in western Montana (Arno 1966). Alpine timberline species were not damaged, however, evidently because they had completed their growth spurt for the season and the new foliage had already "hardened off," or completely matured.

Biologists and climatologists throughout the Northern Hemisphere have long recognized that the arctic and alpine limits of tree growth generally correspond to the location of the 50°F (10°C) "isotherm" (line on a map where a given average temperature occurs) for the warmest month, usually July. Sites where the mean July temperature is colder than 50°F are usually beyond timberline, while those having mean July temperatures substantially warmer than 50° are near forest line or within the forest proper. This correlation holds for cold timberlines in all the diverse climates of North America, and Eurasia north of the tropics.

Still, the correlation is only approximate, as it is only an unsophisticated measurement of the heat budget received by trees for growth. The effect of temperature on plants is very complex and includes direct influences on numerous biological processes—such as, germination, growth, and photosynthesis—which have different temperature minimums and optimums (Tranquillini 1979). In fact, leaf temperatures, rather than free-air temperatures, would serve as a more refined index of temperature's effect on tree growth. Russian scientists have evidently measured both leaf and free-air temperatures at alpine and arctic timberlines with interesting results. The investigators summed (added together) all of the daily mean air temperatures above 50°F (10°C) at a large number of timberline sites. By doing so they discovered that polar timberline was correlated with a sum of mean air temperatures totaling about 600 to 700°C; for alpine timberlines the figure was only about 200 to 300°C. They discovered by correlating *leaf temperatures,* however, that both polar and alpine timberlines occur where the annual sums of daily leaf temperatures above 10°C reach about 800°C. Thus, it appears that cooler mountain air temperatures at alpine timberline are compensated for by marked increases in leaf temperatures. This increase evidently happens because solar radiation intensities are greater at alpine timberline than at polar timberline.

Although the elevation of timberline is much greater at the equator than far to the north or south, elevation does not vary in a constant ratio with latitude (Daubenmire 1954). Along the Cordilleran Chain (Rocky Mountain System) in Canada and the western United States, the 50°F isotherm and the alpine timberline rise in a curved relationship, increasing at a slower rate with decreasing latitude. This is thought to reflect the greater influence southward of maritime air masses.

On a rough average for the interior of western North America, temperature in the mountains decreases 3.3°F per 1000-foot rise in elevation; but in the maritime mountains the average lapse rate is closer to 1.4°F per 1000 feet (Baker 1944). Daubenmire (1954) calculated that northward across the mid-latitudes in the Rockies, Coastal, and Appalachian Mountains the tendency is for timberline to drop about 500 feet in elevation per 100 miles (360 feet per degree of latitude).

An interesting feature of air temperatures at alpine timberlines is illustrated below by graphs of daily summer temperatures from sites at the krummholz line (9365 feet), forest line (8000 feet), and a nearby lower timberline (3370 feet) in western Montana (Arno 1970). During July and August, which is the principal growing season at upper timberline, daily low temperatures at the krummholz line averaged only about 3°F cooler

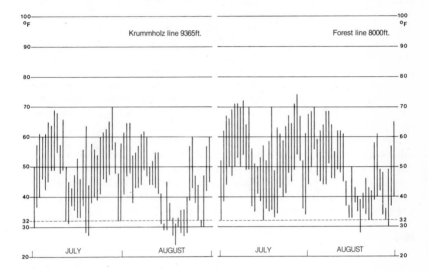

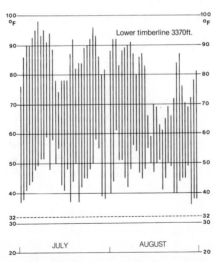

Daily temperatures at upper and lower timberline sites in the Montana Bitterroot Range

than at lower timberline in the broad valley 6000 feet below. The big contrast between summer temperatures at alpine timberline versus the lowland valley was the result of daytime heating. During July and August daily high temperatures in the valley averaged 27°F warmer than those at krummholz line and 21°F warmer than those at forest line.

The climate at these same alpine timberline sites can be put in perspective by comparing average monthly temperatures at tree line (8700 feet) with those at the lower timberline valley station (Stevensville climagraph, page 21), which has temperatures similar to those of populated areas in much of the northern United States and southern Canada. Such a comparison indicates that for seven months of the year the alpine tree line endures temperatures equivalent to cold winter conditions in the valley below. The remaining five months at tree line are comparable only to spring or autumn in the valley. The warmest month (July) at tree line has an average temperature (51°F) similar to that of early May in the valley.

Although most timberline conifers are extremely frost-hardy during fall, winter, and spring, the same species become frost-sensitive in midsummer, and their new needles and shoots can be damaged by temperatures as mild as 27°F, depending upon the species (Tranquillini 1979). Above the krummholz line such frosts are frequent enough throughout the summer so as to prevent new growth from surviving.

Wind

Although summer warmth generally defines the ultimate altitude to which any tree growth can ascend, severe winds impose an additional restriction on tree growth at many alpine timberlines. Violent winds with gusts of hurricane velocity occur rather frequently during all seasons on exposed ridges and peaks. Winds are thought to be the chief cause of dwarfing and krummholz formation at most alpine timberlines.

At two locations along the windy Front Range in Colorado (Pikes Peak and Niwot Ridge) average wind speeds were recorded continuously in the subalpine forest, at tree line, and in the alpine tundra (Bates 1924 and Marr 1961). Average wind speeds were greatest in January, when they measured about 10 mph in clearings in the subalpine forest, about 17 mph at tree line, and in excess of 25 mph in the tundra. Mean January wind speed at Denver on the nearby Great Plains is about 12 mph.

Wind is even more of an environmental force at timberline in the White Mountains of New Hampshire. Average *annual* wind speed at a tree-line site there is about 20 mph (Reiners and Lang 1979), and since winter wind speeds generally average twice those of summer, one might expect the January *average* to be a blustery 27 mph.

Still, average wind speeds are only indicative of the relative strength of this growth-shaping force. Perhaps a few examples of wind measurements from the timberline sites on Saint Mary Peak in Montana will illustrate the magnitude of this force. The exposed peak at krummholz line experienced major windstorms with hourly average winds in excess

Wind-trained Engelmann spruce and limber pine above 11,000 feet in Rocky Mountain National Park, Colorado.

of 40 mph quite often during the winter months and occasionally during the summer (Arno 1970). Gusts of 60 to 100 mph were associated with these storms. The site at forest line was in a protected cirque basin that usually experienced only light winds; however, during some of the major storms, winds literally "boomed" as they swept down into the cirque. During one summer windstorm, such a gust lifted a sturdy and well-ventilated 250-pound weather station from its position in a small opening, snapping two guying cables, and hurling the structure against trees 90 feet away.

Wind has two principal ways of damaging trees at upper timberline. One is inflicting mechanical injury to the branches and crown. Not only are trees broken by the hurricane-force gusts, but they are also battered by ice pellets and their own flailing limbs. Secondly, warm, dry winter winds called chinook or foehn winds help create a phenomenon known as "winter drought" which involves desiccation of foliage. A sudden warm, dry wind can soon evaporate glaze or rime ice protecting the exposed tops of stunted trees and then dehydrate the foliage. Boughs projecting above the snowpack cannot adequately replace lost moisture because their roots and lower stems are at or near freezing, and roots are only able to absorb water very slowly at such temperatures (Daubenmire 1959). The foregoing hypothesis on the role of wind in "winter desiccation" has been challenged as a result of recent physiological studies that indicate death of krummholz shoots is often caused by intense winter sunshine in still air! (See Chapter 2.) Still, on some sites, especially near lower timberline, the role of wind as a desiccating force seems undeniable.

A striking manifestation of winter drought known as "red belt," is a prominent feature at lower timberlines along and east of the continental divide. Sudden, warm winter winds, chinooks, occasionally kill entire stands of conifers growing on exposed sites. As at upper timberline, death or severe defoliation results when the air becomes warm and dry while roots remain frozen or chilled and are unable to replace lost moisture (Bega 1978). It is not uncommon on the lower mountain slopes for chinooks to raise the temperature from 0° to 50°F in two hours. Occasionally, competing frigid and warm air masses push each other back and forth, causing temperatures to fluctuate wildly within a 24-hour period.

Usually the extreme drying conditions that result in red-belt damage are confined to localized bands on the lower- to middle-elevation slopes. Sometimes treetops that project into the red-belt zone are killed, while the lower portions of the same trees' crowns are not injured. Some tree species (notably ponderosa pine, lodgepole pine, and Douglas-fir) are quite susceptible to red-belt desiccation, while others growing in the same stands near lower timberline (especially limber pine) are unaffected. Apparently each species has a different capacity to conserve moisture in the foliage (through regulation of stomata, or minute "breathing pores") and to replenish it through root absorption.

On wind-exposed ridgetops and saddles at upper timberline, prevailing summer winds may be partly responsible for the development of asymmetrical or "wind-trained" trees. For instance, Lawrence (1939) discovered that prevailing winds in the Columbia River Gorge train tree growth by applying continuous pressure (from a westerly direction) on

Limber pine growing in the lee of rocks at 11,500 feet in Rocky Mountain National Park, Colorado.

succulent new growth. However, at upper timberline the primary shaping force is probably the violent gusts, especially those hurling sleet and ice particles, that prune growth off the windward side of trees. Individual, erect trees are occasionally found growing high above the tree line in a sheltered nook behind and beneath a rock outcrop. They testify to the inhibiting effect of wind on tree growth at upper timberline.

In many areas the entire timberline zone is made up of wind-pruned growth forms, ranging from somewhat stunted trees at forest line to patches of cushion krummholz only a foot high growing in the lee of rocks at the edge of the tundra.

Certain sites well below the normal elevation of forest line sometimes are so wind lashed that they support only dwarfed, flagged, and even krummholz trees. Such sites include especially rugged and isolated mountain peaks and major mountain passes that funnel and concentrate the wind. These unusually low, wind-depressed timberlines are often inhabited by species not normally found at true alpine timberlines ("climatic timberlines"), such as Douglas-fir, quaking aspen (*Populus tremuloides*), and Rocky Mountain lodgepole pine.

One of the major effects of wind at timberline is as an agent that transports snow from exposed to sheltered slopes. In drier, inland environments, especially, this action removes snow protection and reduces soil moisture on the windward slopes; both of these effects can inhibit tree growth. Some exposed, convex (rounded) slopes never accumulate any appreciable snowpack and thus are unable to support trees. These sites become the montane or subalpine grasslands known as "balds" that are often surrounded by dense forest located on slightly less exposed slopes. The fact that these balds occur on exposed upper slopes on southern or western aspects testifies to the drying effect of wind and solar heating. In some semi-arid mountain ranges, high-elevation forests are largely replaced by mountain grasslands on windward slopes, and wind-transfer of snow may be responsible.

Thus, wind is an important factor affecting tree growth on exposed sites at alpine timberlines throughout most of North America. However, as we will see, wind is of little consequence in the formation of arctic timberline and at alpine timberlines in the Far North. Wind is not a critical factor at most lower timberlines, and it is of minor importance at most tropical timberlines, including those on the Mexican volcanoes (Daubenmire 1954, Beaman 1962).

Snow

Snow accumulates in considerable quantities at most alpine timberlines in North America and has both beneficial and detrimental effects upon growth and survival of trees. In contrast, at the arctic timberline and at most lower timberlines, snow depths are modest, and snow is not a prominent factor influencing tree growth.

Clare F. Cox (1933) studied the alpine timberline on James Peak in Colorado and observed that, "The presence or absence of the tree species appears frequently to be a matter of enough but not too much snow." This

Ridgetop krummholz in summer (top) and winter (middle), and diagram (bottom) showing wind direction and snow deposition. Subalpine fir at 6550 feet in Mount Rainier National Park, Washington.

statement applies to many alpine timberlines. The snowpack is beneficial to trees in protecting them from extreme cold, from freezing and thawing, and from drying winds. The krummholz community as a whole must depend upon a certain depth of snowpack to protect it from drying out and from sustaining mechanical damage in winter. Branches that project above the normal level of the snowpack are likely to be killed by winter drought or by ice blasting during winter storms.

In coastal and inland-maritime mountain ranges heavy sheaths of snow and rime ice encase exposed trees at upper timberline throughout most of the winter. In extreme cases individual trees 40 or 50 feet tall may be shrouded in a massive cloak of snow and ice weighing a ton or more. Subfreezing moisture-laden air builds these tree encasements into bizarre or ghoulish forms known as "snow ghosts." One effect of such snow insulation may be to allow maritime trees like mountain hemlock or Alaska-cedar to escape injury during occasional outbreaks of subzero polar air. However, the extreme weight of snow and ice can also break branches and tree trunks, especially if in combination with high winds.

When slender young trees are piled high with clinging snow and ice the result will be snowbreak, unless their trunks are supple enough to bend prostrate. This is a prevalent problem for trees growing on steep

Subalpine fir "snow ghosts" atop 7000-foot Big Mountain near Whitefish, Montana

slopes where the snow creeps or slides. Subalpine fir and mountain hemlock up to three inches in diameter can endure annual flattening and then spring back up when the snowpack deteriorates during the following June. When tree trunks grow too large to survive annual flattening, they must become strong enough to support the snow loads without breaking.

Evidence of "snow creep" is prevalent at the base of most trees growing on steep slopes high in the mountains. This evidence is the "pistol butt" or "snow knee" growth form, or characteristic downslope sweep at the base of the tree trunk. It can be caused by continual downslope pressure from creeping snow when the tree is a sapling (Daubenmire 1959). Although unstable soil could be responsible for this growth pattern in conifers, many timberline sites have a dense mat of low undergrowth that virtually stabilizes the soil. Thus, snow creep seems to be the probable cause of the pistol butts on these sites (MacMahon and Andersen 1982).

Snow slides and avalanches scar, flatten, and break tree trunks on many slopes, locally lowering timberline in large basins and wiping out or mowing down vertical swathes of forest along the valley walls. However, avalanches do not control the level of timberline over large areas.

Many visitors to alpine timberlines in the early summer notice the "black-body effect," in which clusters of trees, being dark objects, absorb solar heat and cause the snowpack to melt around them much sooner

Trees confined to humps and ridges in Upper Marmot Lake Basin, Olympic Mountains, Washington

than it does in the small openings between trees. Still, snow may linger so late as to prevent establishment of new trees. The early ecologist C. H. Shaw (1909b) observed that late-lingering snow in sheltered valley heads in the Selkirk Mountains of southeastern British Columbia keeps the upper limit of conifers down to an elevation of about 5900 feet. Here the highest conifers, Engelmann spruce and subalpine fir, grow as trees because wind exposure is not a factor. However, the conifers ascend to 7200 feet on exposed shoulders between the basins, where the snowpack is kept thin by the wind and sunshine. Krummholz can develop on these exposed sites because they have a sufficiently long growing season. Zoologist C. Hart Merriam (1899) described a similar pattern of tree growth on the ridge spurs and intervening basins of Mount Shasta. In fact, this phenomenon is prevalent throughout the maritime mountain ranges of western North America.

Another snow-related curiosity at alpine timberline is the matted, black, moribund appearance of some conifer boughs that emerge in summer from the wet snowpack. This is the effect of snow-mold fungi (principally *Herpotrichia* spp.) which occasionally cover nearly the entire crowns of small trees and, more often, kill lower limbs. These black-felt snow-mold fungi have the remarkable capacity to grow in the mixture of ice and water just at the freezing point, which is the usual temperature of late-lying snowpack. In Colorado, snow mold has been found to infect the lee side of large krummholz cushions, where the protecting snowdrift remains longest (Wardle 1968, Marr 1977). Thus, while a hostile microclimate attacks the windward end of a krummholz island, snow mold may be killing the snow-protected, leeward end!

However, the primary effect of excessive snow at timberline is to prevent tree establishment in sites where air temperatures are adequate for tree growth. Where snow covers the ground until mid- or late summer, it can critically shorten the growing season. In snowy basins, especially in the maritime mountains, groves of conifers are confined to the top of humps or rocky outcrops where the snowpack is relatively thin.

Occasionally, sequences of drier-than-normal winters (with below-normal snowpack) may have allowed conifer seedlings to become established in otherwise treeless sites. Such "episodic regeneration" of conifers in subalpine meadows occurred largely between 1930 and 1944 at Paradise on Mount Rainier (Franklin and Dyrness 1973). Once the trees are established they may be able to survive indefinitely. Their growth as saplings is quite slow but may speed up when they become large enough to project through the spring snowpack and absorb solar heat. Lower-than-normal snowfalls are not the only factor necessary for triggering episodic regeneration, however. A good seed crop (occurring infrequently in timberline stands), unusually mild frost conditions, and adequate summer moisture may also be necessary for successful regeneration.

Naturalist W. P. Taylor (1922) concluded that snow has a more important effect upon the upper limit of tree growth at Mount Rainier than does temperature. This deduction may also apply to much of the timberline terrain in the Cascades, Olympics, and coastal ranges of British Columbia and southern Alaska, where annual snowfall averages more

Subalpine fir invading meadows on Mount Rainier, Washington

than 500 inches. However, inland from the crest of the coastal ranges and the Cascades, excessive snowfall is much less widespread and is confined to the wettest mountain areas (such as the British Columbia Selkirks) or to cirque basins where winds deposit extra snow.

The potential magnitude of wind-augmented snowfall is evident in the deep cirque basin harboring Grinnell Glacier in Montana's Glacier National Park. Here, a precipitation gauge below the glacier at the moderate elevation of 6113 feet (well below the usual elevation of alpine timberline) collects an average of 147 inches of annual precipitation, although the surrounding mountain country apparently receives about 60 inches. Conversely, even the snowiest coastal mountains have steep south-facing slopes and windswept ridges that do not accumulate enough snow to limit tree growth.

In all areas, but especially in mountains of the semi-arid West, winter snowpack recharges the soil water reserve, providing a prolonged supply of water for plant roots. This snowpack is the only dependable water supply for upland sites in the semi-arid West, and the distribution of forest often coincides with that of areas harboring snow. Part of the reason that forest growth coincides with snowpack, however, is that winds deposit more snow in the timber than in either the alpine tundra or in the grasslands below. Also, the forest shades its underlying snowpack, and thus slows the melt.

Precipitation and Moisture

Over much of the terrain in the western United States, annual precipitation is too meager to support forests. The dearth of moisture generally is responsible for the formation of lower timberlines. (However, a few of the lower timberlines in high-desert valleys result from severe cold-air ponding in basins, which prevents tree establishment.) Also, the lower elevational limits of many subalpine tree species are apparently related to insufficient moisture. Where adequate moisture does occur at lower elevations, the subalpine trees are often unable to compete with fast-growing "montane" (lower elevation) species. Most subalpine trees grow well in temperate-zone gardens where they need not compete for water and nutrients.

Inadequate precipitation and accompanying soil drought seldom limit the upper or northern advance of the forest; however, these factors are influential in determining which species will make up the timberline stands. For instance, mountain hemlock might be abundant at timberline in the southern Sierra Nevada of California if a much greater quantity of precipitation fell during the summers.

Moisture requirements of the primary forest types in northern Arizona and northern New Mexico are shown below. Growing-season temperature requirements are also estimated. This simplified depiction of moisture and temperature requirements by species is indicative of the more complex real-world limitations on tree growth.

A certain amount of annual precipitation is required at any site before a forest can grow; but the critical level varies greatly with the temperature (related, of course, to latitude and altitude), the type of soil or geological substrate, and the seasonal distribution of the precipitation itself. For example, annual precipitation of as little as five inches is adequate for tree growth in central Alaska or northern Canada, where

	Moisture		Temperature
Forest zone	Annual precip. (inches)	Evaporation June – Sept. (inches)	Mean for June – Sept. (°F)
pinyon-juniper woodland	12–20	30–40	65–69
ponderosa pine	18–25	18–26	59–63
Douglas-fir	22–34	12–16	56–58
Engelmann spruce	27–36	10–13	50–56

Estimated moisture and temperature data for different forest types in northern Arizona and northern New Mexico (adapted from Pearson 1931 and 1941).

"evapotranspiration" (water loss to the atmosphere by evaporation and transpiration from plants) is minor and soil drainage is poor, often because of underlying permafrost. At middle elevations in the southwestern United States, however, 18 inches or more annual precipitation is necessary for forest growth. And, in the subalpine zone, where temperatures are cool, bristlecone and limber pine can grow on certain favorable soil types when annual precipitation averages as little as 12 inches. The relatively low-elevation bristlecone pines (growing at 9000 to 10,000 feet) have a shorter growing season than those at tree line, since they can grow only until they exhaust the available soil moisture resulting from the winter's precipitation.

Another example of the intertwined effects of moisture and temperature is found in the high, semi-arid valleys of the Rockies. Here, sufficient moisture to support the most drought-tolerant forest trees (for example, ponderosa pine) may occur only at relatively high elevations (such as 7000 feet), where the growing season is too brief for that species. The next most drought-tolerant tree (e.g., Douglas-fir) requires more moisture and thus would have to tolerate still colder (higher) sites. In northwestern Colorado and parts of Wyoming and Alberta, the ponderosa pine zone and most of the Douglas-fir zone are absent, apparently because of the extremely dry, cold conditions. Remember, too, that the ultimate effect of a dry-cold climate occurs locally in Nevada and other western states, where some of the high (subalpine) mountains support no forest.

Often at lower timberline, trees grow in a widely spaced, parklike stand or even on a "savanna," defined as a grassland with scattered trees. As moisture increases upslope, the sites are able to support a more heavily stocked stand. Deep-rooted trees such as ponderosa pine often grow well on dry upland sites, once they overcome the tremendous difficulties of initial establishment and their roots reach the water-bearing subsoil. It may take an unusual sequence of events, such as a good seed crop followed by a few years of favorable moisture conditions, for saplings to become established. Yet, once that precarious early life is successfully completed, the odds shift markedly, making subsequent growth and development far more likely.

Although the drought-resistant trees of lower timberline are tenacious once established, the size of their growth rings is strongly related to the amount of annual rainfall. As we will see later, the width patterns of their annual growth rings have recorded the "Dust Bowl" drought of the 1930s and the sequences of dry, average, and wet years, going back hundreds and even thousands of years in some timberline species.

Soils and Geology

Soils and underlying rock types strongly influence rooting abilities of trees. They also affect available moisture for tree growth and are critical factors at the lower or drought-caused timberlines. Seedlings of various pines, Douglas-fir, and other conifers develop deep, extensive root systems rapidly and are able to take up moisture readily in coarse-textured soils (Daubenmire 1959). In fine-textured soils, moisture is less available to conifers, and seedling roots fail to reach the layer retaining available

Stunted ponderosa pine on the first rocky ridge at the foot of the Front Range west of Fort Collins, Colorado

moisture in mid-summer. Also, competition from grasses and other fibrous-rooted plants is much more severe on fine-textured soils.

An example of the combined effect of soil type and precipitation is evident in the distribution of ponderosa pine forests in eastern Washington and Oregon (Franklin and Dyrness 1973). Pine can grow on sandy or stony soils where annual precipitation is only 12 inches (or occasionally as low as 10 inches); but pine and other conifers are unable to establish themselves on the deep, silty soils of the Palouse prairie area unless annual precipitation totals nearly 25 inches. A similar phenomenon can be seen while driving west from the shortgrass prairie near Denver or Fort Collins, Colorado. Conifers (stunted ponderosa pine) appear abruptly when the traveler reaches the first rocky outcrop of the Front Range.

An example of geology as a critical factor at timberline is the ponderosa and Jeffrey pine (*Pinus jeffreyi*) stands growing in the sagebrush desert some distance east of the northern Sierra Nevada (Billings 1950). In every case, these stands are confined to a mineral-deficient volcanic rock that sagebrush does not occupy.

In contrast, soil rarely acts as the primary limiting factor at upper or northern timberlines, where moisture is generally adequate. This should be apparent to anyone who has seen the large trees growing atop boulder fields and out of cracks in massive granite bedrock in some of North America's moist but rocky mountain ranges.

Still, the chemical composition of the "substrate," or underlying rock, often helps determine which species will inhabit a given site at the alpine timberline. For instance, in the semi-arid White Mountains of east-central California a narrow band of forest, made up of Great Basin bristlecone pine, extends to both higher and lower elevations on the basic (alkaline), dolomite rock substrate than on the slightly acidic sandstone or granite (Wright and Mooney 1965). Conversely, big sagebrush (*Artemisia tridentata*), which is considered to have cold tolerances similar to that of timberline conifers, ascends about 1000 feet higher in elevation on sandstone and granite (to 12,200 feet), than it does on dolomite.

The greater success of bristlecone pine on dolomitic substrates seems to be related to the better availability of moisture in these soils, the tolerance of bristlecone pine for low nutrient availability, and the lack of competing vegetation (Wright and Mooney 1965). Dolomitic surfaces are light-colored and thus reflect the sunlight and stay cool, reducing moisture stress. On the other hand, sagebrush apparently is intolerant of the low nutrient status of dolomitic soils but is more drought tolerant than bristlecone pine.

In central Colorado, Engelmann spruce and subalpine fir ascend to unusually high elevations on basic, calcium-rich limestone substrates (Curry 1962). Ecologists long ago noted the tendency of certain species to grow only on basic, calcium-rich substrates at their upper or northern limits (Daubenmire 1959). White spruce and Siberian larch (*Larix sibirica*) are considered to be such "calciphytes" at the arctic tree line. In contrast, black spruce and alpine larch seem to prefer or even require acidic rock substrates at timberline (Larsen 1974, Arno and Habeck 1972). Such species are termed "calcifuges."

"Ultramafic" (ultrabasic) rocks produce unique forest communities and strange timberlines at several locations in the far western United States. These rocks yield soils rich in iron and magnesium and poor in calcium, nitrogen, and phosphorus. Rocky Mountain lodgepole pine is the dominant timberline tree on this rock type on the west peak of Twin Sisters Mountain (Kruckeberg 1969). This peak rises above the luxuriant maritime forest near Bellingham, Washington, in an area where lodgepole pine is scarce. In addition, whitebark pine and subalpine fir spread down to lower-than-normal elevations on this ultramafic site. To the southwest, across Puget Sound, a similarly strange timberline dominated by large, sprawling lodgepole or perhaps shore pines (*Pinus contorta* var. *contorta*) occurs atop Mount Townsend on a manganese-rich volcanic rock formation.

In some of the drier ranges of the Northern and Middle Rockies, dense lodgepole pine – subalpine fir forests give way abruptly, across a straight-line boundary, to luxuriant grass-forb (broadleaved herbs) communities with scattered clumps of Douglas-fir, whitebark pine, or limber pine. These sharp vegetation boundaries usually coincide with a shift in substrate: the dense forest grows on acidic rocks like granite, argillite, or shale, and the herbfields with scattered dry-site trees occupy the adjacent limestone.

But why do these different rock types support such contrasting vegetation? In addition to the markedly different chemical compositions of the soils on these substrates, much of the limestone weathers to a coarse, droughty soil. As a result, soil scientist Herbert Holdorf of the U.S. Forest Service has noted that while sites on granitic substrates can support lodgepole pine if annual precipitation exceeds 16 inches, similar sites on limestone require nearly twice as much precipitation for lodgepole to survive. In moist mountain ranges west of the Continental Divide, however, annual precipitation is sufficient to allow generally similar tree communities to develop on both sides of adjoining acid rock and limestone substrates.

Frozen Ground

A continuous zone of permanently frozen ground hundreds of feet thick underlies most of North America's arctic tundra. In summer, thawing is confined to a thin mantle of surface soil called the "active layer," except in gravelly areas such as along stream channels where thawing extends down 10 feet or more. In northern Alaska and northwestern Canada the southern boundary of continuous permafrost coincides approximately with the northern limit of the arctic timberline or forest-tundra zone (Hunt 1967, Larsen 1974). Southward from this boundary, permafrost becomes discontinuous or patchy, and the seasonally active layer of surface soil becomes thicker.

Permafrost restricts growth of all tree species but not all to the same extent. In northern Canada shallow-rooted black spruce can grow on a boggy, one-foot-thick active layer above permafrost. In northeastern Siberia a species of larch (*Larix dahurica*) forms vast swamp-forests atop continuous permafrost in a climatic zone second only to Antarctica in winter severity. The larch's shallow root system utilizes only the surface foot or so of muskeg soil which thaws in summer (Eyre 1963). However, jack pine (*Pinus banksiana*) of the Canadian boreal forest does not spread northward into the forest-tundra zone, perhaps because it forms a deep tap root and seems unable to grow even in a thick active layer above permafrost.

White spruce, balsam poplar (*Populus balsamifera*), and Alaska paper birch (*Betula papyrifera* var. *humilis*) are somewhat tolerant of permafrost. They can grow on sites where permafrost is three to four feet below the surface (Hustich 1966); but they grow much faster on sites where the active layer is deeper, such as along river courses where running water thaws the soil.

Much of the varied pattern of tree growth in the forest-tundra zone of northwestern Canada is undoubtedly related to the micro-relief of the surface topography and to the thickness of the active layer. For example, in the lower Mackenzie River Valley black spruce are mostly confined to sides of small hummocks that rise above the permafrost and that have adequate but not excessive moisture.

In contrast, permanently frozen ground is not extensive at most *alpine* timberlines. This is the case even in Alaskan mountains; evidently permafrost does not form as readily and does not preserve well in rugged mountainous topography. Also, the snowpack at alpine timberlines insulates the ground and generally prevents deep penetration of frost. Thus, despite air temperatures that average well below freezing during the winter half of the year, the soil scarcely freezes in most stands at alpine timberline.

"Patterned ground" and tundra with subalpine fir and alpine larch at 9100 feet in Montana's Anaconda-Pintler Range

The most significant exception to this general rule is windswept krummholz sites above tree line. Here, snow protection is very localized and confined to the crowns of the individual krummholz cushions. Thus, soil temperatures *between* the shrublike trees drop well below freezing and perhaps to lethal temperatures for tree roots. Wardle (1968) recorded extreme minimums of 14°F in the soil beneath a windswept and largely snowfree krummholz site in the Colorado Front Range.

At windswept alpine tundra sites, the upper few feet of soil characteristically freeze each winter, and although seasonally frozen ground does not by itself limit tree growth, it greatly increases the danger of winter desiccation. At arctic timberlines, where winter desiccation is not a widespread problem, the rooting zone reaches temperatures of a few degrees below freezing in winter. Ironically, the permafrost, below, acts as a moderating influence, since it remains only a few degrees below freezing year-round.

Repeated freezing and thawing on snowfree sites causes "patterned ground" at cold timberlines and especially in the tundra zone. In moist, silty or organic soils such as in meadows or bogs, frost action creates small, regularly spaced hummocks. In ground containing stones, the stones are likely to be transported to the edges of the hummocks or mounds, creating a "rock net" pattern. In any case, daily freeze/thaw cycles in moist ground damage roots of tree seedlings and probably prevent tree regeneration from becoming established in some frosty basins.

Still another form of ground frost limits tree growth in the mountains of central Alaska and no doubt elsewhere (Spurr 1964, R. Haugen*). The *annual* freeze/thaw cycle of perennially frozen ground, together with lingering snow patches, creates an excess of moisture in the soil which then creeps downslope. This imperceptibly slow movement called "solifluction" causes great injury to tree roots. Low-growing tundra plants are better adapted to survival than trees under such conditions. In solifluction, soil moves down over an impermeable surface (permafrost or bedrock). This phenomenon occurs only on moderate slopes, since the water runs off steeper slopes.

Robert Curry (1962) reports an interesting observation of permafrost very deep in the mountainside beneath a timberline stand of Engelmann spruce near Climax, Colorado. Permafrost was found at depths of 50 to 130 feet in a sealed mine tunnel beneath this forest at 11,000 feet elevation. This permafrost is evidently a relict of an earlier, colder climate. Similarly, the boulder piles or "talus" near timberline on north-facing slopes may contain a core of persistent ice that melts slowly, supplying moisture to trees throughout late summer.

Rarified Atmosphere

One might suspect that the rarified atmosphere could in some way limit tree growth at the highest elevations. For instance, ecologists have long recognized that atmospheric rarity tends to increase evaporation (Cooper 1908); however, lower temperatures generally offset this effect (Shaw 1909a). Also, physiologists in Europe and North America have measured transpiration water losses of the same species of trees growing at different elevations and have found that high-elevation trees generally use less water. Also, they discovered that the stomata (pores in the leaves) of timberline trees tend to be almost completely closed during winter, thus preventing evaporation (Tranquillini 1979).

Another manifestation of the increasingly thin air at higher altitudes is a diminishing quantity of carbon dioxide—a key ingredient (along with water and sunlight) for photosynthesis. Carbon dioxide availability decreases with altitude but is probably not limiting for most high-mountain species (Billings and others 1961). Moreover, even at the world's highest timberlines, dwarf shrubs and herbs extend to still higher altitudes, and yet research has not indicated that trees require more carbon dioxide than lesser vegetation.

Light Intensity

High-elevation timberlines, particularly those in relatively dry, sunny climates, are exposed to high intensities of solar radiation. In winter, reflection from snow amplifies radiation up to double the intensity

---

*R. K. Haugen 1966: personal correspondence. Earth Sci. Div., U.S. Army Cold Regions Res. & Engineering Lab., Hanover, New Hampshire.

experienced at low elevations (Tranquillini 1979). While it is not known that ultraviolet radiation causes much damage to trees at timberline (Caldwell and others 1980), high intensities of visible light in winter or summer can cause loss of chlorophyll, or "chlorosis."

Austrian physiologist Walter Tranquillini (1979) has studied the chlorosis (a pronounced yellowing of needles) that occurs in winter on the sunny side of timberline conifers. Normally this lost chlorophyll is replenished by new production the following summer. After extreme damage, however, replenishment is no longer possible in light-sensitive species, notably in European spruce (Collaer 1934).

Engelmann spruce seedlings planted in full sunlight at elevations of 9000 to 11,000 feet in Colorado also showed symptoms of marked chlorosis (Ronco 1970). This condition appeared first in the older needles, and by the end of the first summer the yellowing had spread to the new growth. The seedlings died during the first winter, sometime after they were covered by snow (a sharp contrast to the symptoms of winter desiccation). Evidently the chlorosis and death were caused primarily by "solarization"—a phenomenon in which photosynthesis is inhibited by high light intensities. Carefully controlled experiments indicated that moisture (and nitrogen) deficiencies were not the primary cause of chlorosis and death in the sun-exposed spruce seedlings. Seedlings in the same sites that were given artificial shade did not become chlorotic. Still, even a modest amount of moisture stress contributes to this damage, since seedlings on the same site that were kept in pots and watered suffered less chlorosis. As seen in this experiment, the heating effect of intense sunlight on a seedling is great and can produce a strong evaporative demand, and therefore water is lost from the foliage.

Thus, it appears that excessive sunlight on exposed sites near or above 10,000 feet limits regeneration of certain sensitive species. These species can regenerate on northern exposures or within forest stands where shading from other trees occurs. Perhaps this sensitivity to strong radiation is responsible for the abrupt transitions from dense, stunted forest to alpine tundra that occur in some areas (Tranquillini 1979).

In contrast to light-sensitive species, the mountain pines, which are sun-tolerant species, show little or no chlorophyll reduction in winter, and this seems to be related to their ability to form open stands on southern exposures at the highest timberlines. Subalpine fir, the most widely distributed timberline dweller in North America, becomes rather scarce on open south exposures at tree line in Colorado; might this be the result of solarization? Or, perhaps drought is responsible.

Available Tree Species and Genetic Types

Each tree species that forms part of the timberline in different regions of the world has its own special limits of tolerance to the vicissitudes of climate, whether in high mountains, high latitudes, or semi-arid lower slopes. And yet, despite the contrasting species that make up arctic and alpine timberlines throughout North America and most of the Northern

Hemisphere, the elevations of these timberlines show a remarkably consistent relationship with summer warmth.

In the eastern Himalaya this critical level of summer warmth seems to apply uniformly to very different types of trees (Swan 1967). Three kinds of trees, each with differing altitudinal limits in other parts of Asia, coincide to form a common timberline at 13,500 feet, where the mean July temperature is very close to 50°F. These trees are an evergreen conifer, the fir *Abies spectabilis*, a broadleaved deciduous birch, *Betula utilis*, and two broadleaved evergreen *Rhododendron* trees. In other areas where these trees diverge at timberline, at least one species assumes a timberline approximating the July 50°F isotherm.

Where a factor other than summer warmth restricts some of the timberline species to a lower elevation or latitude, one unusual species will often extend beyond and form the ultimate limit of tree growth near the 50°F isotherm. For example, in northeastern Siberia the larch *Larix dahurica* extends hundreds of miles north of the limits of evergreen trees to form a timberline near the 50°F isotherm. The evergreens are evidently kept out of this region by extreme winter desiccation.

Occasionally in tropical or Southern Hemisphere mountain ranges, upper timberlines develop at abnormally low altitudes because of the lack of a cold-hardy tree flora. A striking example of this situation is found in the Serra do Mar Mountains of Brazil, where the upper timberline occurs at the modest elevation of 6400 feet (Clausen 1963). However, this treeless summit area experiences only slight frosts even in winter, and 10 months of the year have mean temperatures above 50°F. Only tropical tree species are present in this region, and none have evolved a significant degree of cold-hardiness.

The tree species growing together at timberline often respond differently to limitations imposed by the local climate. For example, bristlecone, limber, and whitebark pines often develop into erect trees among krummholz of subalpine fir and Engelmann spruce in the Rocky Mountains, evidently because the pines are better able to withstand winter desiccation.

Even within a species, genetic differences allow some races (strains) or individuals to grow at timberline where others cannot. For example, Tranquillini (1979) cites evidence that the crown form of European spruce is genetically controlled. At timberline in the Alps, the spruce trees have narrow crowns—probably an adaptation to protect against heavy snow loads—whereas at lower elevations the same species typically has a broad crown.

Clausen (1963) hypothesized that at upper timberline the treelike form of a given species may be replaced by its genetically different dwarf or "elfinwood" race or "ecotype." However, to confirm that krummholz forms are genetic races, they would have to be transplanted or otherwise propagated on more moderate sites. Horticulturists have frequently found, to their dismay, that dwarf trees from timberline grow luxuriantly once re-established in a fertile, low-elevation garden!

Available Seed

Lack of viable seed might result in the formation of upper timberline, since stunted trees, and especially krummholz, seldom produce much of a seed crop. Thus, one might theorize that timberline results from conditions too harsh for seed production rather than from conditions too severe for tree establishment and growth. Lack of viable seed may be of some consequence locally at the arctic timberline where winds consistently blow from the tundra into the forest, as they do along the east coast of Hudson Bay (Savile 1963). Seed dispersal would also tend to be more critical at arctic timberline than at others because of the great width of this forest-tundra zone.

Seeds need to be carried only half a mile or so in order to spread from stands at forest line to the *alpine* tundra. Strong upslope winds are common enough at most alpine timberlines to ensure some of this sort of seed dispersal. For example, in California's Sierra Nevada, I found the relatively heavy seeds of foxtail pine lying in alpine snowfields 1000 feet above the highest possible seed source. These seeds, like those of most timberline trees, have a membranous wing that facilitates wind transport. (As I will discuss, the large, wingless seeds of some species are transported by animals.) Moreover, the substantial amount of exposed mineral soil in many alpine areas provides an excellent seedbed for conifers. This is of little benefit, however, where the climate is too severe for seedlings!

Lack of a seed source undoubtedly prevents trees from growing in some favorable habitats that have become isolated because of past climatic changes. In the semi-arid Great Basin, for instance, ponderosa pine or other tree species may have died out on certain isolated mountain ranges during unfavorably dry climatic periods since the Wisconsin Glaciation (ending about 12,000 years ago). Subsequently, the climate on some of these mountains may have again become suitable for ponderosa pine; but the species has been unable to re-colonize because the nearest ponderosa stands (seed source) are over 100 miles distant, across arid lowlands (Critchfield and Allenbaugh 1969).

A comparable explanation was proposed by ecologists Dwight Billings and A. F. Mark (1957) to account for treeless balds high up on some peaks in the southern Appalachians. In this region of North Carolina and Tennessee, the theoretical climatic timberline at present would occur at an elevation considerably higher than the tallest peak (6684 feet), which is occupied by spruce-fir forest. However, the highest summits are today above the limits of eastern hardwood species, and according to the above hypothesis some relatively high peaks lost their spruce-fir forest during a warmer climatic period. Thus, Big Bald (5516 feet) is today capped, in the potential spruce-fir zone, by a large, grassy bald that developed as the hardwood forest retreated downslope with climatic cooling. Spruce is invading many similar balds where seed sources are available, but the nearest spruce seed source is about 15 miles from Big Bald. Overall, the Appalachian balds involve several different vegetation types and settings and isolation through climatic change does not completely explain their existence. Various other factors are no doubt involved in their formation, including repeated burning and heavy grazing (Gersmehl 1973).

Major Disturbances

Various disturbances can influence the position of timberline. In pre-cipitous mountain areas that receive heavy snowfalls, snow avalanches are so prevalent and destructive that they prevent normal development of subalpine forest on most of the landscape. Examples of this condition can be found in Glacier National Park, Montana, and locally in some areas of the Canadian Rockies, the Colorado Rockies, the Wasatch Range of Utah, the North Cascades of Washington, and the European Alps. In these areas, avalanche swathes make up a major part of the high-elevation landscape, and these strips are occupied by a mosaic of plant communities, including small crippled conifers and resilient shrubs such as Sitka alder. Still, even these avalanche-permeated areas support patches of normal forest and timberline stands on convex ridge spurs and occasional moderate slopes.

Volcanic activity is another factor that locally depresses timberline. Even before the disastrous May 18, 1980, eruption, the alpine timberline on Mount Saint Helens, Washington, was remarkably low. Forest line occurred at about 4400 feet, about 1100 feet lower than on nearby Mount

A band of trees near tree line escaped burning by a wildfire that swept through the subalpine forest near Cathedral Peak in Washington's Okanogan Cascades.

Hood (Franklin and Dyrness 1973). This Saint Helens timberline was also unusual because it was composed largely of species not normally found at timberline—including lodgepole pine, western white pine (*Pinus monticola*), Douglas-fir, black cottonwood (*Populus trichocarpa*), noble fir (*Abies procera*), and western hemlock (*Tsuga heterophylla*). Comparison of timberline on photos taken in 1897 with its position prior to the 1980 eruption suggested that trees were advancing at a discernible rate onto the coarse pumice. Of course, a new, much-lower timberline will result from the 1980 eruptions, although it probably will advance rapidly up the lower slopes of the volcano unless additional massive eruptions occur. Similar depression of timberlines have been noted elsewhere throughout the world on the slopes of active volcanoes.

Fire is another disturbance that can locally depress upper timberline or raise the level of lower timberline. Because of the generally sparse,

Nearly a century after the erect limber pines burned, only krummholz has developed on this windswept ridge on Red Mountain, near Lincoln, Montana.

discontinuous fuels and cool/moist conditions, large, destructive fires are not common at most alpine timberlines. However, the prevalence of lightning strikes and high winds allows many fires to ignite and a few of them to spread, especially along exposed ridges. Many of the larger fires affecting timberlines spread up from the forests below.

In the Medicine Bow Mountains of south-central Wyoming a fire in 1809 destroyed a timberline stand (at 10,500 feet), and the site is now occupied by moist alpine tundra (Billings 1969). This reversion to low-growing vegetation evidently results from the exposure of the site to the full force of strong winds. The winds remove snow that is needed to protect tree seedlings in this harsh, continental climate.

Similarly, over a century ago, fire leveled a stand of tall alpine larch trees in the upper part of Larch Valley (7500 feet elevation) in Banff National Park, Alberta. The result has been a reversion to tundra, with a slow re-invasion of krummholz conifers on the exposed site. In less-continental climates, where wind-exposure is not as severely limiting, tree growth may become re-established somewhat sooner after fire. For instance, in the Montana Bitterroot Range (inland-maritime climate), three different ridgetop fires (50 to 200 years ago) have resulted in re-invasion of krummholz whitebark pine where erect trees had formerly grown. On wind-sheltered slopes, erect tree growth apparently develops more readily after fire.

Most often, only clumps or isolated trees are burned in fires at timberline. It is true that the large pines at upper timberlines in western North America frequently contain considerable amounts of dead, weathered, resinous wood that allow them to torch out when ignited by lightning; but often, fires have difficulty spreading to nearby trees because of the open nature of the stands, moist conditions, and the rocky terrain with sparse surface fuels. In the timberline parkland of the moist mountain ranges, fires that are allowed to burn naturally, frequently creep slowly and sinuously from one tree grove or stringer to the next, failing to burn the meadows and snow glades in between. Often, some trees are killed while others survive these ground fires that burn slowly and fitfully — depending on weather conditions — for as long as a few weeks before being doused by driving rain or wet snow.

Fire, driven by strong winds, is considered a major destroyer of stands of black and white spruce at the arctic timberline across northern Canada (Viereck and Schandelmeier 1980, Payette 1980). Burned sites may revert to tundra for an indefinite period of at least a few centuries under the present climate. Some timberline stands that burned 900 and 3500 years ago are still in tundra, and tree line has retreated as much as 175 miles as a result of fires in some areas (Bryson and others 1965). A similar, essentially permanent displacement of tree line by fire occurs in Siberia, and the resulting plant community has been termed "pyrogenic tundra" (Kryuchkov 1968).

At *lower* timberlines, prior to the advent of organized fire suppression, fires were usually of low to moderate intensity, and they passed beneath open-growing trees, killing few of them. Occasionally, severe fires occur, and in these cases tree regeneration may be so slow that a grassland or

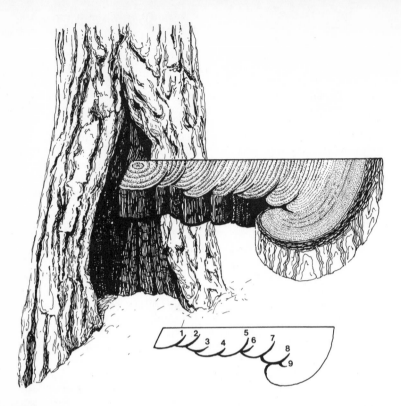

Multiple fire scars show a pattern of frequent surface fires prior to 1900 on this cross-section from a ponderosa pine near the lower timberline. Similar patterns have been traced back to A.D. 1500 on the oldest pine trees and stumps.

shrub community gains control of the site. In many areas, lower timberlines have advanced downhill or stands have dramatically thickened because of fire suppression and heavy grazing (Arno and Gruell 1983). In presettlement times, Indian- and lightning-caused fires tended to keep conifers from invading mountain grasslands.

Biological Factors

Insects and diseases are generally not important in determining the position of timberlines, although they occasionally cause severe damage to timberline tree species. Some stands of whitebark pine in moist mountain ranges are being devastated by white pine blister rust (*Cronartium ribicola*), a disease which was accidentally imported in the early 1900s on a shipment of infected western white pine seedlings brought from Europe. However, in much of whitebark pine's range, in drier mountain regions, blister rust has had little effect, apparently because dry summer conditions are unfavorable for the fungus. Even in the moist mountain ranges, a small percentage of the trees is resistant and will probably ensure that whitebark will not be totally destroyed (Hoff and others 1980).

A century of change at the Douglas-fir lower timberline near Tower Junction in Yellowstone National Park, Wyoming. Original scene is from an 1885 photograph; retake is 1970.

One of the most destructive insects at upper timberline also concentrates on whitebark pine. Vast forests of mature whitebark in the Northern Rockies were killed by outbreaks of mountain pine beetle (*Dendroctonus ponderosae*) between 1909 and 1940. This native beetle's larvae overwinter in the inner bark, and they tunnel around the circumference of the trunk while feeding, thereby girdling and killing the tree. But only large, vigorous trees have a suitably thick inner bark, so younger trees are spared. In the late 1970s new outbreaks of mountain pine beetle killed most of the large whitebark pine in mountains west of Glacier National Park, Montana. In these moist mountain ranges the combination of blister rust infection, mountain pine beetle outbreaks, and suppression of forest fires is changing the composition of timberline stands.

Animals that plant tree seeds are important factors at some timberlines. Certain jays harvest and cache immense quantities of seed from various pines [whitebark, limber, pinyons, ponderosa, Jeffrey, and foxtail pine], especially near upper and lower timberlines. Also, the berrylike cones of several species of juniper, which grow at lower timberline, are inadvertently planted across the landscape by various kinds of birds that devour them. Juniper seed does not readily germinate unless its fleshy covering is dissolved by passing through the digestive tract of birds or other animals. These animal tree planters (discussed more fully in Chapter 2) disperse seeds over a broader range of sites on the landscape than seeds would otherwise reach, but they probably have little effect on the position of most timberlines.

Alpine timberlines have been lowered in many parts of the world by human activities such as overgrazing, clearing for pasturage, woodcutting, and deliberate burning. In the European Alps, for instance, timberlines have been lowered by 330 feet or more, and their tree and undergrowth communities have been altered greatly by a millennium of human activities. In contrast, alpine and arctic timberlines of North America have been left largely unchanged by ancient and modern man. Some alpine areas in the western mountain ranges were heavily impacted by sheep grazing in the late 1800s and early 1900s, but this covered only a few decades in most areas and, overall, recovery of the natural vegetation has been good. Timberline tree growth was much less affected than the intervening meadows.

Interacting Factors

Our discussion of individual factors affecting timberlines should not imply that temperature, wind, snow, and other influences act independently. Careful study of any particular timberline will usually reveal a combination of causal agents. The "ridgetop ribbon forest" formation provides a striking example of such interactions.

This odd timberline formation occurs at several locations in the Northern Rockies, but it is especially common along the crest of ridges averaging 7800 feet in elevation near the Idaho-Montana border about 90 miles south of Missoula (Arno 1966, Daubenmire 1981). Several ridges attain this elevation and extend in a southeasterly-to-northwesterly di-

"Ridgetop ribbon-forest" on the Montana-Idaho divide northwest of Lost Trail Pass. Grassland slope is at left.

rection; thus, they have broad slopes facing southwest and northeast.

Along the very crest of each ridge grows an almost perfect windrow (10 to 30 feet wide) of short, stout trees. This thin strip or "ribbon forest" (Billings 1969), is composed of mature whitebark pine and subalpine fir averaging 30 to 40 feet tall. Prevailing winds blow from the southwest, and on the windward side of the ribbon forest lies a broad band of semi-arid mountain grassland. In contrast, the leeward side of this strip of trees is bordered by a narrow "snow glade" (70 to 150 feet wide) filled with a moist sedge (*Carex*) meadow which gives way abruptly downslope to a dense subalpine forest. One of these ridgetop ribbon forests, north of Medicine Point, extends unbroken for a mile.

Walking a transect perpendicularly across one of these ridgetops, from the southwestern to the northeastern slope, allows us to examine the reasons for vegetation change. Starting on the southwestern slope several hundred yards below the crest, we climb up through an open stand of whitebark pine and Douglas-fir that gives way to a bunchgrass "bald" on the exposed upper slope. This bluebunch wheatgrass-Idaho fescue (*Agropyron spicatum-Festuca idahoensis*) grassland is similar in composition to those found in semi-arid lowlands all across the inland Northwest. The bunchgrass community reflects dry site conditions that result from direct exposure to both strong winds and the afternoon sun. Although this site is a few hundred feet below the usual elevation of forest line, the wind produces such exposed conditions in winter and severe drought in summer on this rounded southwestern slope that not even krummholz can exist! The unusual harshness of this site's local climate (microclimate) is apparent when we gaze out across the mountain landscape, which, except for a few bunchgrass balds, consists of an unbroken blue-green conifer forest stretching to the horizon.

During winter the wind blows snow across this open grassland and deposits it in a huge drift, complete with an overhanging cornice, just over the ridgetop. At the very crest of the ridge lies a narrow strip of habitat favorable for tree growth. This strip is covered by the thin portion of the snowdrift, which provides adequate moisture for trees along with protection at surface level from the winter winds (necessary for seedling development).

Just a few yards away on the leeward slope, however, snow accumulates to 20 feet in depth. This snowdrift prevents tree growth by lingering too long into the growing season and, on its lower edge, by creeping and sliding, thus breaking off woody stems. The narrow band of habitat under this drift is a snow glade inhabited only by sedges, mountain heath (*Phyllodoce empetriformis* and *Cassiope mertensiana*), and other low-growing plants characteristic of the moist meadows at timberline. Along the lower edge of the snow glade lies a narrow "cripple zone" of saplings and small trees which are periodically crushed or broken by sliding snow. However, just a few yards farther downslope stands a dense subalpine forest of well-developed subalpine fir, Engelmann spruce, whitebark pine, and lodgepole pine.

2
Strategies for Survival

Timberlines represent the response of trees to increasingly harsh environmental conditions. Around the Northern Hemisphere a few dozen tree species, mainly conifers, have evolved diverse strategies for growth and survival in these inhospitable environments.

PHYSIOLOGICAL LIMITS

Growth and Ripening of Shoots

Ripening of new growth is a critical process among trees at cold timberlines. If new shoots fail to mature fully during the brief, cool summer, they will be susceptible to both frost damage in autumn and desiccation in winter (Tranquillini 1979). The ripening or maturation process, known as "hardening off of shoots," involves the completion of growth and the loss of succulence. Succulence is a "soft" appearance that results from high water content, incompletely lignified cell walls, and a thin "cuticle" (the waxy covering that protects mature leaves) (Wardle 1974). Ripening markedly reduces the water content of the foliage in general and allows space for ice crystals to form between cells without causing damage.

Two consecutive processes are involved in ripening: (1) the completion of growth, including that of individual cells and their walls, which depends upon adequate summer warmth; and (2) development of "hardiness" or the characteristic degree of cold tolerance attainable by a given species or race (Wardle 1974). Provided that the growth process is completed, the slight frosts of early autumn will bring about the full development of hardiness.

The ultimate cold limit of tree growth occurs at the altitude or latitude where the summer temperatures barely allow for growth and ripening of shoots during most years.

Limits of winter hardiness have been tested for many North American trees by artificially freezing buds and twigs (Sakai and Weiser 1973). Species that inhabit cold timberlines in the Far North, northeastern United States, and Rocky Mountains survived freezing to −76°F or colder, once hardened by lighter frosts. As might be expected, however, the maritime timberline species from the Pacific Coast withstood freezing only to between −4 and −40°F, depending on the species.

Winter Desiccation

Winter desiccation is a lethal loss of moisture from leaves when the roots are chilled and unable to supply moisture. This is an important cause of death in unripened shoots at the alpine limits of tree growth, especially in inland climates. Winter desiccation can be identified by the orange-brown color of dead shoots, which are those exposed to direct sunlight or strong winds. In contrast, frost damage generally appears as drooping, and then shrivelled and blackened, new shoots.

On the windy eastern slopes of the Continental Divide from Alberta to Colorado one occasionally finds a stand of krummholz where the upper half of each shrubby tree consists of orange, dried-out foliage. During winter the lower portions of this krummholz were encased in snowpack and thus protected from winter drought. Naturalist Enos Mills (1920) wrote about walking for hours through the remains of such a top-killed krummholz forest in Colorado.

If trees are to survive, winter transpiration must be fully controlled, because chilled and frozen roots and stems are physically unable to replace water lost from the leaves except at a very slow rate. When the cuticle layer encasing new conifer needles does not develop fully, because of an inadequate growing season, this foliage will be unable to control transpiration losses in winter (Baig and Tranquillini 1976). Such winter desiccation is evidently the principal reason that alpine conifers from the snowy maritime mountains often cannot survive when cultivated in northern cities, where winter transpiration demands are sometimes high despite frozen soil.

The process of winter desiccation in conifers has been investigated in the mountains of the northern Japanese island Hokkaido (Sakai 1970). On exposed southern slopes the surface soil and the lower stems of conifers remain solidly frozen all winter, while upper stems and leaves were heated to about 62 and 48°F respectively, on sunny days. This caused intense dehydration by late February. While many species of trees can withstand very low temperatures, few have been able to evolve the high degree of hardiness necessary to survive winter desiccation at continental timberlines (Wardle 1974).

Although strong, warm, dry winds (chinooks) are a cause of winter desiccation (red-belt damage) in some of the lower timberline trees, the species at continental alpine timberlines appear to be resistant to damage from this source, provided that their new growth ripens fully during the previous summer. Warm, dry winds are normally considered to be a major desiccating force, but still air and bright sunlight (strong radiation) at similar temperatures and relative humidity cause much more pronounced drying of hardy conifers (Marchand and Chabot 1978, Tranquillini 1979). The different effect occurs because drought-resistant conifers are able to close their stomata during high winds. Moreover, strong winds cool the leaves so that they remain at about the same temperature as the air. This reduces the vapor pressure within the leaves, lessening the tendency for water to evaporate. Conversely, bright sunshine reflecting off snow, and

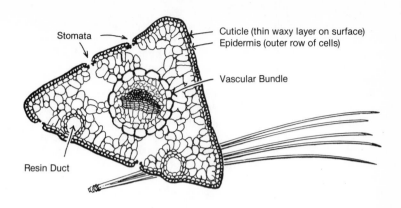

Cross section of a white pine needle (after Salisbury and Ross 1978).

relatively warm, still air often occur in late winter or early spring, when roots and lower stems are frozen. Under these conditions leaves may be heated 18°F above the air temperature, causing increased water loss (Marchand and Chabot 1978, Richards 1981). Wind speeds of only one mph generally reduce the differences between leaf temperatures and free-air temperatures and thus may reduce water loss in winter. However, abrasion of exposed krummholz foliage by ice-blasting winter winds evidently increases desiccation damage (Hadley and Smith 1983).

Large trees are better able to meet water demands in winter than small trees that are not buried in the snowpack, evidently because large trees have sizeable water reserves in their trunks, which can replenish leaf water losses (Tranquillini 1979). Large trees—even those growing in relatively open stands—also tend to ameliorate their climate by reducing wind, solar radiation, and extremes of temperature, thereby making the microclimate more favorable for tree growth. Thus, when stands of erect trees at timberline are destroyed by fire or cutting, regeneration is often retarded because of the more severe microclimate, including conditions of winter drought. However, the importance of winter drought relative to other limiting factors is not fully known.

Photosynthesis

Photosynthesis is the underlying process responsible for the ripening (maturation) of shoots and for resistance to winter desiccation. In this process, carbon dioxide gas (from the atmosphere) and water (taken up by the roots) are converted in the leaves (with light energy, and in the presence of chlorophyll) to glucose and oxygen. Glucose is a simple sugar that is used as an essential material from which other more complex substances are formed. This organic carbon "building material" is manufactured in shorter supply at the cold limits of trees because photosynthesis is a temperature-dependent process.

A complementary process called "respiration" oxidizes or transforms the simple sugar, creating water vapor, carbon dioxide, heat, and chemical energy. Together these processes convert light energy into chemical energy for use by the cells to maintain the plant's vital processes, including growth.

Annual tree growth depends upon a favorable balance of photosynthesis in excess of the energy needs for respiration. To keep functioning throughout the year and to grow as well, the tree must assimilate enough carbon (from carbon dioxide) during the short growing season to produce a surplus of the organic matter necessary for growth of leaves, cones, shoots, trunk, and roots. Losses of organic matter occur each year with respiration and with the dieback of the oldest leaves (in evergreen conifers), branches, roots, and cones. The balance between production and all losses indicates the annual biomass increase of the tree. In temperate-zone forests, annual above-ground biomass increases (i.e., net primary production) average roughly seven tons/acre/year (Hanley 1976, Spurr and Barnes 1980), whereas a comparable measure in tree-line stands of whitebark pine would be about one to two tons/acre/year (Forcella and Weaver 1977). Some trees that have become adapted to survival in exceptionally harsh environments, notably Great Basin bristlecone pine, are able to forego formation of an annual growth ring when drought is severe.

Experiments have shown that trees of the upper timberline carry out their peak rates of photosynthesis at relatively low temperatures com-

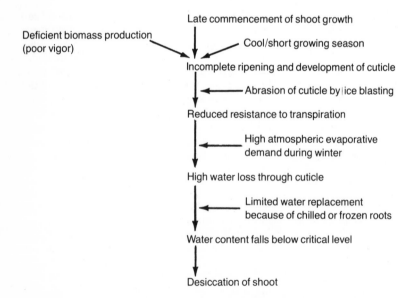

Model of the relationships leading to desiccation of exposed shoots of krummholz (modified from Tranquillini 1979).

pared to their counterparts of the same species growing in warmer climates (Tranquillini 1979). But there are limits to the temperature minimums required for significant photosynthesis, and leaf temperatures must generally be above 46°F for substantial rates of photosynthesis to occur (Vowinckel and others 1975, Tranquillini 1979). A winter dormancy prevents photosynthesis among alpine trees, even during brief warm periods, but there is no corresponding dormancy of respiration, and winter respiration losses (of glucose) can be considerable.

One might be tempted to hypothesize that the rapid decrease of tree stature or the total elimination of woody plants, upwards in the timberline zone, is primarily due to inadequate photosynthetic production. However, total photosynthetic production is not completely consumed by respiration even at the very limit of tree growth (Tranquillini 1979). Instead, it appears that limited photosynthetic production can result in incomplete ripening of shoots. The diagram opposite depicts how these factors are thought to interact, resulting in winter desiccation damage to exposed shoots of krummholz.

Important as photosynthesis seems to be as a physiological limitation, most authorities who have studied photosynthesis and carbon assimilation of timberline trees caution that various other limitations on tree growth (such as the ability to regenerate) are important in determining the position of many tree lines (e.g., Schulze and others 1967, Wardle 1974, Marchand and Chabot 1978).

GROWTH FORMS

Certainly the most prominent feature of alpine timberlines is the variety of growth forms and clumpy patterns that trees assume in order to survive in the windy, cold, snowy climate (Clausen 1965). Trees become progressively shorter, grow in groups, and exhibit unusual crown shapes. Individual species take on distinctively different growth forms. For example: subalpine fir develops tall trees with sharp, spirelike crowns, as well as clusters of stunted trees ringed by skirts, and on the most exposed sites, krummholz cushions; bristlecone and foxtail pines generally maintain erect, spreading crowns on the highest, most-exposed sites; and alpine larch often forms a slender, single 40-foot tall trunk and grows amidst krummholz of subalpine fir and whitebark pine.

Large Tree Forms

Visitors to the cold timberlines may be surprised to find remarkably large trees growing in the lower part of this ecotone (transition zone) near forest line. They will find, however, that Engelmann spruce in moist, wind-sheltered basins at about 11,000 feet in elevation make up some of the biggest timber in Colorado. Throughout this species' range, large old trees near forest line commonly attain diameters of 3 feet and heights of 100 feet or more.

Unlike their stunted counterparts at tree line, the large trees near arctic or alpine forest lines seldom propagate vegetatively through layering. Their size may be partially attributable to more ample growing space

than is available in the dense boreal or subalpine forests below, to plentiful moisture, and to longer intervals between stand-replacing fires (hence, the greater ages often attained).

The narrow, spirelike crowns of high-elevation spruce and subalpine fir accumulate only modest snow loads and offer less wind resistance than the broader-crowned trees of lower-elevation forests. In contrast, whitebark, limber, foxtail, bristlecone, and Sierra lodgepole pines (and to some extent mountain hemlock) near forest line form broad, spreading crowns, often on trunks 3 feet or more in diameter and 70 or more feet tall. The supple boughs of these pines can withstand strong winds and generally do not provide platforms where large snow-loads can accumulate. Alpine larch often becomes a large tree at forest line; its long, spreading, flexible branches shed their leaves at summer's end.

Stunted Trees and Tree Islands

Higher in the alpine timberline ecotone, or kampfzone, trees begin to show the effects of their "struggle" for existence by their noticeably stunted stature (attaining average heights at maturity of less than 50 feet)

(Opposite) Large foxtail pine at tree line (10,500 feet) on Alta Peak in Sequoia National Park, California. (Below) Large Engelmann spruce near forest line (10,800 feet) in Rocky Mountain National Park, Colorado

Stunted subalpine fir on a ridgetop at 5900 feet in Mount Rainier National Park, Washington

and by their growth in clumps. Stunted-tree forms occur frequently at the arctic and lower timberlines as well.

Most stunted forms probably result from severe wind exposure and repeated desiccation or frost damage to growing shoots. Individual trees on sites exposed to consistent, strong winds often develop a one-sided, wind-trained upper crown caused by the wind-blasting and desiccation of branch buds on the windward side during winter and, perhaps, by the

Tree islands, often with whitebark pine in the center and subalpine fir clustered around, on a broad ridge (8200 feet) in Montana's Little Belt Mountains

pressure of continuous wind against actively growing shoots.

The lower branches of stunted trees on exposed slopes often form a luxuriant horizontal band of growth extending several feet out from the lower crown itself. This "skirt" of branches develops beneath the level of the winter snowpack in response to a warmer, wind-sheltered microclimate.

Two kinds of clumped tree growth occurs. One, represented by species such as whitebark and limber pines, tends to produce multi-stemmed trunks at ground level in the stunted-tree zone. The other, more extensive group form is the "tree island," in which dense clusters or small groves of stunted trees develop because clustering enhances their chances of survival. The dense clump provides wind-shelter, mutual mechanical support, ameliorated temperature extremes, higher humidity, and a black-body effect resulting in earlier snowmelt. In some species this clumped growth is largely the result of vegetative reproduction through layering.

The tree island is often started with the development of an erect tree of one of the hardiest timberline species (e.g., one of the pines, mountain hemlock, or alpine larch). Later, seedlings of various species become established around the original tree. Less hardy or wind-resistant species are often shade-tolerant and thus able to prosper in the shelter of the original

"Ribbon forest and snow glade" patterns of subalpine fir at 5200 feet on Hudson Bay Mountain near Smithers, British Columbia

or "patriarch" tree, sometimes ascending through the overhead crown as if it were a trellis.

Over many decades or centuries a tree island may continue to expand through establishment of seedlings or vegetative saplings. When the original tree at the center of a tree island finally succumbs at an old age, the established tree island will develop a hollow center and be termed a "timber atoll" (Griggs 1938).

Sometimes an unusually tall and vigorous individual of a shade-tolerant species provides the shelter for a cluster of its own kind. In some cases, notably with subalpine fir, the original tree might also be termed a "mother tree" since virtually all the surrounding stems are its "offspring," or a second generation produced vegetatively. Such a tree island is a genetically identical clone. The second-generation saplings arise through layering, or rooting of lower branches that are pressed against moist ground and that, after taking root, begin to produce erect stems. After these new roots develop, the limb connection to the parent tree dies out and the offspring becomes independent (Wardle 1968). This layering and atoll formation process can continue through at least three generations in subalpine fir.

Tree islands commonly develop on topographically favorable microsites such as atop hummocks within a snowy basin or on the crest of a ridge. Another fascinating variation of the tree island is the extensive parallel "ribbon forest and snow glade pattern" which covers broad uplands in the timberline zone of the Rocky Mountains (Billings 1969, Arno 1970). Unlike the ridgetop ribbon forest described earlier, this formation consists of many parallel bands of stunted trees. These average perhaps 15 feet in width and extend perpendicularly to the prevailing winds. These ribbon forests are separated by bands of moist meadow vegetation (snow glades). Ribbon forests are essentially elongated tree islands that function like snow fences. The glades in between are piled high with drifts that persist until mid-summer and thus prevent tree establishment.

Flagged Krummholz

Above the tree line on windy slopes, conifers are reduced to progressively shorter krummholz (shrubby) forms. Flagged krummholz has erect, wind-battered stems ranging from about 6 to 12 feet in height. The flagged stems protrude from the snowpack in winter and are thrashed and ice-blasted to such an extent that even the bark on the windward side is abraded and polished. Often only a tuft of foliage remains on the leeward side near the tip of the stem (the "flag"), and a band without foliage occurs immediately below the flag—in the zone where ice particles are blasted most heavily across the surface of the winter snowpack. Below the erect stems lies a large, luxuriant cushion of foliage that is normally encased in (and protected by) the winter snowpack.

While it is relatively easy for low cushion growth to survive, only a few erect shoots are produced that do not soon succumb to winter desiccation. Flags represent the few stems that were able to grow quickly enough (over several years) through the severe ice-blasting zone to live. Even so, flags

Krummholz of whitebark pine at Kearsarge Pass in California's Sierra Nevada

survive only marginally; they are plastered with glaze ice and thrashed thoroughly many times each winter.

On certain wind-exposed slopes, generally on warm aspects, krummholz forms dense thickets that are difficult to walk or climb through. Not all species form krummholz, however, and some, such as Great Basin bristlecone pine, form krummholz only in certain mountain ranges (LaMarche and Mooney 1972).

Cushion Krummholz

A variety of wind-shaped forms of stunted trees and krummholz in Colorado have been classified in relation to wind direction and velocity (Marr 1977a, Davis 1980). Cushion krummholz is the most severe wind-caused deformity of tree growth. It ranges in size from a miniature stunted conifer shrub only a few inches high and a foot long growing in the shelter of a rock to a massive, sprawling, circular mat 50 feet across and 3 feet high, again representing a single conifer.

Some cushions remain in one place throughout their few hundred years of existence. Often, their shoots grow densely toward the point of critical wind exposure and there form a perfect hedged surface, as if trimmed by a meticulous gardener. Other cushions, especially those in certain locations exposed to strong winds from only one direction, move downwind at a measurable rate. Moving krummholz stringers of Engelmann spruce and subalpine fir in the Colorado Front Range become established as seedlings in a depression or rock-sheltered microsite, then grow in the leeward direction and out of the protected spot (Marr 1977b). As they continue to spread, through layering, in the leeward direction, utilizing the small measure of shelter they have created, their windward end (or starting point) eventually dies out. Thereafter, the wind-exposed end dies back a little more each year.

A massive krummholz cushion of Alaska-cedar on Mount Angeles in the Olympic Mountains, Washington

Prostrate tree form of lodgepole pine on Gray Wolf Ridge in the Olympic Mountains, Washington

Thus, the entire krummholz stringer moves downwind, somewhat as a gravel island in a river moves downstream, at rates ranging from about 7 to 23 feet per century (Marr 1977b). Weathered remnants of krummholz stringers can be found extending in a windward direction from the current living growth; these skeletons suggest that some krummholz cushions moved at least 50 feet over a long period of time.

Some krummholz islands die back on the windward end faster than they grow to the leeward and are eventually eliminated. Others grow more rapidly than they recede and thus become large. However, after attaining a certain critical size, they will produce a large snowdrift which persists long enough into spring to allow snow-mold fungus to develop and to kill the leeward branches.

Despite the meager amount and somewhat transitory nature of the shelter provided by moving krummholz, a scientist in Colorado found that mountain gooseberry (*Ribes montigenum*) grows within the krummholz but never out in the wind-lashed tundra (Marr 1977b). Similarly, other undergrowth species from the subalpine forest ascend into rigorous alpine habitats only by growing within the protective crown of a krummholz tree.

One other form of low krummholz is the totally prostrate tree that sometimes develops among the timberline pines. A good example of this is the stand of lodgepole pine (*Pinus contorta* var. *latifolia?*) atop Gray Wolf Ridge in the Olympic Mountains (Arno 1966). These stout trees become progressively shorter toward the ridge crest, and ultimately, in a windy saddle, they develop trunks 1 to 2 feet thick and 20 feet long growing straight and horizontally leeward along the stony ground. An increment

Alpine willow at 10,700 feet in Yosemite National Park, California

borer (a hollow drill used for determining the age of trees) revealed that some of these prostrate trees are about 300 years old.

The ultimate reduction in stature (an escape from the adverse elements) is achieved by dwarf birch and especially by certain species of willow that grow beyond the alpine and arctic limits of conifers. Willows (*Salix*) and birches (*Betula*) are widely distributed throughout the Northern Hemisphere, and although they are most familiar as trees and tall shrubs, they form dwarf shrubs in the Arctic and in some alpine areas. The dwarf arctic birch, *Betula nana,* forms dense mats of low shrubs six inches to three feet high at and far beyond the arctic timberline. But several species of willows are even more prostrate and hardier, extending as far north as land goes and high into the alpine tundra.

Willows have achieved this hardiness partly by becoming ground-level plants with branch systems appressed against or embedded in the surface soil. Consequently, they are less exposed to the frigid winter air. In summer, they send up leafy shoots and erect catkins only an inch or two above the surface, making maximum use of the solar heat absorbed at ground level. As a result of this growth form, alpine willows often resemble a lawn! Extensive surface mats of willow are a major component of the tundra landscape on moist alpine sites from Colorado and California to northern Canada and Alaska. An exceptionally fine example of this growth form is the "turf" of willow that completely covers a soggy, sediment-filled cirque lake basin at Royal Basin in the Olympic Mountains (Arno 1966).

Woodland Formations

Often approaching lower timberline and sometimes at alpine timberline, the forest remains dense while the trees gradually become short and then give way abruptly to treeless terrain. Such a band of dense, stunted forest or woodland often separates the taller subalpine forest from the alpine tundra in the coastal mountains of southern Alaska. Bands of dense, stunted forest are also prevalent at timberline in the White Mountains and on other high peaks in northern New England (Reiners and Lang 1979). Relatively smooth topography and uniform soil conditions (as opposed to rugged, broken terrain) tend to favor development of this growth form at the alpine timberline. Ample moisture also seems to be necessary. At upper timberlines this stunted woodland is usually made up of the same species found in the subalpine forest, although in southern Alaska, Sitka alder often forms a band of scrub above the conifer tree line.

In contrast, lower timberlines have more diverse and extensive woodland formations, although some of these are also made up of stunted forms of the same species found in the forests immediately above. Perhaps the most striking example of this is the woodland of stunted ponderosa pines at the foot of the Colorado Front Range, which merges gradually into a taller ponderosa pine forest with increasing elevation. More often, however, the woodland formations that occur at lower timberline in the semiarid West represent a distinct vegetation zone dominated by different species than the forest proper. Examples include pinyon pine, juniper, and oak woodlands, and chaparral. The lowermost forest is often made up of ponderosa pine or interior Douglas-fir, attaining heights of 50 to 100 feet, and in many northern inland areas (e.g., in Idaho and Montana) this forest gives way directly to grassland or sagebrush without an intervening woodland. The woodland zone becomes increasingly broad and diverse (sometimes consisting of two or three different bands of vegetation) southward in the western United States, where the forest proper retreats to relatively high elevations because of the intense heat, evaporation demand, and soil drought.

REGENERATION

Seed Crops and Dispersal

Timberline tree species can regenerate under conditions that would be intolerable for seedlings of most forest species. Still, seed-produced regeneration depends upon a sequence of favorable events, and at timberline this schedule is seldom fulfilled: (1) a good seed crop must be produced; (2) adequate numbers of seeds must be dispersed to suitable seedbeds or microsites; and (3) favorable weather conditions, such as lack of severe summer frost or drought, must prevail for the first few growing seasons.

Good seed crops occur at intervals of about 3 to 10 years at forest line and considerably less often at tree line. Even when there is a good seed

Week-old seedling whitebark pine in a clump of alpine tundra plants

crop, only a very small proportion of viable seeds reach microsites suitable for establishment. Where exposure to wind or solar heating is severe, the seed may need to land in a small depression or the lee of a rock to have even a slim chance of becoming established. In arctic and moist alpine timberlines, a nearly continuous mat of lichens, heath, and other low-growing vegetation prevents seeds from reaching a suitable seedbed. Wildfire or other disturbance may be required to temporarily reduce the competition from low-growing plants or to expose a mineral soil seedbed (Black and Bliss 1978). Black spruce, a tree of the arctic timberline, has cones that hang on the upper boughs and retain some of their viable seeds for several years. These cones can be opened fully by the heat of a fire so that their remaining (stored) seed is cast upon the ashy seedbed (Fowells 1965).

Because of the extremely harsh climate, seedlings at tree lines develop comparatively slowly, both in shoot growth and hardening and also in root growth (Tranquillini 1979). Ironically, because of severe climate, seedlings develop poorly as well, which in turn renders them ill-equipped to cope with those environmental conditions. The hardiness of the seed itself sometimes becomes a disadvantage. Seeds of subalpine fir, Pacific silver fir (*Abies amabilis*), California red fir (*A. magnifica*), and mountain hemlock become active at such low temperatures that they sometimes germinate and perish on the surface of wet snowpack (Franklin and Krueger 1968, Arno 1966).

Young seedlings are also vulnerable to being uprooted by frost heaving on moist sites, to being girdled by overheating at the ground surface on southern exposures (especially at lower timberline), and to being gnawed by rodents or other animals. A beneficial fungus-rootlet relationship seems to be essential for successful establishment of trees at timberlines and on other severe sites (Tranquillini 1979, Spurr and Barnes 1980). Such fungus-root associations are called mycorrhizae; they vastly increase the efficiency of tree rootlets in taking up water and nutrients from the soil. Evidently mycorrhizae are available at essentially all timberline sites, and so the absence of mycorrhizae may not be a real limiting factor for seedling establishment.

Considering the numerous hazards and constraints on seed-based regeneration, it is a wonder that seedlings *do* become established. A little seed contains only a small amount of stored food for its embryo, so the embryo needs nearly perfect growing conditions to germinate and survive. Obviously there must be mitigating factors that favor seed-based regeneration. One such factor is that enormous quantities of seed are occasionally produced by most timberline species (often within the contiguous forest), and winds or animal agents can disperse these into many of the potentially suitable microsites. Species with small seeds usually bear staggering numbers of them. Small seeds almost invariably have large wings or tufts of cottony material (e.g., in willow and cottonwood) which allow them to be carried great distances in the wind.

Large-seeded species are generally aided in dispersal by birds and sometimes by rodents or even livestock. This category includes several species of junipers found near lower timberline in the semi-arid West. The most widespread are western juniper (*Juniperus occidentalis*), Rocky Mountain juniper (*J. scopulorum*), Utah juniper (*J. osteosperma*), one-seed juniper (*J. monosperma*), and alligator juniper (*J. deppeana*). Birds and other animals readily gobble up the small, bluish, berrylike fruits of junipers and distribute the seeds across the landscape. Juniper seed does not germinate readily unless its fleshy covering is dissolved by passing through an animal's digestive tract (Nichol 1937). The rich juniper fruits cling to the trees all winter, making an excellent food source, and evidently birds are the principal agent responsible for scarification and dissemination of juniper seed (Phillips 1910).

Two species of birds, the Clark's nutcracker (*Nucifraga columbiana*) and the pinyon jay (*Gymnorhinus cyanocephalus*), "plant" pine seeds at alpine and lower timberlines in western North America. Tree species involved include whitebark, limber, ponderosa, Jeffrey, and the various pinyon pines. The nutcrackers and jays attack the ripening cones of these trees, deposit as many as 100 of the nutlike seeds in their sublingual (throat) pouch, and then fly off to a caching site where they bury small groups of seeds in the soil at a depth of about one inch, suitable for germination (Ligon 1978, Tomback 1978, Lanner and Vander Wall 1980). Although the birds feed on seed caches heavily throughout much of the year, many caches are left unharvested, and they in turn produce small clumps of pine seedlings the following summer.

It seems significant that the Clark's nutcrackers and pinyon jays plant seeds of whitebark, limber, and pinyon pines in open areas on southern exposures, often in bare mineral soil. Clark's nutcrackers cached an estimated 13,600 limber pine seeds per acre in an open, burned area in the Raft River Mountains of northern Utah (Lanner and Vander Wall 1980). In such areas, seeds are retrievable for a long period because of more rapid snowmelt. Moreover, these sites are nearly ideal for germination of the pines!

This avian planting program is quite successful, judging from the frequent small clumps of pine saplings in burns and other open areas far from a seed source. In the northeastern Olympic Mountains, lone whitebark pine trees and saplings grow along alpine ridges that are often a few miles from the nearest possible seed source (Arno 1966). Another suggestion of planting by Clark's nutcrackers is illustrated by the numerous clumps of whitebark seedlings that occur in a low-elevation ponderosa pine forest (3800 feet) where my family lives, south of Missoula, Montana. The nearest whitebark pine seed source is over two miles away, above the 7000-foot level on a mountain range. We often observe Clark's nutcrackers feeding on the ponderosa pine seed in this forest early in autumn. Apparently the birds bring pouches full of whitebark pine seeds down from the high ridge.

It has long been known that at alpine timberlines in Europe and Asia nutcrackers (*Nucifraga* spp.) are critically important in caching—and thus in dispersing and planting—seeds of mountain pines such as Swiss stone pine (*Pinus cembra*), Siberian stone pine (*P. sibirica*), and Japanese stone pine (*P. pumila*) (Turcek and Kelso 1968). In western North America, nutcrackers and pinyon jays have probably evolved a mutually beneficial relationship with large-seeded pines in which the birds provide a primary means of seed dissemination and planting, while the trees provide the birds an abundant and highly nutritious food (Ligon 1978). In addition, an abundance of developing green cones can stimulate breeding by pinyon jays (Ligon 1974). The seeds that are eaten are the price the trees pay for reliable dispersal and planting.

Anticipation of good cone crops apparently also affects litter sizes in Douglas squirrels (*Tamiasciurus douglasi*) in British Columbia (Smith 1970). Tree squirrels harvest and store great quantities of cones, from a number of tree species, in rotten logs and in the ground, but these hoards apparently do not result directly in many successful new seedlings. However, chipmunks, ground squirrels, deer mice, and other rodents pilfer the cone hoards, as well as picking up loose seeds, and then make small seed caches in the surface soil, some of which remain to germinate.

Seedling Invasion

Another intriguing aspect of seed-initiated regeneration is the invasion of conifer seedlings into meadows, heathland, and snowdrift sites at upper timberline as well as into the semi-arid grasslands at lower timberline. Ecologist Jerry Franklin and others (1971) studied this phenomenon at timberline meadows and heathland on Mount Rainier and elsewhere in

Douglas-fir invading the former grassland on the south slopes of the Tobacco Root Mountains, Montana. The distinct lower timberline in the distance is on the north slope of the Ruby Range.

the Cascades. They found that most of the conifers became established in relatively dry periods (centered on the "Dust Bowl" 1930s) when glaciers were markedly retreating. Subalpine fir and mountain hemlock are the principal invaders, but their growth has been slow in these snowy glades. Farther inland, alpine larch saplings of similar age can be found invading certain snow-glade sites (Arno 1970, Franklin and others 1971).

Similar invasion by Engelmann spruce, lodgepole pine, and whitebark pine occurs in meadows near forest line in Wyoming's Wind River Range (Dunwiddie 1977). This invasion began about 1890 but was most intense between 1940 and 1963 and nearly ceased thereafter. Cattle grazing was heavy between 1890 and 1937, and it apparently triggered some of the invasion by reducing competing meadow vegetation; but the grazing cattle also trampled many seedlings. Cattle numbers were markedly reduced after 1937, and this aided tree invasion because meadow vegetation was still removed but with a minimum of trampling damage to new seedlings. Grazing ceased after 1962 and this essentially ended the invasion. However, grazing would not be a factor in some of the steep, rocky, heath-covered snow-glade sites that have been invaded by conifers in the Cascades and Northern Rockies.

The limited invasion at upper timberlines differs from the widespread and fast-growing conifer encroachment commonly found at lower timberlines in the semi-arid West. The thickening and expansion of forests at lower timberlines is generally related to grazing that reduced competing vegetation and to fire suppression that has allowed young trees to escape burning. Even before organized fire suppression was developed in the early 1900s, heavy grazing had reduced the amount and continuity of cured grass fuel, thereby reducing the frequency and intensity of the grass fires that had kept out the conifers.

Layering

Layering is the form of vegetative reproduction in which lower branches of certain tree species take root where they are pressed against moist ground. Horticulturists often propagate trees that cannot readily be grown from cuttings by inducing them to layer and then severing the branch connection and transplanting the rooted branch. In natural stands not all rooted branches develop into new erect stems, but (particularly if the main trunk dies) they have the potential to form a new tree of identical genetic characteristics. Many trees of moist, snowy sites—including true firs, spruces, mountain hemlock, and Alaska-cedar—have developed the ability to spread through layering. Black spruce at the arctic timberline appears capable of maintaining its populations indefinitely through this means alone. This may be necessary in some areas where dense surface vegetation, such as the caribou lichen (*Cladonia* spp.), presents a formidable barrier to seedling establishment (Savile 1963). Black spruce is also well adapted to sexual reproduction, which is necessary following stand-destroying wildfires that render layering impossible.

Swampy-site conifers such as black spruce, tamarack, and balsam fir commonly layer, while species typically confined to well-drained sites (e.g., white spruce and many pines) do not. Layering of balsam fir and black spruce occurs in wet lowland boreal forests as well as at the alpine timberlines in New England.

Generally, in the mountains of western North America layering becomes a significant form of regeneration only near the alpine tree line. However, occasionally subalpine fir and Engelmann spruce will layer at relatively low elevations on moist sites. A striking example of this is found near the lower timberline near Jenny Lake in Jackson Hole, Wyoming. Here, the early-day timberline ecologist Robert Griggs (1938) described a hollow-centered timber atoll as being 60 feet across but with an open interior 30 feet in diameter. This layered doughnut-shaped cluster was vacant in the center and so dense around the edges that, when an entrance hole and gate were made, the compound served as a horse corral!

COMPETITION AND SUCCESSION

Competition among different species of plants for light, water, minerals, or any other environmental commodity results in vegetation change. Competition is most intense between plants having similar life forms and environmental requirements (Billings 1966)—an example of this would be competition among several species of evergreen conifers in a dense subalpine forest.

Competition is a driving force in the process of vegetative change known as succession. Over a long period of time without any major disturbance (such as severe wildfire, insect epidemic, violent windstorm, avalanche, or logging) certain species become dominant because they are able to regenerate beneath a dense overstory canopy. Often one or two of these "shade tolerant" tree species are capable of maintaining dominance indefinitely in the absence of disturbance. They are termed "climax" or "potential climax" species.

Secondary Succession

When a dense forest is destroyed by wildfire or other major disturbances, fast-growing "shade intolerant" species have an opportunity to become established. In fact, a series of increasingly tolerant tree communities may arise after major disturbance, ultimately giving way (after a few centuries) to the climax community type. This process of vegetation change on a single site is called succession, and the revegetation of a formerly occupied site is termed secondary succession.

A simplified example of secondary succession in subalpine or subarctic forests is the initial establishment of a fireweed (*Epilobium angustifolium*) and grass community, followed by a young stand of intolerant trees such as lodgepole or jack pine and aspen. This in turn gives way to tolerant but slower-growing spruce or fir as climax is approached.

At arctic and alpine timberlines, competition and succession take place in an intricate mosaic pattern. For instance, tree islands are pioneered by hardy but intolerant pines which provide shelter for the more tolerant spruce, fir, or hemlocks that eventually replace them. Up near the

Subalpine fir growing up through the protective canopy of a hardy alpine larch in the Montana Bitterroot Range

Sapling of krummholz whitebark pine growing beneath the shelter of a krummholz snag

krummholz line, however, succession may scarcely be detectable. Here, environmental stresses are so severe that disturbance never ceases.

Consider the following example of forest succession after wildfire on a site between forest line and tree line. Re-establishment of vegetation is slower than it would be below forest line, and alpine tundra species appear in the initial community. Tree seedlings require a few decades to re-establish themselves in the open, exposed site, which has a microclimate nearly as severe as that of alpine tundra. (Some of these "deforested" sites will remain open indefinitely.) The hardiest shade-intolerant species become well established first, but eventually (over a few centuries) the tolerant species become co-dominant.

However, climax conditions cannot be attained because of the mechanical damage and desiccation caused by strong winds, massive loads of ice and snow, summer frosts, and other factors. These stresses maintain a dynamic equilibrium at the forest frontier. As a result, any tree species that is hardy enough to survive the harsh growing conditions will be able to remain as a member of the climax community. Thus, the effect of competition among species is subdued at timberline, and although succession toward climax proceeds in the patches of forest or tree islands, it is periodically re-started when other patches are broken down and openings are invaded by seedlings.

Lower timberlines are also tension zones where an unfavorable climate hampers forest succession. As we have seen, however, in the past many lower timberlines were kept at slightly higher elevations because of recurring wildfires. The frequent fires of pre-1900 times generally favored development of grass or shrublands rather than forests. During the twentieth century lower elevation forests have spread downslope into former grass and shrublands. This forest growth apparently represents the climax condition under the present climate.

Primary Succession

Another basic type of vegetational development is commonly found at alpine timberlines in recently glaciated or volcanically devastated areas or wherever new geologic material is exposed. This is primary succession and it applies to the initial colonization of formerly unvegetated sites. Textbooks often portray primary succession on a rocky, glacial site as beginning with lichens and then mosses. Over long periods of time (perhaps centuries), organic material is built up and the rock is sufficiently weathered so that grasses and other herbs, and later, shrubs, and finally trees can develop. However, exploration of sites near retreating glaciers in coastal Alaska and the Northwest will reveal that timberline trees often colonize glacial moraines, fresh talus, or glacially scoured bedrock. One prerequisite for tree invasion on recently deglaciated sites (near the snouts or flanks of retreating glaciers) is that the growing season must be sufficiently warm. This requirement is often met near the tongues (lower extensions) of glaciers in the snowy but mild coastal mountains.

Examples of prompt development of tall Sitka alder shrubs followed by subalpine conifers can be observed near retreating glaciers on Mount Hood in Oregon, Mount Rainier and Mount Baker in Washington, and near glaciers flowing down from Alaska's Juneau Icefield, as well as those emptying into Glacier Bay. At Glacier Bay detailed studies of primary succession were begun by pioneer ecologist William S. Cooper (1923) and have been expanded in recent decades (e.g., Lawrence 1958). Several years after glacial retreat, the prostrate shrub mountain-avens (*Dryas drummondii*) and then Sitka alder become the dominant vegetation. These species, especially alder, fix atmospheric nitrogen, thereby enriching the soil. This fertilization allows black cottonwood, Sitka spruce, and western hemlock to grow vigorously up through the alder thickets. Although such soil enrichment no doubt hastens forest development, subalpine trees, most notably alpine larch, often invade high-elevation glacial moraines without preliminary occupation by mountain-avens, alder, or appreciable amounts of other nitrogen-fixing plants (Arno and Habeck 1972).

Timberline trees involved in primary succession can readily be seen in the Sierra Nevada and other high mountain areas that have vast expanses of glacially scoured bedrock. Bedrock domes and canyon walls have small fissures in which fine materials and moisture accumulate. These cracks often support scattered trees of several species — gnarled, ancient Sierra junipers (*Juniperus occidentalis* var. *australis*) are characteristic in the High Sierra. Virgin talus slopes or boulder piles at the foot of towering cliffs are similarly colonized by subalpine trees even though only a minimum of lesser vegetation has developed. Fresh talus is a particularly common site for alpine larch in the inland Northwest.

3

Timberlines through Time

Since timberlines are distinct vegetational boundaries dependent on certain levels of temperature and moisture, they can serve as a useful guide for identifying past climatic changes. Timberlines can function as climatic indicators in various ways. During the most recent Pleistocene glacial period (ending about 12,000 years ago) a cold, wet climate in the Southwest and the Great Basin allowed forest trees to spread to lower elevations than their present lower timberlines. Fossil remains of forest trees, including Douglas-fir, have been found in caves that occur far below and often great distances away from modern forests. These fossils include pollen, leaves, and twigs deposited in nests (middens) of woodrats and in layers of the dung of large Pleistocene herbivores that became extinct several thousand years ago. The giant ground sloth, nearly as large as an elephant, ate only plants and left large deposits of now-fossilized dung in southwestern caves. Plant remains in these deposits, in what is now a desert shrub or pinyon-juniper zone, clearly indicate that lower timberline was 1500 to 2000 feet lower during the late Pleistocene and until about 8700 years ago (Spaulding and Petersen 1980).

Fossil foliage of the subalpine trees bristlecone and limber pine dating from this "pluvial" (rainy) period have been found in ancient woodrat ("packrat") middens at the relatively low elevation of 6300 feet on Clark Mountain in California's Mojave Desert, southwest of Las Vegas (Mehringer and Ferguson 1969). These midden specimens were determined by radiocarbon dating to be about 29,000, 24,000, and 12,500 years old, and they constitute a remarkable find since no alpine timberline species presently exist on or near this small mountain range. Based upon the current elevational distribution of bristlecone and limber pines in the nearest subalpine mountain range, 50 miles to the north, it appears that subalpine forests occurred at least 2000 feet lower during the pluvial period.

Dates of fossil dung, fossil wood, or any other once-living material can be obtained by measuring the ratio of radiocarbon to normal carbon. Radiocarbon is the radioactive form of carbon (carbon 14) present naturally in the atmosphere. It and normal carbon (carbon 12) are absorbed by all living things; when they die, the radiocarbon decays at a very slow but measurable rate. However, as will be discussed later, radiocarbon dating is only approximate and has been much improved by cross-referencing objects dated in this manner to wood samples of known age taken from ancient timberline trees.

Another use of timberline as a climatic indicator lies in measuring the timing and magnitude of the major warm period (the Hypsithermal) since the last ice age. Remains of large trees above the current alpine timberlines in the Great Basin, the Cairngorm Mountains of Scotland, and at numerous locations north of the current polar timberline indicate that the climate was substantially warmer a few thousand years ago (Wardle 1974). Dates of the Hypsithermal vary by region.

Existing timberline trees can also be used to detect short-term fluctuations in temperature and precipitation. For instance, a forestry researcher (Keen 1937) studied width patterns of annual growth rings in old-growth ponderosa pine stands in semi-arid eastern Oregon. By cross-dating ring-width records (chronologies) from several trees, he was able to develop a master chronology extending back almost 700 years. After comparing these growth patterns with available weather records, he concluded that the drought, or warm-dry period, extending from 1908 through the 1930s was the most severe in the life span of these trees.

Evidence from Bristlecone Pine

The most definitive work on climatic changes in relation to tree growth has been performed using Great Basin bristlecone pine in eastern California and Nevada. Often in this area, pinyon pine and juniper form a woodland on the lower slopes of the mountain ranges rising out of the high desert. Then, there is a treeless sagebrush belt. This gives way upslope to the narrow belt of forest formed of bristlecone and limber pines, extending from about 9000 to 11,500 feet.

Near their lower limits on the dry southern exposures between 9500 and 10,000 feet, bristlecone pines are especially sensitive to variations in annual moisture (Ferguson 1968). These otherwise barren, gravelly sites receive as little as 12 inches of annual precipitation, yet they support the oldest and most climatically sensitive trees. In the White Mountains, east of California's southern Sierra Nevada, many living bristlecone pines on dry sites have been found, through increment borings, to be over 4000 years old. The oldest known is somewhat over 4600 years.

The relative widths of growth rings in these dry-site bristlecone pines are closely correlated to variations in available moisture and, hence, to variations in annual precipitation. The ring-width patterns are consistent from tree to tree; thus, researchers (dendrochronologists) have been able to construct master chronologies, based on living trees, stretching back over 4000 years. They have also extended the master chronology for the White Mountains back an additional 5000 years (bringing the total chronology to about 9000 years) by using snags and remnants of former trees. These ancient fragments come from trees that died thousands of years ago. Snags of some bristlecone pines that *died* 2000 years ago are still standing; their pitch-impregnated wood does not decay in the cold, dry desert environment.

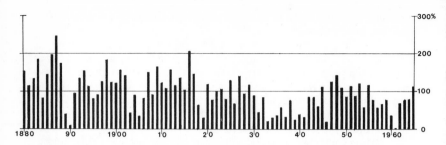

Pattern of annual growth for Douglas-fir trees at lower timberline near Helena, Montana. 100% line = average growth (data from Stokes and others 1973).

Bristlecone pine ring-width chronologies correlate well with those derived from other drought-sensitive tree species growing on dry sites and with those derived from 200-year-old sagebrush plants. Similar tree-ring chronologies, based upon several species, have been developed for areas throughout the semi-arid western United States and adjacent regions of Canada (Stokes and others 1973). These chronologies serve as indicators of annual variations in moisture for well over 500 years.

Samples of precisely dated bristlecone pine wood have been used to test the reliability of radiocarbon dating, which has led to the development of correction factors for improving the accuracy of the latter. Also, ring-width patterns from logs in prehistoric dwellings have been matched with regional tree-ring chronologies, and the result is a precise determination of the years the trees were cut for construction of the dwellings.

The 9000-year bristlecone pine master chronology has been computerized to simplify its use in correlation tasks. However, the ring-width patterns of sensitive trees are so distinctive that patterns from wood remnants of unknown age can be visually fitted into the master chronology. Missing growth rings are rather common in increment cores from drought-stressed trees and may even extend around the entire circumference of a tree. Nevertheless, missing rings can readily be detected through comparison to ring-width patterns in a master chronology (Stokes and Smiley 1968).

Another bristlecone pine tree-ring chronology is an index derived from *temperature*-sensitive trees that grow at the alpine tree line (LaMarche and Stockton 1974). Scientists have also noted the presence of "fossil stands" of bristlecone pine above present upper timberlines in the White Mountains and the Snake Range. These remnants indicate that the forest extended at least 330 feet in elevation higher than at present during a warmer climatic period from 4000 to 2000 years ago (LaMarche and Mooney 1967, 1972).

In their splendidly illustrated book *Timberline Ancients,* David Muench and Darwin Lambert (1972) explain still other types of scientific interpretations of past events that have been discovered through the study of bristlecone pine. These include the identification of natural geological

Remnant of whitebark pine among tundra vegetation

erosion rates of one foot per thousand years on some sites, detectable through studying the position of tree root systems. Another discovery was that severe summer frosts damaged cells in certain growth rings (precise years) at various times during the last 2500 years.

Evidence from Pollen Deposition

Bog and lake sediments also yield information on the changing positions of timberlines. Researchers known as palynologists study the pollen "rain," or sediment deposits, contained in cores extracted from bogs and ponds that date back to the Pleistocene glaciation. Some subalpine bogs in the Rockies started out as frigid glacial pools 12,000 years ago, and in some cases layers of sediments 25 to 40 feet thick accumulated during this period. Throughout the Northwest, distinctive bands of volcanic ash appear in such sediments. Most prominent is material from the explosion of Mount Mazama (now Crater Lake, Oregon) about 6700 years ago. This eruption left ash deposits as much as 8 to 12 inches thick in bogs in the Northern Rockies (Mehringer and others 1977b).

The bog at 7000-foot Lost Trail Pass on the Idaho-Montana divide (adjacent to the ski area parking lot) has provided a record of vegetation and climate since the Pleistocene glaciers melted 11,500 years ago. For the first few centuries after meltwaters formed the glacial pond here, there is little sign of organic material in the sediments, which are glacial gravels and silts (Mehringer and others 1977a). Then, sagebrush (perhaps an alpine form) and a scattering of spruce pollen appear, suggesting that timberline trees had migrated upslope and perhaps northward to the vicinity. Between about 7000 and 4000 years ago, the pollen rain and "macrofossils"—such as needles, seeds, and twigs—in the sedimentary core indicate that a Douglas-fir forest occupied the site. This was during the Hypsithermal or warm period. The current, colder climate supports a subalpine fir-lodgepole pine forest at Lost Trail Pass.

Fluctuations of upper timberline in Jasper National Park, Alberta, have recently been estimated based on sediment cores and fossil logs collected in the alpine tundra (Kearney and Luckman 1983). Timberlines evidently reached as much as 650 feet higher than present ones between 8700 and 5900 years ago, during the Hypsithermal Period, while the lowest timberlines recorded during the past 8700 years are those of the last few centuries.

Fluctuations of alpine timberline in the LaPlata Mountains of southwestern Colorado were determined using sediment cores (Petersen 1976, 1981). Findings suggest that over the last 10,000 years timberline was higher than at present during three short periods, whereas it dropped below its present level during eight periods. Studies of sedimentary cores at lower elevations in the LaPlata Mountains have given insight into the changing positions of drought-caused, lower timberlines. For instance, Ken Petersen's analysis suggests that soon after the year 1150 A.D. there was a dramatic reduction in summer rainfall and a cooling of summer temperatures in the Four Corners region of Colorado, Utah, Arizona, and New Mexico. The cool and dry summers resulted in a shrinking forest zone, in that lower timberline rose while alpine timberline descended. This climatic change apparently contributed to abandonment of the area by the corn-growing Anasazi Indians and hence the abandonment of the cliff dwellings at Mesa Verde.

Movement of Arctic Timberline

Evidence of movement at the arctic timberline includes peat bog sediments far out in the tundra that contain tree pollen (Ritchie and Hare 1971). Ancient tree trunks and beaver-gnawed wood have also been found far north of the modern limits of trees and of beavers in northwestern Alaska. Fossil tree pollen and a 5000-year-old, rooted white spruce stump (dated by the radiocarbon method) were discovered on Canada's tundra-covered Tuktoyaktuk Peninsula (Ritchie and Hare 1971). This indicates that during the Hypsithermal warm period 8500 to 5500 years ago, the arctic timberline was about 217 miles farther north than it is today. Evidently, during the Hypsithermal the cold, cloudy weather associated with the "Arctic Front" was displaced northward from its current average summertime location (Kay 1978). This produced markedly warmer summers than at present at the arctic timberline. Average daily temperatures for the summer months were about 9°F higher than at present, and the growing season was about 30 days longer.

In much of northern Canada and Alaska the arctic timberline has migrated southward during the past 5500 years in response to colder summer conditions. The northern limit of trees in Canada is often defined by severely stunted white or black spruce growing in what appear to be vegetatively reproduced groups confined to sheltered locations in valleys (Nichols 1976). These diminutive trees were originally derived many centuries ago from sexually produced seedlings, but today they rarely bear viable seeds and yield only small quantities of pollen. In the forest-tundra zone of the Northwest Territories, black spruce has failed to regenerate after wildfires; whereas further south, this species readily regenerates after wildfires (Black and Bliss 1980). The northernmost stands evidently represent a "stranded" northward extension of forest line which gained that position during a warmer period in the eighteenth and early nineteenth centuries.

Evidence from many investigations of recent timberline positions in Alaska, Canada, and the Soviet Union suggests that in some regions timberline is advancing northward, while in others it is retreating or merely maintaining its position. Probably the most dramatic advance of a northern timberline is that of the Sitka spruce migrating westward into the maritime tundra on Kodiak Island, Alaska. Sitka spruce is advancing at the rate of about one mile per century, following the westward-creeping 50°F isotherm (for July), which becomes the limiting factor about 250 miles beyond the present tree limit (Griggs 1934 and 1937). The uniqueness of this forest advance is suggested by the fact that peat bogs on Kodiak Island received no spruce pollen between the last Pleistocene glaciation and the recent deposits.

No doubt some of the vagueness in scientific knowledge concerning movement of arctic timberline can be attributed to its exceedingly slow response to climatic changes. In the case of a climatic warming trend, for instance, an *alpine* timberline might be able to advance, via seed-produced regeneration, in a few decades to the nearby higher position of the climatic limit. In contrast, it would take the diffuse polar timberline vastly longer to adjust to comparable warming because it would have to migrate hundreds of times as far. Thus, alpine timberlines are more sensitive to a marked climatic change.

4
Human Uses of Timberline

Mankind and domestic animals have caused extensive, often severe, damage to upper timberline environments throughout most of the world, sometimes with catastrophic consequences for human life and agriculture. Because large human populations have developed only in recent times in North America, damage to this continent's timberline ecosystems has been far less conspicuous than in the Old World or in the Andes of South America. In much of the world, intensive use and exploitation of alpine and arctic timberlines have taken place over several centuries, or even millenniums.

Like former grasslands and lower-elevation forests, *lower timberlines* are within the primary zone of human occupancy throughout the earth. In most of the world it would be difficult to find even small segments of lower timberlines in any semblance of their "natural" or "primeval" condition. In fact, those terms would be hard to define meaningfully, since human impacts (man-caused fires, clearing, cultivation, heavy grazing) have been concentated in such environments for thousands of years. In contrast, lower timberlines in the western United States and adjacent Canada are exceptional in often bearing some resemblance to their pre-European settlement condition. Most of these areas have been logged and heavily grazed, but often the forest has regenerated and become denser than in early days.

Only in the last decade or two has intensive development spread along the lower timberlines of western North America. This has come largely in the form of suburban and rural subdivisions and is an outgrowth of the greatly expanding human population in the intermountain West. Between 1970 and 1980 this eight-state region experienced the greatest surge of growth, on a percentage basis (37 percent), of any region in the United States. Land prices, speculation, subdivision, and development will no doubt continue in this manner, and lower timberlines will be converted into cultural environments. Significant exceptions to this trend could be made in sizeable areas of public lands, especially in national forests, where the management direction is generally to maintain and utilize natural vegetative communities. Even in these areas, however, severe impacts in the form of mineral and petroleum exploration and development, pipelines, major roads, transmission lines, and other development will occur in increasing numbers.

Some protected natural areas have been established, and hopefully large areas of public lands at lower timberline will be retained in moderately used grazing, timberland, and wildlife habitat status. At most lower timberlines in the mountain West, periodic use of prescribed fire will be necessary to stimulate wildlife forage and perpetuate vigorous tree growth. (As was discussed on page 51 and 52, the combination of heavy grazing and fire suppression has brought about an unprecedented thickening and decadent growth in many stands at lower timberline.)

In the Mediterranean-Middle East region, "desertification" of the landscape, including lower timberlines and dry forest types, has occurred through 7000 years, as is vividly described in the classic report by W. C. Lowdermilk (1953) of the U.S. Soil Conservation Service. Vast mountain forests in this large region have been reduced to small groves surviving in the fenced grounds of monasteries. These include the formerly great forests of ancient Phoenicia, dominated by the cedar of Lebanon (*Cedrus libani*). Only four small groves of this famous Lebanese cedar forest have survived. Most important of these is the Tripoli grove which 300 years ago had been reduced by rapacious goat grazing to just 43 scattered trees. About that time a little church was built in this grove and a stone wall erected to keep out the goats. Afterwards, the veteran trees seeded in a fine stand that filled most of the compound.

Most nations of the Middle East have made some attempt to re-establish ancient forests, but success has been very limited because it is nearly impossible politically to control grazing. Also, severe erosion over the millenniums has degraded the mountain soils, making them drier, stonier, lower in nutrients, and thus poor substrates for tree establishment.

Similar human influence extends to upper timberline in much of the world, with bad consequences for mankind. For instance, Lowdermilk (1953) describes the degradation of high mountain forests and upper

Hauling firewood

timberlines in the southern French Alps, where population pressure pushed cultivation and development far up the steep slopes. Excessive disturbance of this high mountain landscape unleashed torrential floods that for more than a century ravaged productive Alpine valleys, killing many inhabitants.

Since the mid-1800s ambitious programs of reforestation, to restore natural upper timberlines, have been conducted with remarkable success in the southern French Alps (Douguedroit 1978). Still, a great deal of timberline restoration needs to be accomplished throughout the European Alps in order to reduce the avalanche menace. In the 1950s increasing numbers of researchers came to realize that a continual downslope retreat of upper timberline was responsible for recurring avalanches that inundated many Alpine villages. In the Tirolean Alps of western Austria, human activities caused timberline to retreat about 330 feet in elevation between 1774 and 1880, and the area of forest shrunk to half (Hampel 1961 as cited by Wardle 1974). The bleak consequences of excessive tree cutting and overgrazing at timberline in the Alps have been summarized by Friedrich-Karl Holtmeier (1973):

> In the alpine valleys the situation has deteriorated. Widespread deforestation of former times has increased the frequency of avalanches and catastrophes by torrential washes. Villages and communication systems are very often heavily endangered. In these densely populated valleys, where the people today are living mainly from tourism, the economic development depends on the effective prevention of avalanches. Endangered villages, roads, etc., must be protected immediately by artificial avalanche walls.... Large areas must be reforested to prevent avalanches and snow- and earth-slides. But since the local climate and also the soil deteriorated when the forest was cleared, it was very difficult today to reintroduce the forest in these areas.

Similarly disastrous deforestation of upper timberlines threatens villages in some of the rugged fiord valleys of northern Norway (Holtmeier 1973). At the nearby arctic timberline in Lapland, the Lapps are not allowed to cut pines, but destruction of birch groves for fuel, coupled with uncontrolled grazing, continues.

Impacts on upper timberlines have often brought severe consequences in the poorer, "Third World" countries. In the Himalayas, for instance, overpopulation of nearby lowland cities has resulted in a human migration to the mountains. This leads to further deforestation, overgrazing, and expansion of terraced fields to higher and steeper mountainsides, as described by Bayard Webster (1982):

> These impacts in turn trigger massive soil erosion, flooding, landslides, mudslides and avalanches that wipe out crops and livestock and kill humans in scores of settlements. Ironically, the changing contours of upland areas also create problems such as silting and crop losses in the lowland areas from which many mountain residents migrated in the first place.

Terrace agriculture near Annapurna in Nepal

In North America impacts at upper timberlines are more recent but could potentially become severe within a few decades. The effects of human exploitation and development are compounded at alpine timberlines by the often violent forces of nature and the exceedingly slow recovery rates of bulldozed sites or trampled vegetation. Arctic timberline generally does not occur on potentially hazardous steep slopes. Instead, it is underlain by permafrost, and frost action greatly hampers rehabilitation of bulldozed sites.

The principal values of upper timberlines can be characterized as follows. Alpine timberlines are of vital importance as a source of high-quality water for metropolitan and agricultural use. They provide year-round snow accumulation and water storage areas. Alpine and especially arctic timberlines are very important wildlife sanctuaries. The latter are part of the breeding grounds for much of North America's migratory waterfowl. Upper timberlines are biologically rich ecotones that have high values as reservoirs of species and genetic diversity. In arctic regions, strong sociological ties exist between the native peoples and their environment. Alpine timberlines also have strong values for European-Americans as areas in which to experience the raw, primeval forces of nature that still underlie mankind's very existence.

A comprehensive evaluation concluded that despite considerable efforts expended to rehabilitate damaged alpine and arctic environments, ecosystem recovery rates by both artificial and natural means have been extremely slow at best (Brown and others 1978b)! This finding also applies well to cold timberlines.

Overgrazing has thus far had the most widespread impact on alpine timberlines in North America (Brown and others 1978b). Long-term damage from livestock grazing, principally sheep, is common at upper timberline in Utah, Colorado, Wyoming, and Idaho. Paired photographs illustrate past grazing damage and moderately successful rehabilitation of subalpine and timberline grasslands in the Wallowa Mountains of northeastern Oregon (Strickler 1961). By the late 1930s sheep grazing in the Wallowas had reduced the grazing capacity of the subalpine grassland to 8 percent of its estimated potential. The area of ground surface covered by vegetation was reduced to 25 percent of potential, and accelerated erosion had resulted in soil losses averaging 521 tons per acre. After two decades of restricted grazing and other rehabilitation efforts, accelerated erosion had been arrested and a modest recovery of vegetation was recorded; however, the pregrazing era conditions evidently cannot be restored in the foreseeable future.

The livestock forage resource at upper timberline and in alpine tundra has a minor commercial value, and in recent times the sheep herds on open ranges have dwindled for economic reasons. Hopefully, public land managers will be able to further reduce the grazing pressure in timberline and alpine communities.

Outdoor recreation is another category of impacts on alpine timberlines in North America, and its effects have grown rapidly in the past 30 years. Heavy recreational impacts are associated with off-road vehicles and with concentrated use by pack stock on trails and campsites. But considerable trampling damage and tree injury are also associated with auto tourism and even with hikers on heavily used trails. Water pollution problems have become a widespread concern at back-country campsites where there are no sanitation facilities. Hacking down of snags and live trees for firewood has reached alarming proportions at many popular timberline campsites. In response to this destruction, the U.S. National Park Service began prohibiting campfires at some popular back-country sites in California's High Sierra Nevada in the early 1960s. A compendium of reports dealing with recreational impacts in subalpine environments arose from a recent conference in Seattle, Washington (Ittner and others 1978). Also, David Cole and G. S. Schreiner (1981) have compiled an annotated bibliography on back-country recreational impacts and implications for management and rehabilitation.

Expansion of existing mass-recreation sites and development of new ones, such as ski resorts and summer condominium tracts, threaten some upper timberline areas in North America. In the long run, from both economic and ecological perspectives, it probably would be wise to confine such mass developments to the forest zones considerably below the alpine timberline.

Mineral and petroleum exploration is yet another rapidly expanding impact category at both alpine and arctic timberlines. Disturbances associated with exploration, mining, drilling pads, construction sites, work camps, and networks of access roads are among the most disruptive of human activities at upper timberlines. Large areas of such disturbance have spread through the Absaroka and Beartooth mountains of south-central Montana, where rehabilitation specialists have found it exceedingly difficult to achieve even a modicum of revegetation (Brown and others 1978a and b). Their findings make it clear that rehabilitation in the traditional sense is not attainable, and this realization should cause the public to question whether it is worth permanently disfiguring such magnificent landscapes for some unproven chance to make money in minerals. Unfortunately, the public has very limited legal rights to control mineral or petroleum exploration or development on public lands, especially outside of designated wilderness areas.

The effects of direct human impacts on tundra and upper timberline environments is summed up by R. W. Brown and others (1978b):

> The floristic evolution of these regions reflects an almost total lack of man's influence.... Yet, in the short span of one century, man's impacts are almost everywhere. In his search for minerals, fossil fuels, forage for livestock, and even for the restitution of his soul, man has left a trail of destruction and debris behind him that may remain for centuries.

Recently an *indirect* impact of modern man has begun to produce a dramatic effect in subalpine and timberline forests of northeastern North America—in the Adirondacks, the Green and the White mountains of New England, and the Laurentian Mountains of Quebec. Air pollution in the form of "acid rain" (more precisely, acid deposition) is now believed to be largely responsible for extensive mortality of high-mountain conifers (Vogelmann 1982). Death of spruce trees is conspicuous on the windward slopes at high elevations throughout the northeastern United States. Almost half the spruce on Camels Hump in Vermont's Green Mountains have died since 1965, and many of these trees were over 300 years old. In Europe, mounting evidence indicates that acid deposition is killing large numbers of high-elevation conifers. In West Germany alone, thousands of acres of spruce and fir forests are dying (Roberts 1983).

That acid deposition has damaged or destroyed fish life in hundreds of lakes in northeastern North America and in Europe has been firmly established, but only recently has its impact on forests been studied

(Hutchinson and Havas 1980, Cowling 1982). Acid deposition is a modern-day product resulting from massive combustion of fossil fuels, mainly coal, in our industrialized civilization. This produces millions of tons of sulfur and nitrogen oxides that combine with water in the atmosphere to make sulfuric and nitric acids that continually rain down on the landscape.

Just how acidic the rain has become can be determined by comparing it with precipitation from pre-industrial times. Annual layers of frozen precipitation preserved in the Greenland Ice Cap can be used as this pre-industrial control (Vogelmann 1982). Studies have revealed that rain now falling on the northeastern United States is at least 30 to 40 times more acidic than pre-industrial precipitation. Compounding the excess acidity is the plethora of toxic heavy-metal pollutants also being showered on the forest landscape. Acid rain appears to combine with aluminum already present in the soil, transforming this metal into a soluble toxic form which is then taken up by tree roots, severely damaging or killing them and, at the least, impairing the tree's uptake of water.

While the effects of acid deposition are complex and not fully understood, gaining control of this global pollutant will be an infinitely greater challenge than its study, because to gain control will require international cooperation among the industrialized nations. Increasingly acidic precipitation has recently been detected in mountain areas of western North America and Asia; this may be the forerunner of problems for subalpine forests in many areas. Acid deposition's potentially massive damages to terrestrial and aquatic ecosystems can only be prevented through a large scientific effort to detect its occurrence and unravel the detailed mechanisms through which it kills.

While this has been by no means an exhaustive survey of human impacts at upper timberlines, it illustrates the need for increasing protection of these rigorous but easily damaged environments. North Americans are fortunate to have comparatively healthy upper timberlines, while corresponding environments in much of the rest of the world have been degraded. The principal long-term values of North America's upper timberlines are great as undamaged watersheds, sanctuaries for wildlife, untrammeled natural areas supporting diverse species and genetic forms, and rugged wilderness environments where nature continues to dominate in a world that has otherwise become greatly altered by the forces of civilization. All these aspects of upper timberlines are precious. Their values for exploitation and resource extraction are relatively low and fraught with logistic difficulties and dangers of ecosystem degradation. It seems that the prudent approach in resource management would be to emphasize protection of the natural values at North America's upper timberlines.

Part Two

EXPLORING TIMBERLINE

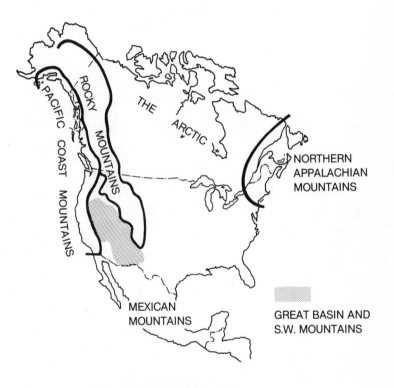

Alpine timberline in the Pacific Coast Mountains

5
Pacific Coast Mountains

This region supports alpine timberlines at increasing elevations along the coastal mountain ranges from south-central Alaska to southern California. In south-central Alaska (60°N) the maritime timberlines form at elevations below 2000 feet, while in western Washington (48°N) they average nearly 6000 feet and in central California (37°N) they commonly attain 11,000 feet. The coastal mountains form a more-or-less continuous chain bordering the Pacific shore for over 2500 miles. Alpine timberlines occur on the coastal mountains of Alaska and British Columbia, the Olympic Mountains of Washington, the Cascades stretching from southern British Columbia to northern California, the Klamath Mountains of northwestern California, the Sierra Nevada of central California, and a few isolated high peaks near Los Angeles.

The dominant climate of this region is maritime in the north, with a dry-summer or "Mediterranean" climate becoming prevalent southward in Oregon and California. In the Alaskan coastal mountains abundant precipitation falls the year around; southward, a gradually lengthening summer dry period develops. The effects of this drought are mitigated to a large extent by the heavy snowpack that persists into July at most alpine timberlines.

On the western slope of the Alaska and British Columbia coastal mountains and the Cascades of Washington and northern Oregon, the subalpine forests and timberlines are distinctively maritime. They are dominated by Sitka spruce (in Alaska), mountain hemlock, subalpine fir, Alaska-cedar, and, occasionally, Pacific silver fir (see graphs page 96).

In contrast, the inland slope of these ranges, and both slopes of the mountains in southern Oregon and California, have drier climates. These are continental climates to the north and inland-maritime and even semi-desert climates to the south. The inland-slope timberlines are dominated by white and black spruce in Alaska and northwestern Canada and by subalpine fir, Engelmann spruce, whitebark pine, and, locally, alpine larch in the region extending from southern British Columbia to central Oregon. In southwestern Oregon and California a variety of maritime, inland, and southwestern conifers comes together at upper timberline. These include mountain hemlock, whitebark pine, Sierra lodgepole pine, foxtail pine, limber pine, and smaller amounts of several other species.

Lower timberlines occur on the dry, inland slope of the Cascades and

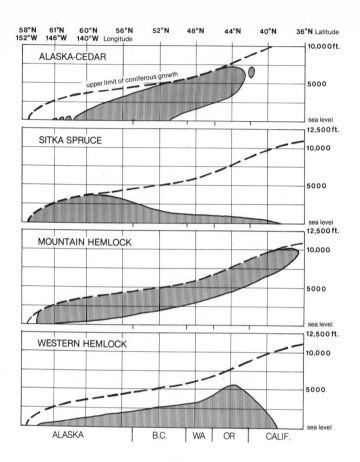

Elevational distributions of three timberline tree species and one lower-elevation (montane zone) conifer along the Pacific Coast Mountains

on both slopes of the Sierra Nevada and mountains of southern California. From Oregon northward, ponderosa pine is the primary forest tree at lower timberlines, giving way to sagebrush, grasslands, or western juniper (*Juniperus occidentalis* var. *occidentalis*) woodlands on drier sites. In California, however, diverse assemblages of conifers (including ponderosa pine), oaks, and other broadleaves form the lower boundary of the forest. Often a zone of broadleaved woodland or a pinyon-juniper woodland occurs below the forest belt.

Lower timberlines can also be found in the dry valleys of western Oregon and occasionally northward on exceptionally dry sites to Victoria and the San Juan Islands, although land clearing and development makes it difficult to determine the position of natural forest boundaries. Oregon white oak (*Quercus garryana*) is the most characteristic tree of these coastal lower timberlines.

Alaska Coast Range

The coast of south-central and southeastern (the Panhandle) Alaska is a fiord-mountain country where luxuriantly forested slopes meet the cold, blue waters of the North Pacific Ocean. On the coast of south-central Alaska the forest forms a narrow band extending from tidewater to 1000 or 1500 feet in elevation. In the Alaska Panhandle, forest is more extensive, occasionally reaching as high as 3000 feet. Throughout these regions, the forest borders countless spectacular inlets and covers thousands of coastal islands and peninsulas. The forest belt is broken in many places by glaciers flowing down to the sea from large mountain icefields. Avalanche chutes filled with dense Sitka alder shrubfields also project downward into or through the narrow forest zone. Also, large patches of bright-green brushy alders extend a few hundred feet above the timberline conifers. Thickets of Sitka alder (*Alnus sinuata*) cover large areas of the maritime coast from the Aleutian Islands to British Columbia, but some forms of this species (formerly known as *A. crispa* and *A. fruticosa*) grow inland all across northern Canada and Alaska, and throughout northeastern Siberia (Little 1979).

Mountain hemlock krummholz below Chilkoot Pass near Skagway

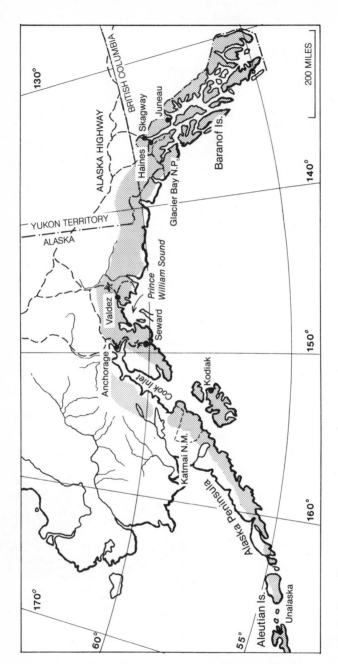

Alaska Coast Range

The climate of the Alaskan southern coast is cold and wet. Mean annual precipitation at low elevations ranges from about 55 inches up to 221 inches at Little Port Walter on Baranof Island. An abundance of precipitation falls in every month of the year. Annual snowfall in the timberline zone is copious, although records are available at only one site, 2722-foot Thompson Pass on the highway to Valdez. Thompson Pass is in alpine tundra about 500 feet above even the limit of scrubby Sitka alder; however, the mean annual snowfall of about 550 inches is probably similar to that experienced at timberline.

Sitka spruce extends farther west along the coast of southern Alaska than any other forest tree, reaching into Katmai National Monument on the Alaska Peninsula and to nearby Kodiak and Afognak islands (Viereck and Little 1972). Small groves of Sitka spruce were planted by the Russians as early as 1805 at Unalaska, 600 miles southwest of the natural forest boundary in the Aleutian Islands. These trees are still growing and have produced cones (Griggs 1936).

At the western limit of spruce, on Kodiak Island, the oldest trees have attained diameters in excess of 4 feet and heights of 75 feet. They grow in scattered stands from sea level up to an elevation of 1300 feet. These spruce are migrating into southwestern Alaska's "coastal tundra," which is not comparable to the cold-environment alpine and arctic tundras of Alaska (Griggs 1936). Ecological relationships of the coastal tundra are little known. Dense thickets of Sitka alder, salmonberry (*Rubus spectabilis*), wild rose (*Rosa nutkana*), and a variety of ferns dominate in the lower terrain. A more usual arctic-alpine muskeg plant assemblage occupies the poorly drained sites. The mean temperature during the warmest summer month at Kodiak is 55°F, whereas at Cape Sarichef, near Unalaska, the warmest month averages only 50°F.

In south-central Alaska, from Cook Inlet to the north end of the Alaska Panhandle, the maritime forest forms a narrow, broken band along the shore, consisting mainly of three coniferous trees—Sitka spruce, western hemlock, and mountain hemlock. Although Sitka spruce occupies the shoreline all the way to northern California, it is unique in being a timberline dweller only at the north end of its distribution—exclusively in Alaska.

Most mountain conifers grow at progressively higher elevations toward the south. In contrast, Sitka spruce occupies the entire forest belt in coastal Alaska and extends higher as krummholz than other conifers, while southward it becomes increasingly confined to wet lowlands in the coastal fog belt. Apparently this species, known also as "tideland spruce" in the "Lower 48 States," can tolerate mountain upland sites only in Alaska, where summers are very rainy and cool.

As a coastal *lowland* dweller from Alaska to Oregon, Sitka spruce attains immense size on favorable sites. Old-growth stands in fertile, sheltered valleys contain spruce trees over 10 feet in diameter and 250 feet tall at modest ages of 300 to 600 years. But this tree is also among the first to colonize Alaskan glacial moraines, and it alone forms krummholz on nunatacks (rocky peaks) protruding through the Juneau Icefield (Heusser

1960). From tidewater to upper timberline, Sitka spruce faces stiff competition from more shade-tolerant hemlocks. Mountain hemlock is the potential dominant climax species in the upper half of the forest zone, while western hemlock has a similar role in the lowland forest. However, spruce is the most abundant species above tree line as well as in the immediate vicinity of tidewater—sites where the hemlocks grow with difficulty. Alaska-cedar is a minor component of alpine timberlines from Prince William Sound south and eastward through the Alaska Panhandle and thence to Oregon.

Another conspicuous feature of the south-central Alaskan timberlines is "slope muskeg" or alpine bog vegetation that forms even on moderately steep slopes in areas of massive seepage. Also, south-central and southeastern Alaska have an abundance of low-elevation terrain recently released from glacial ice. The primary succession following glacial retreat at Glacier Bay National Monument is probably typical of other glacial sites. Here, the glaciers retreated so rapidly in the past 200 years that they left a gap of many miles between the edge of the ice and the forest. As a result, establishment of forest reproduction near the ice has taken 50 to 100 years instead of the 5 to 10 years that would have been sufficient if a seed source were near (Lawrence 1958).

Seward's fiord from Mount Marathon, with a zone of bushy Sitka alder upslope from the forest

Subalpine fir at Deep Lake, near Chilkoot Pass

Dwarf willows, black cottonwood, and Sitka alder are the first shrub and tree species to invade after glacial retreat. The showy, mat-forming mountain-avens and Sitka alder are fast-growing pioneer plants that fix nitrogen and thus enrich the site. At first, cottonwood seedlings are nearly prostrate and have yellow, nitrogen-deficient foliage; but as nitrogen becomes available, the cottonwoods begin to grow up through the alder thickets, which themselves may be 25 or 30 feet tall. After 60 years, spruce and hemlocks are growing vigorously beneath the alder (Lawrence 1958). About 170 years after the ice melts, alder has been replaced by Sitka spruce up to 110 feet tall with annual growth rings one-third of an inch wide. Mosses and litter are almost a foot deep. A sphagnum mat gradually develops to such thickness on some sites that aeration (oxygen) is cut off to the tree roots, and after 6000 to 10,000 years, large areas have gradually reverted to muskeg.

The coastal timberlines are readily visited at a number of points because of their modest elevation and close proximity to coastal towns. The Portage Glacier Recreation Area in the Chugach National Forest, 50 miles southeast of Anchorage, is a good place to observe one-sided, wind-deformed Sitka spruce and krummholz below the 1000-foot level. Hiking and running trails lead up Mount Marathon above Seward and its fiord, Resurrection Bay. These paths make transects through a mountain hemlock-Sitka spruce subalpine forest, with spruce krummholz extending to 1800 feet and bushy Sitka alder ascending somewhat higher. Above the 2000-foot level lie heathlands and luxuriant alpine tundra, as well as perpetual ice and snow on the mountains encircling Resurrection Bay.

On 3000-foot Mount Roberts, rising directly above Juneau, a hiking trail climbs through a narrow timberline where in some spots 50- to 80-foot mountain hemlock and Sitka spruce adjoin alpine heath. In early summer, this and other coastal timberlines are good places to observe ptarmigan hens and their chicks. The highways from Moose Pass to Seward, from Thompson Pass down to Valdez, and the road leading south from the Yukon Territory to Haines all traverse maritime timberlines. At low passes, white spruce from the inland forest often meets Sitka spruce and mountain hemlock; however, in most areas the Coast Range is so high that the maritime and inland forests are separated by miles of alpine or glacial terrain.

In the southern part of the Panhandle, subalpine fir regularly becomes a member of the timberlines, and it increases in abundance southward in coastal British Columbia. At the north end of the Panhandle, subalpine fir crosses over the Coast Range divide from the inland slope in a few areas, notably near Skagway (which has a relatively dry climate) at the head of Lynn Canal, where it descends from timberline at 3000 feet to sea level (Viereck and Little 1972). Forests of subalpine fir and Sitka spruce (an unusual combination) can be seen east of Skagway on the Klondike Highway. These forests give way to picturesque timberlines of the same species, along with mountain hemlock, below 3290-foot White Pass.

British Columbia Coastal Ranges

The inland slope of the Coast Mountains immediately east of the Alaska Panhandle lies within British Columbia and supports timberlines similar to those of the Boreal Rockies discussed in Chapter 7. Our current subject is the 550-mile-long segment of the coastal (and insular) mountain chain extending south from the tip of the Alaska Panhandle to the Fraser River Canyon near Vancouver, British Columbia. This complex system of mountains abuts the North Pacific Ocean, forming spectacular steep-walled fiords, but also extending nearly 100 miles inland. Additionally, isolated alpine peaks jut above the maritime forests on the Queen Charlotte Islands and on Vancouver Island.

Throughout this broad mountain chain, high peaks rise above 7000 feet and project well up into alpine tundra and glacial zones. In the central portion at about 52°N, several peaks exceed 10,000 feet, including Mount Waddington (13,177 feet), the highest point in British Columbia. Glaciers drape the upper slopes, but none of them flows down to the tidewater as in Alaska. However, Mount Waddington's Franklin Glacier extends about 20 miles, and its snout reaches the 700-foot elevation.

The coastal ranges form a massive barrier that milks most of the precipitation out of the moisture-laden Pacific storm systems. Weather records gathered at stations along a west-to-east transect at 52½°N illustrate this pattern. Bella Bella, on the coastal archipelago, receives an average annual precipitation of 106 inches. Ocean Falls, at the base of the

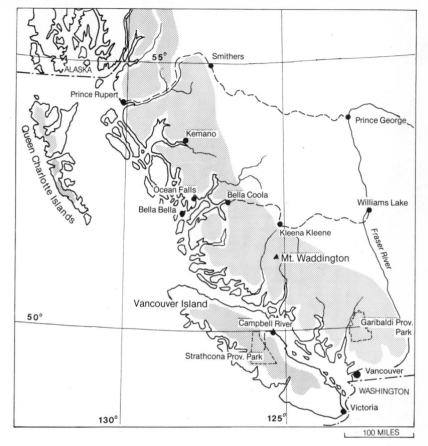

British Columbia Coastal Ranges

coastal foothills and about 15 miles from the ocean proper, is drenched with an average of 174 inches. Bella Coola, another 40 miles eastward at the end of a fiord, receives 61 inches, while Kleena Kleene, 25 miles east of the Coast Range divide, averages only 14 inches per year.

This west-to-east moisture gradient has a dramatic effect on vegetation. The coastal lowlands and foothills support a "temperate rain forest" made up of the Alaska Panhandle species—Sitka spruce, western hemlock, and western redcedar (*Thuja plicata*)—but also including species not found in Alaska—giant coastal Douglas-fir (*Pseudotsuga menziesii* var. *menziesii*), Pacific silver fir, and, in the south, grand fir (*Abies grandis*). In contrast, immediately east of the coast ranges lies a dry inland forest of Rocky Mountain Douglas-fir (var. *glauca*), lodgepole pine, and quaking aspen.

At higher elevations, near timberline, the west-to-east gradient primarily reflects differences in snowfall. The westernmost or seaward

Mountain hemlock parkland in southern British Columbia

mountains lie under a deluge of snow in all but the summer months. No permanent weather stations exist at these timberlines, but for six winters measurements were made at 5280-foot Kildala Pass near Kemano (53°N). The average seasonal snowfall was 770 inches (64 feet), perhaps the highest average snowfall measured anywhere in the world. This site apparently lies several hundred feet above the krummholz line for mountain hemlock, which is the principal conifer at timberline on seaward slopes. Snow depth reaches a maximum of 12 to 20 feet during April in the coast range timberlines, which are termed the "parkland subzone" of the subalpine mountain hemlock forest by ecologist Vladimir Krajina (1965). In this timberline parkland snow lingers until August, and some patches persist through the entire summer season. As a result, even the snow-tolerant mountain hemlock is largely confined to rock outcrops, humps, or ridges that emerge from the snowpack relatively early.

Mountain hemlock is the main pioneer species in the timberline parkland, partially because of its ability to endure heavy, wet snow loads with little breakage. Alaska-cedar is also common; its drooping foliage (branchlets) resists or sloughs off incipient loads of clinging snow. The slender, spirelike crowns of subalpine fir are likewise not susceptible to snow breakage.

Pacific silver fir—a vigorous and very shade-tolerant component of the subalpine forest—does not ascend high into the parkland. Unlike the timberline species, it does not reproduce vegetatively through layering,

Mountain hemlock parkland early in winter

and much of its seed germinates unproductively on the late-lying snow-pack (Brooke and others 1970).

On the oceanic Queen Charlotte Islands, timberline develops at 3000 to 3500 feet (Heusser 1960). Farther inland, near Bella Coola, this parkland is found at about 4500 to 5200 feet (McAvoy 1931). On the seaward mountain slopes rising above the city of Vancouver, timberline occurs between 4500 and 5500 feet. Inland 40 miles, in Garibaldi Provincial Park, snowfall is much reduced and timberline is formed about 1000 feet higher.

The Black Tusk Meadows area of Garibaldi Provincial Park supports a beautiful timberline parkland with tree islands of mountain hemlock, subalpine fir, Alaska-cedar, and whitebark pine (Brink 1959). Interestingly, each island often contains all four species. The intervening heathlands have been invaded by saplings of subalpine fir and mountain hemlock, most of which date from the dry period between about 1920 and 1940. Growth of these little trees has been exceedingly slow in the snowier period since 1940. However, if any of them do grow tall enough to project above the spring snowpack, they will begin to create a "snow crater," because the snow will melt away from these dark-colored objects first. This may allow the young trees to grow more rapidly.

The timberline heath communities at Garibaldi and elsewhere in the coast ranges bear a profusion of delicate bell-shaped flowers. These include red-flowered *Phyllodoce empetriformis,* yellow *P. glanduliflora,* and the white *Cassiope mertensiana* and *C. tetragona.* Another characteristic

Black Tusk Meadows near Mount Garibaldi

low shrub of these timberline parklands is the delicious huckleberry (*Vaccinium deliciosum*), whose leaves turn brilliant red in September. Partridgefoot (*Luetkea pectinata*) is a ground-layer plant that is covered in summer with masses of cream-colored blossoms. Late-melting snowdrift sites between krummholz islands are inhabited by dense patches of tiny, deep-green, succulent leaves that support dainty white and purplish flowers borne on three-inch stalks. This is the alpine or snowbed saxifrage (*Saxifraga tolmiei*). Well over 150 species of flowering plants occupy the diverse microhabitats in the timberline parkland. These range from marsh marigolds (*Caltha leptosepala*) that grow up through standing water and in moist meadows to a rich assortment of wildflowers to communities of ground-hugging cushion plants on windswept, gravelly fellfields.

The high-country of the British Columbia coastal ranges includes some of the most inaccessible terrain in North America. Much of this area can be explored by boating long distances along the coastline and up the fiords, then clambering through thick forests to reach the high-country. Float planes and even helicopters have become common modes of access in recent years. Areas with easier access include the southern end of the coastal ranges, where hiking trails lead up some of the 5000-foot-high seaward mountains immediately north of Vancouver. Also, Provincial

Highway 99 north of Vancouver provides access to trails that climb into the splendid timberline parklands of Garibaldi Provincial Park.

The 7000-foot-high alpine peaks on Vancouver Island are reached by hiking trails that join a paved road that itself has climbed westward into Strathcona Provincial Park from the town of Campbell River. A 300-mile-long winding gravel road leads from Williams Lake in south-central British Columbia over the coastal ranges to Bella Coola. This route crosses the high-country of the central coastal ranges in Tweedsmuir Provincial Park. The highway from Prince George in central British Columbia to Prince Rupert on the coast just south of the Alaska Panhandle provides views and local access to timberlines on peaks rising above the Skeena River Valley. A road to the ski area on Hudson Bay Mountain near Smithers reaches a 5000-foot-high inland-slope timberline of spirelike subalpine fir and meadows, with extensive krummholz and alpine tundra above.

Olympic Mountains

The Olympics are a cluster of rugged, snow-capped mountains, less than 50 miles across, that juts above western Washington's Olympic Peninsula and is bordered on three sides by tidewater. This small but impressive knot of mountains harbors the southernmost glacial, alpine-

Above forest line at 3800 feet in the misty western Olympic Mountains

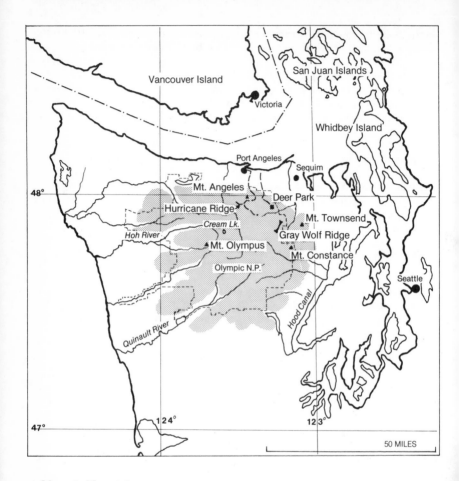

Olympic Mountains

tundra, and timberline environments along the immediate coast of the
North Pacific Ocean. The Olympics lie 60 miles west across Puget Sound
from the massive Cascade Range and have high-country vegetation generally similar to that of the western Cascades. However, timberlines in this
small coastal range are unique in several respects.

The climate of the Olympic Peninsula is strongly maritime and has
helped produce temperate rain forests of gigantic conifers (Douglas-fir,
Sitka spruce, and western hemlock) and clubmoss-draped maples (*Acer
macrophyllum*). Such rain forests fill the major westside valleys, where
annual precipitation averages 120 to 150 inches. These valleys and others
in the Olympics radiate from a central mountain mass that includes
glacier-clad Mount Olympus (7965 feet), whose slopes receive about 200
inches of precipitation in the average year. This area is the wettest place in

the 48 contiguous United States, and it may also have the lowest regional snowline, or average elevation of persistent snow (6000 feet), for its latitude in the Northern Hemisphere (Danner 1955). As an indication of the tremendous snowfall, some small glaciers lie wholly below the upper limit of erect trees. The western, southern, and central portions of this range milk so much precipitation from the maritime storms that the northeastern Olympics remain rather dry. The town of Sequim, beneath the northeastern peaks, receives only 17 inches of annual precipitation — less than that of any other area on the Pacific Coast north of central California.

In the western and central Olympics, forest line usually develops between 4000 and 4500 feet, and the krummholz line forms near 6000 feet on warm exposures. Some years, large snowfields persist through the summer in timberline stands as low as 4500 feet. Mountain hemlock, subalpine fir, and Alaska-cedar are the principal timberline trees, often crowding together in dense, integrated stands of krummholz. Lingering snowpack generally restricts tree growth except on exposed ridges and steep southern slopes. On the latter sites, wind and cool summer temperatures probably inhibit growth of the krummholz conifers.

Several of the Pacific Coast trees reach their largest dimensions in the western and central Olympics, including the world's record Douglas-fir

Deep snow country at 5000 feet on the Queets-Quinault Divide in the western Olympics

(14½ feet in diameter and 221 feet tall). Timberline trees also attain record sizes here. The largest known subalpine fir grows in the central Olympics at the forest line in Cream Lake basin. This huge tree, nearly 7 feet in d.b.h. (diameter at breast height—4½ feet above the ground) and 129 feet tall, has a rotten, hollowed-out trunk that an enterprising mountaineer put to use as a cache cabin by affixing a small door to the entrance hole! The largest-known Alaska-cedar grows in a snow-deluged subalpine forest at only 3000 feet. This heavily buttressed, shaggy-barked giant, 12 feet thick and 120 feet tall, grows in a "hillside bog" along the trail below Three Lakes, north of the Quinault rain forest.

In the northeastern rain-shadow zone, forest line averages about 5500 feet and krummholz line is near 6500 feet. Tree communities are quite diverse, although subalpine fir is generally the most abundant timberline dweller. Mountain hemlock is common but often confined to moist northern slopes and basins, where, on rocky hummocks, it often forms a large patriarch surrounded by vegetatively spreading limbs and saplings. It is absent from the driest areas and from certain highly mineralized geologic types in the northeastern Olympics.

Alaska-cedar is largely confined to springs, streamsides, and other moist sites in this area, but it sometimes reaches great size. It also forms krummholz cushions on exposed rocky peaks, higher than any other tree species reaches. One of these cushions atop Mount Angeles is 50 feet in diameter and has a dead center like a timber atoll. This dwarfed tree may

Exposed root of Alaska-cedar on Mount Angeles, Olympic Mountains

be a thousand or more years old, like some of the large streamside Alaska-cedars. Another isolated krummholz Alaska-cedar on Mount Angeles has a large root that has been exposed by geological erosion for 75 feet across a loose, rocky slope. Beyond this exposed portion, the still-living root descends into the infertile substrate. One stand of Alaska-cedar krummholz on Gray Wolf Ridge extends up an east-facing cliff to the exceptionally high elevation of 7200 feet.

Whitebark pine inhabits only the northeastern, rain-shadow portion of the Olympic Range. Even within this limited area whitebark is rather scarce and is found sprinkled along lofty ridges, mostly between 5800 and 6800 feet. Individual large, sprawling shrubs of whitebark pine often grow in the rocky crags two or more miles from the nearest seed source, suggesting they originated from a Clark's nutcracker's seed cache. Some stands, such as the one at Constance Pass, have been largely killed by white pine blister rust (*Cronartium ribicola*), an introduced disease that primarily infects western white pine.

Lodgepole (*Pinus contorta* var. *latifolia*) and possibly shore pine (*P. contorta* var. *contorta*) are also prominent at timberlines in the Olympic rain shadow. Dense stands of treelike lodgepole pine have arisen on dry exposures near Deer Park as a result of severe wildfires in the past 250 years (Fonda and Bliss 1969). Succession to the more shade-tolerant subalpine fir was apparently retarded by the dry, exposed microclimate in these burned sites. But another, more unique form of *Pinus contorta* growth is also found in the northeastern Olympics. Squatty, heavily limbed trees with thick bark, characteristic of shore pine occur near tree limit on some of the high ridges, such as at Mount Townsend. Farther upslope, this form grows as scattered, sprawling krummholz trees, often providing shelter for cushions of subalpine fir. The trunks of these stout, bushy *Pinus contorta* are arched over a few feet off the ground. The dense canopy creates a microsite beneath it that supports understory plants normally confined to the subalpine forest far below.

Another inland species was recently discovered among the northeastern Olympic peaks. Three stands of Engelmann spruce have been reported in moist subalpine valleys, well below forest line (Fonda and Bliss 1969). Interestingly, the largest stand (35 acres), along Cameron Creek, contains a spruce 7 feet in d.b.h. and 179 feet tall. This is the second largest Engelmann spruce known, despite the fact that this species occupies tens of millions of acres in the Rocky Mountains.

The Olympic rain shadow extends east and northward to Whidbey and the San Juan Islands, where lower timberlines give way to dry grasslands on south-facing slopes (Franklin and Dyrness 1973). Principal trees of the lower timberline and savannas are stunted Douglas-fir, Pacific madrone, Oregon white oak, shore pine, and Rocky Mountain juniper. This rain shadow area is the juniper's sole occurrence west of the Cascades (Little 1969).

The only paved road providing access to upper timberline in the Olympics leads to 5220-foot Hurricane Ridge in Olympic National Park south of Port Angeles. This area lies in the northeastern Olympics where subalpine fir is the major timberline species, among lush meadows of lupine (*Lupinus* spp.), Indian paintbrush (*Castilleja* spp.), and glacier and avalanche lilies (*Erythronium grandiflorum* and *E. montanum*). These lilies have the startling habit of pushing up through the edge of melting snowpatches. At Hurricane Ridge a visitor can readily observe classical wind-timber and krummholz formations, including timber atolls and flag-topped trees with luxuriant skirts of lower branches. Some of the most picturesque wind-timber trees on the ridge spur immediately north of the visitor center are battered Douglas-firs, an unexpected timberline component. The Hurricane Ridge timberlines can be visited during winter, since the road is generally kept open on a daily basis for skiers and snowshoers; but as its place name implies, this area should be avoided in bad weather! A branch road winds nine miles eastward through timberline stands to tree line at 6200-foot Obstruction Point.

Elsewhere, a network of hiking trails joins roadheads all around the periphery of this cluster of mountains and leads into fascinating timberline country.

Northern Cascade Range
(Washington and British Columbia)

The Cascades are a complex chain of mountains stretching 700 miles from southern British Columbia through Washington, Oregon, and northern California to Mount Lassen. The Columbia River cuts westward through the Cascades at 45½°N and the resulting Columbia Gorge, whose base elevation is less than 100 feet, is the only major break in this large mountain range. The Columbia Gorge also forms the boundary between Oregon and Washington, and the large segment of the Cascades discussed here lies north of the gorge, in Washington and British Columbia.

Although alpine timberline occurs on high peaks throughout the northern Cascades, it becomes a major life zone in the "North Cascades"— a broad stretch of rugged high-country lying between Snoqualmie Pass, east of Seattle, and the Canadian border. North of Snoqualmie Pass the Cascades are geologically complex. Great expanses of granitic rock occur, interfingered with sedimentary and volcanic geology. Two large volcanoes, 10,778-foot Mount Baker and 10,568-foot Glacier Peak, rise up amidst the non-volcanic crags. Major peaks and ridges attain 7500 to 9500 feet, often soaring 6000 feet above nearby valley bottoms. This glacially sculptured landscape still harbors hundreds of small mountain glaciers. The high, alpine terrain extends several miles north of the border, into Manning Provincial Park and the Ashnola River drainage of British Columbia. Farther north, only isolated high peaks reach the elevation of timberline.

South of Snoqualmie Pass, the Cascades are primarily composed of volcanic rock (andesite and basalt), and three large volcanoes dominate the landscape: Mount Rainier (14,410 feet), Mount Adams (12,307 feet), and the famous Mount Saint Helens (formerly 9677 feet, but reduced to 8400 feet by the 1980 eruption). Rainier and Adams are ringed with a splendid band of timberline parkland. This parkland also spreads along

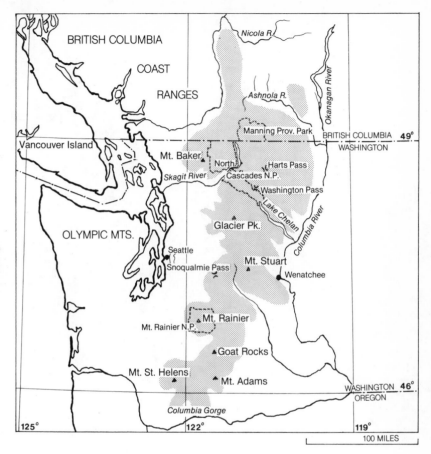

Northern Cascade Range

the Cascade Crest east of Mount Rainier National Park and extends 30 miles southward through the Goat Rocks Wild Area.

As in the Olympic and Canadian Coast ranges, a pronounced climatic change occurs eastward across the Cascades. In fact, a 1000- to 1500-foot rise in timberline accompanied by marked changes in vegetation can be seen by traveling 30 miles eastward in these mountains. This phenomenon results from the decreasing influence eastward of the maritime climate, with its heavy snowfall and generally cool, cloudy summers. For instance, forest line develops near 5000 feet on the western slope of the Cascades near Snoqualmie Pass, while it averages 6500 feet in the Stuart Range, 30 miles to the east. On the northern side of Mount Baker on the maritime slope just south of Canada, forest line occurs below 4500 feet; whereas 75 miles eastward, in the Okanogan Cascades rain-shadow zone, a comparable ecotone is found at 7000 feet on cool exposures. At Harts

Avalanche-damaged subalpine fir on Lime Ridge in the Northern Cascade Range's Glacier Peak Wilderness

Pass, on the Cascade divide between the two climatic extremes, northern slopes have forest line near 6000 feet.

At the maritime end of this transection across the North Cascades, the weather station at Heather Meadows (4150 feet) on Mount Baker records 516 inches of snowfall and 110 inches of total precipitation in the average year. Both measurements would probably be higher in the timberline belt, a few hundred feet higher. Mountain hemlock, subalpine fir, and some Alaska-cedar make up the timberline, which is a parkland of tree islands surrounded by luxuriant heath and meadows. The road to 4630-foot Austin Pass often remains blocked by snowdrifts in mid-August. Glaciers are common, many extending down into the timberline zone. Temperatures are cool year-round, but even in mid-winter they seldom drop to 0°F.

Forty-five miles eastward at Harts Pass annual precipitation is estimated to be 60 to 70 inches. Timberline here is primarily of subalpine fir, with lesser amounts of whitebark pine, alpine larch, and Engelmann spruce. Only traces of the maritime trees, mountain hemlock and Alaska-cedar, can be found. Subalpine meadows are prevalent, but not as lush as those to the west. A few tiny glaciers persist, usually at 8000 feet in the uppermost sheltered cirques on the tallest peaks.

Another 30 miles eastward, atop the Okanogan Cascades, annual precipitation is reduced to about 30 inches. Timberline is made up of whitebark pine, alpine larch, Engelmann spruce, and subalpine fir, with the fir largely confined to moist sites. Subalpine meadows are restricted to especially moist areas, but dry herbfields are extensive. By late summer, snowpatches are rare even on the 8000-foot peaks. Extremely cold-dry conditions can occur in winter, occasionally with temperatures dipping below −30°F. Immediately east of the Okanogan Cascades, the terrain drops off steeply into the hot, dry Okanogan Valley, where annual precipitation is only 11 inches and a lower timberline is formed where ponderosa pine gives way to sagebrush and bunchgrass communities, on sites not converted to agriculture.

Stands of alpine larch are a distinctive feature of the North Cascades, since this timberline dweller does not occur elsewhere in the Pacific Coast mountains. This deciduous conifer grows as far south as the Wenatchee Range, west of the city of Wenatchee, and extends a dozen miles north of the border into British Columbia. It is largely confined to the highest elevations along the crest and eastern slope of the North Cascades. Yet,

Subalpine fir and mountain hemlock on Sahale Arm in North Cascades National Park

within its limited distribution, this distinctive tree becomes abundant on the rugged granite peaks between 6000 and 7500 feet. Alpine larch stands among the lofty crags can be spotted from the valleys below or from aircraft around October 1, when they turn golden prior to losing their leaves. This species forms the highest band of tree growth on northern exposures and is often found at the foot of alpine glaciers, bordering the highest cirque lakes, and growing on boulder piles (talus), where few other plants exist. These trees are generally long lived and can eventually attain large size despite extremely infertile "soils" and harsh climate. The largest known alpine larch grows on a north-facing talus slope at 6200 feet, high above Lake Chelan. This veteran is 75 inches in d.b.h. and 94 feet tall and has a great, spreading crown. Although it may well be 1000 years old, it probably will not survive another century because it is supported only by a thin shell of sound outer wood that encases a massively heart-rotted trunk.

Alpine larch and subalpine fir on north-facing slope in the Northern Cascade Range

Another distinctive feature of upper timberlines in the Cascades is the luxuriant meadow and heathland interspersed with the tree groves and islands. Jerry Franklin and Ted Dyrness (1973) have classified this parkland vegetation into five broad groups, each having several community types: (1) heath communities of *Phyllodoce, Cassiope,* and *Vaccinium deliciosum* cover gentle slopes and well-drained soils; (2) moist meadows are made up of a diverse assemblage of forbs such as *Valeriana sitchensis, Lupinus latifolius,* and the sedge *Carex spectabilis*; (3) dwarf sedge communities consisting of a lawnlike mat of *Carex nigricans* occupy sites having a short growing season due to late-persisting snowbanks and cold, wet soils; (4) pioneer low-herbaceous communities, ranging from alpine saxifrage (*Saxifraga tolmiei*) on snowbed sites to cushion plants on windswept, gravelly ridges, survive on raw, exposed sandy or gravelly sites; and (5) dry grasslands dominated by fescue (usually, *Festuca viridula*) are a conspicuous element of the parkland mosaic in the rain-shadow areas of the Cascades and the Olympics.

Subalpine marsh and rivulet communities are also part of the timberline mosaic. These are dominated by several species, including scarlet monkeyflower (*Mimulus lewisii*), marshmarigolds (*Caltha* spp.), grass-of-Parnassus (*Parnassia fimbriata*), colts foot (*Petasites frigidus*), alpine fireweed (*Epilobium alpinum*), black alpine sedge (*Carex nigricans*), and the rush *Juncus drummondii.*

Nowhere are parkland communities more richly represented than at Mount Rainier, where they encircle the base of the massive glacier-laden volcano. Forest line averages about 5200 feet on Mount Rainier, with scrub line generally about 6800 feet. The Rainier timberline consists largely of subalpine fir, mountain hemlock, and Alaska-cedar, along with whitebark pine and Engelmann spruce on the drier, northeastern side of the mountain. Pacific silver fir is also common in the lower part of the parkland here and elsewhere in the Cascades; however, it is evidently less hardy than the other trees. Most individual mountains have timberlines at lower elevations on their cooler, northeastern slope; but Rainier is so gigantic that it creates a rain shadow on its northeastern side (Yakima Park vicinity), resulting in less snowfall and therefore a higher timberline.

The weather station at 5550-foot Paradise Ranger Station on Mount Rainier's southwestern slope provides a detailed record for a maritime timberline. Average annual precipitation is 106 inches and annual snowfall is about 600 inches (50 feet), but this station was deluged with a world-record of more than 90 feet of snowfall during the winter of 1971-72. Although Paradise is just a few hundred feet above forest line, considerable snowpack often remains on the ground in mid-July. This is usually reduced to scattered patches by August, however. Were it not for this copious blanket of potential ground water, soils could become droughty in late summer, since July and August are often rather dry. In the rain-shadow zone, snowpack disappears much earlier, and less summer rainfall occurs; thus, soil drought can become a critical factor determining the distribution of tree, heath, and meadow species. Interesting tree and

Timberline parkland at 5800 feet on Mount Rainier in the Northern Cascade Range. Little Tahoma Peak in background.

krummholz islands consisting of combinations of subalpine fir, whitebark pine, mountain hemlock, and an occasional Alaska-cedar or Engelmann spruce can be seen along the road to Yakima Park on the northeastern side of the mountain.

Most of the parkland zone encircling Mount Adams, and in the Goat Rocks southeast of Mount Rainier, is comparatively dry and is similar to the rain-shadow country on Rainier. An unusual feature at Goat Rocks (Heart Lake Basin) is that noble fir (*Abies procera*) ascends into the parkland with whitebark pine and subalpine fir.

Prior to the May 1980 eruption, timberlines on Mount Saint Helens were odd because they were exceptionally low (forest line was at about 4400 feet) and composed largely of species seldom found at upper timberline—for example, lodgepole pine (the dominant species), western white pine, Douglas-fir, black cottonwood, noble fir, and western hemlock (Franklin and Dyrness 1973). Unlike the relatively stable alpine timberlines elsewhere in the Cascades, the forest on Saint Helens was rapidly advancing upward. This ascent was dealt a massive setback with the cataclysmic eruption of 1980; but if the mountain settles down for a century or so, forest growth will advance once again up Saint Helens' slopes. (Interestingly, much of the timberline on the mountain's southern slope survived the 1980 eruption.)

Countless hiking trails provide access to timberline habitats throughout the Cascades of Washington and British Columbia. Paved roads reach the parkland on Mount Rainier, Mount Baker, and at 5480-foot Washington Pass in North Cascades National Park. Unpaved forest roads lead to the timberline on Mount Adams, at Harts Pass, and at several other points. In British Columbia, a major highway crosses through Manning Provincial Park on the Cascade divide immediately north of the international boundary. A park road leads to the 6500-foot level on Blackwall Peak, just above forest line, where nature trails wind through meadows and open groves of Engelmann spruce, subalpine fir, whitebark pine, and a northern "outlier" population (a disjunct population of a species beyond the general distribution limits) of alpine larch.

Southern Cascade Range
(Oregon and California)

South of the Columbia Gorge, the Cascades form a broad, moderately high, heavily forested chain of mountains stretching 250 miles without a break. Then, near the Oregon-California border (42°N), the Klamath River Valley cuts across the range, and 80 miles farther south the Pit River Valley does likewise. These high, open valleys are the only interruptions in the Cascade-Sierra Nevada backbone between the Columbia Gorge and southern California's Mojave Desert.

The southern Cascades are composed of volcanic rock—for the most part gently sloping lava flows that have been eroded by stream channels and, in the highest areas, by glaciers. In Oregon, the Cascades form a

Krummholz whitebark pine, mountain hemlock, and Shasta red fir on pumice at Mount Shasta in the Southern Cascade Range

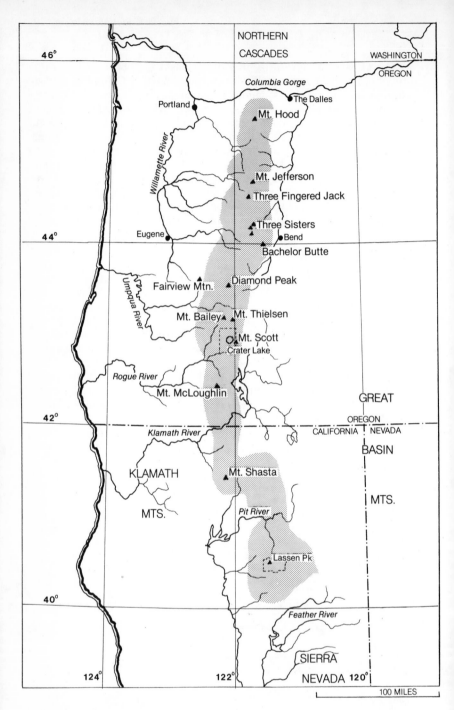

Southern Cascade Range

50-mile-wide mountain upland covered by a dense carpet of montane and subalpine forests. From the Klamath River southward, a drier, more open montane forest covers most of the Cascade Range, which merges into the granitic Sierra Nevada at the headwaters of the Feather River.

Along the crest of the southern Cascades, numerous volcanic peaks and cones rise above the forested mountains. The major peaks support timberline habitats and even small areas of alpine vegetation. The principal timberline areas surround the following mountains (north to south): Hood (11,245 feet), just south of the Columbia River; Jefferson (10,499 feet); Three Sisters (10,354 feet); Bachelor Butte (9060 feet); Diamond Peak (8792 feet); Bailey (8361 feet); Thielsen (9173 feet); Scott (8926 feet), in Crater Lake National Park; McLoughlin (9495 feet); and in California, Shasta (14,162 feet) and Lassen (10,466 feet). Additionally, there are areas of timberline vegetation around some of the tallest secondary peaks. Several small glaciers flow down the upper slopes of Mounts Shasta, Hood, Jefferson, and the Three Sisters.

Contrasting regional climates strongly influence forest and timberline development in the southern Cascades. In northern Oregon the western slope of the Cascades has a pronounced maritime climate, with annual precipitation averaging about 100 inches on Mount Hood. However, both annual and summer precipitation, as well as the incidence of cool, cloudy summer weather, decrease southward. For example, at Crater Lake National Park Headquarters (6475 feet) in southern Oregon, average annual precipitation is 65 inches, and comparable high-elevation sites on Mount Shasta are considerably drier. Moreover, only about 1¼ inches of precipitation fall during July and August at Crater Lake, compared to an average of 4½ inches at Mount Rainier, which lies 270 miles farther north. Nevertheless, winter snowfall remains plentiful southward in the Cascades, with Crater Lake recording an average annual snowfall of 516 inches.

The eastern slope of the southern Cascades, like that of the Northern Cascades, lies within a prominent rain shadow. Thus, while luxuriant coastal Douglas-fir and western hemlock forests dominate the western slope, the east-slope forests are sunny, open stands of ponderosa pine. South of the Klamath River, however, even the western slope has an open, rain-shadow forest, since here the Cascades stand in the lee of the prominent coastal range known as the Klamath Mountains.

On Mount Hood, forest line develops at about 5500 feet. It averages 6500 feet on the Three Sisters east of Eugene, near 7500 feet in Crater Lake National Park, and 8000 to 8500 feet on Mounts Shasta and Lassen. In addition to the drier, sunnier summer conditions, another factor involved with this rise in timberline is simply the effect of latitude— warmer climates occur at any given elevation nearer to the equator. From Mount Hood to the Klamath River, mountain hemlock with lesser amounts of whitebark pine and subalpine fir are the primary timberline trees. Pacific silver fir is a major climax component of subalpine forests on the western slope of the Cascades south to central Oregon, and it ascends into the lower part of the parkland. The shade-tolerant mountain hemlock co-dominates the upper subalpine forest belt, along with Pacific silver fir, and forms timberline on moist sites and cool exposures. In contrast, the relatively intolerant whitebark pine primarily inhabits open rocky sites and windswept ridges, and it only becomes a member of the subalpine forest proper in drier mountains east of the Cascade Crest.

Subalpine fir becomes less common at timberline southward in the Cascades. At Crater Lake it is largely confined to the margins of wet meadows, streamsides, and the recesses of deep canyons. The southern Oregon Cascades, along with a few isolated spots in the nearby Klamath Mountains, mark the southern limits of subalpine fir west of the Rocky Mountain states. Although subalpine fir is the most widely distributed timberline tree in western North America (occurring from the Yukon Territory to southern New Mexico), it is nearly absent from California. In the Pacific Northwest, subalpine fir inhabits drier sites than mountain hemlock, which extends far into California. Nevertheless, it appears that subalpine fir is unable to tolerate the dry summer conditions of the California mountains. Hence its confinement to topographically moist and protected sites at its southern limits. Competition from more shade-tolerant species can hardly explain subalpine fir's absence in the timberline zone, where open sites abound.

Whitebark pine on an 8000-foot pumice ridge south of the South Sister, Oregon Cascades

In northern and central Oregon, Alaska-cedar is a minor component of the west-slope subalpine forest; but it is not very common at timberline. In southern Oregon, Pacific silver fir is replaced by Shasta red fir (*Abies magnifica* var. *shastensis*), and southward (in California) this luxuriant, stately fir often reaches forest line but does not ascend as high as its associate, mountain hemlock, or the timberline dweller, whitebark pine.

Increasingly dry summers southward from Mount Hood, coupled with coarse volcanic substrate, bring about a diminishing amount of lush parkland. Moist meadow, heathland, and dwarf sedge communities similar to those described for the northern Cascades are abundant around Mount Hood, but from Mount Jefferson southward, nearly barren pumice flats become common in the timberline zone (Franklin and Dyrness 1973). The sparse vegetation on these pumice sites consists of low, compact perennials with large taproots, such as wild buckwheats (*Eriogonum pyrolaefolium* and *E. marifolium*). The severe diurnal temperature changes, low soil fertility, and dry surface conditions are responsible for the shift from meadows and heathlands to pumice flats.

Well-drained, open sites at timberline in the Mount Jefferson area are being invaded by seedlings of Pacific silver fir, subalpine fir, whitebark pine, mountain hemlock, and lodgepole pine which germinate at the edges of melting snowpack in early summer (Swedberg 1973). The coarse, droughty volcanic soils provide such a harsh environment for young trees, however, that successful establishment is rare. In addition to surface drought, intense frost-heaving in these openings lifts tree seedlings and taprooted perennial herbs, killing them. Even when they have become established, tree seedlings and saplings on sloping sites are subjected to strong shearing forces from the creeping snowpack. Only mountain hemlock stems are sufficiently supple and resilient to resist damage. In dense groves near forest line, mountain hemlock forms essentially pure stands. The closed hemlock canopy and thick layer of needle litter prevent regeneration of other conifers, and even undergrowth vegetation is sparse.

Mount Hood supports a majestic timberline parkland that can be reached by car in two locations. A paved road leading to Timberline Lodge at the 6000-foot level on the southwestern side of the mountain provides a popular year-round access above the forest line. The lodge itself is an alpine architectural attraction, built of heavy stone and hand-hewn timbers and studded with carvings and paintings by American artists. It was constructed by the Works Progress Administration and dedicated by President Franklin D. Roosevelt in 1937. A chair lift ascends beyond timberline to provide year-round skiing.

An unpaved road reaches the parkland (6000 feet) at Cloud Cap on Mount Hood's northeastern slope. Cloud Cap Inn, built in 1889 but no longer open as a commercial facility, is an excellent example of early log construction. Hiking trails lead around the mountain, largely through parkland with groves and islands of mountain hemlock, subalpine fir, and whitebark pine and with lesser amounts of Engelmann spruce, lodgepole pine, Pacific silver fir, and Alaska-cedar.

Timberlines on other principal peaks in the northern and central portions of the Oregon Cascades can be reached in day-hikes. An unusual

Timberline Lodge on Mount Hood, Oregon Cascades

alpine timberline is found atop 5933-foot Fairview Mountain southeast of Eugene. This peak is a western outlier of the Cascades at the southern end of the Willamette Valley. It is only 75 miles from the ocean and has a maritime climate with a cool, dry summer (Baker 1951). The summit rises above forest line and is covered with meadows and small groves of mountain hemlock with some Alaska-cedar, but there is no subalpine fir or whitebark pine.

In southern Oregon, roads around the rim of Crater Lake ascend to over 8000 feet and pass through picturesque, broken stands of dwarfed mountain hemlock and whitebark pine. The short hiking trail up Mount Scott leads high into the krummholz zone. Pumice flats with their interesting drought-resistant flora are ubiquitous in the timberline zone on the Crater Lake rim.

In northern California, 14,162-foot Mount Shasta, second only to Rainier in height among all the Cascade Range volcanoes, towers 10,000 feet above semi-arid valleys. Five small glaciers cling to the mountain's upper slopes, above 9800 feet, yet Shasta stands in the rain shadow created by the Klamath Mountains and is distinctly dry compared to the nearby Oregon Cascades, Mount Lassen, or the Klamaths (Cooke 1940). Vehicle access to the timberline on the southern slope of Shasta is open all year over the Everitt Memorial Highway which leads to Mount Shasta Ski Bowl at 7930 feet.

Forest line averages 8000 to 8500 feet on Shasta and the timberline is composed of whitebark pine, mountain hemlock, and Shasta red fir. Krummholz communities of whitebark pine extend as high as 9500 feet, with individuals growing sometimes near 10,000 feet on ridges radiating from Shasta's summit. However, the glacier-carved gorges between these windswept ridge spurs support their highest-dwelling conifers as clumps of erect whitebark pine, Shasta red fir, and mountain hemlock at 8000 to 8500 feet. Snow accumulation, cold air drainage, and shortness of the warm season depress the conifer limit in these basins. The usually montane tree, white fir (*Abies concolor*), has been observed on a ridge south of Horse Camp in the timberline zone (Cooke 1940). The subalpine forest proper consists of dense stands of Shasta red fir and mountain hemlock with extensive mats of mountain manzanita (*Arctostaphylos nevadensis*) covering the ground.

Lassen Peak rises at the southern end of the Cascades, 70 miles southeast of Shasta. Lassen erupted in the early 1900s and is characterized by a raw, rugged, volcanic landscape. A highway through Lassen Volcanic National Park ascends to 8512 feet in the timberline zone.

Krummholz and manzanita mats on a pumice ridge, Mount Shasta, California Cascades

Whitebark pine on Lassen Peak, California Cascades

California red fir (*Abies magnifica* var. *magnifica*) dominates the upper subalpine forest, extending into the lower portion of the timberline. Mountain hemlock and whitebark pine ascend to 9200 feet in scattered, wind-dwarfed forms, and krummholz cushions of pine are reported as high as 10,000 feet. There is no alpine zone as such, but the timberline zone is a main feature of the national park.

Lower timberlines occur at the base of both the western and eastern slopes of the southern Cascade Range. On the western slope they are formed at low elevations in the warm, dry inland portions of the coastal valleys—the Willamette, Umpqua, Rogue, and Klamath valleys. Natural vegetation has been removed or heavily disturbed by agriculture, development, logging, and grazing in these valleys. Suppression of fires has also changed the character of the presettlement landscape at lower timberline. Prior to 1900 these areas were mosaics of open oak woodlands, savannas, and grasslands (Habeck 1961, Thilenius 1968, Johannessen and others 1971, Franklin and Dyrness 1973). Oregon white oak was the principal tree species, along with lesser amounts of Pacific madrone and, in the southern areas, California black oak (*Quercus kelloggii*). Because of fire suppression, undeveloped areas now have denser stands of these species, along with bigleaf maple (*Acer macrophyllum*) and the more shade-tolerant Douglas-fir. Hot, dry summer weather causes extreme soil drought which limits establishment and growth of most trees in these sites, and in the past surface fires, often set by Indians (Weaver 1974), killed most saplings, although larger trees were not damaged. Daily maximum temperatures often surpass 90°F in summer in these valleys, and from June through August precipitation is scant—totaling about two inches in the Willamette Valley and only one and one-third inches in southwestern Oregon.

At the eastern base of the Cascades, lower timberlines are formed in a relatively continental climate. Ponderosa pine is the principal forest tree, generally giving way to sagebrush-grass or a western juniper (*Juniperus occidentalis* var. *occidentalis*) woodland where annual precipitation averages less than 12 inches. However, much of the high basin country (4000 to 5000 feet) immediately east of the Cascades in central and southern Oregon is extremely frosty. Killing frosts occur occasionally in the basin bottoms even in mid-summer. Ponderosa pine cannot survive such frosty growing seasons; only lodgepole pine is capable of enduring the summer frosts and of growing on the dry pumice soils. Lodgepole pine inhabits areas where average annual precipitation is as low as 14 inches (Franklin and Dyrness 1973). Pure stands of lodgepole occupy depressions and broad, level basins, while on every slight hill or rise in topography this species is replaced by ponderosa pine. Lodgepole pine also forms pure stands in central Oregon on sites that have high water tables or are flooded in spring, and these areas are sometimes adjacent to lower timberline.

Western juniper woodlands extend out into the central Oregon desert on sites receiving as little as eight inches of annual precipitation. These juniper types are discussed in Chapter 6.

Klamath Mountains

The Klamath Mountains occupy the northwestern corner of California and the adjacent part of Oregon. This region encompasses the rugged coastal ranges lying west of Interstate 5 from Oregon's Rogue River southward to California's Yolla Bolly Mountains, which lie west of the town of Red Bluff. Only the highest ridges and peaks (7000 to 9000 feet) in the Klamath region support alpine timberline, and except for a few peaks southwest of Ashland, Oregon, these are confined to the California portion.

The Klamath region is densely timbered and its redwood (*Sequoia sempervirens*) forests, confined to the coastal fog belt, have worldwide renown. However, despite their location in the nation's most populous state, the Klamath Mountains themselves and their remarkably diverse forests are little known. The California portion of the Klamath region harbors about 53 species of native trees, including a dozen timberline conifers. Timberline habitats occur on the few highest peaks (above 7000 feet) in the Siskiyou Mountains on both sides of the California-Oregon border. Timberline terrain becomes more common southward atop the Marble, Scott, Salmon, and Trinity mountains. Farther south, the summit of the Yolla Bolly Mountains also exhibits an alpine timberline.

The mountains themselves are old, having been built up during the Paleozoic and Mesozoic eras, over 60 million years ago. The Klamath Mountains are formed from a great mass of ancient, closely folded and faulted rocks, generally metamorphosed (structurally changed under great heat and pressure), and intruded by igneous rocks (Fenneman 1931). The result of their history of repeated sedimentation, vulcanism, and igneous intrusion, uplifting, folding, faulting, and erosion is an extremely complex mixture of rock types. At high elevations there are, for instance, large areas of metamorphic rocks, including schists, gneisses, and marbles, as well as sedimentary sandstones, siltstones, and shales. Granitic rocks are abundant in many locations. Ultramafic (ultrabasic) rocks—peridotite, dunite, and serpentine—occur in stringerlike outcrops, and they support unusual dry-site vegetation (Sawyer and Thornburgh 1977). These highly mineralized rocks yield soils poor in the important nutrients, calcium, nitrogen, and phosphorus.

This exceptional array of rock types provides diverse parent materials for vegetation. Great topographic relief enhances the environmental diversity, since the tallest ridges and peaks tower 5000 to 6000 feet above nearby canyons and valleys. Additionally, there is a pronounced change from maritime to inland climates eastward across the Klamath Mountains. The westernmost ridges and peaks are deluged with over 100 inches of precipitation each year, while the eastern peaks, rising above the semiarid interior valleys of the Klamath and Sacramento rivers, receive only half as much moisture. The dryness of the inland peaks and ridges is accentuated by the dearth of summer rainfall and the hot summers that develop in the adjacent inland valleys. The town of Yreka (elevation 2635 feet) on the eastern slope of the Klamath Mountains records *average* daily

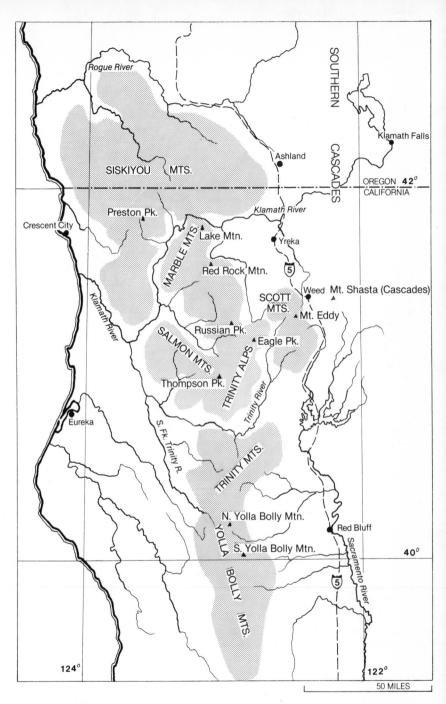

Klamath Mountains

high temperatures of 92°F during July.

But perhaps the most important factor allowing the Klamath region to support such a remarkably rich flora is its "central" location. It lies along the coast at the southern end of the North Pacific maritime forest and at the northern end of the copious California floristic region. Also, the eastern side of the Klamath region adjoins the Cascade Range via a series of mid-elevation ridges. Through this Cascade connection, the eastern Klamaths have been accessible for colonization by inland mountain species during the last few million years.

Ecologist Robert Whittaker (1961) stated that, "All western plant formations dominated by trees occur in the Klamath Region, as in no other area." This region is the "center" of the western forests, in the same sense that the Great Smoky Mountains of Tennessee and North Carolina are known as the center of eastern forests. Thus, the Klamath region is a center toward which mesophytic (warm and moist) forests of the past have shrunk. The result is an accumulation of species having varied ecological histories. Many of the relict stands in the Klamath Mountains occur on serpentine, gabbro, or other peculiar substrates where they have escaped competition from the vigorous conifers that dominate most parent materials—for instance, mountain hemlock and Shasta red fir in moist subalpine forests.

As an index of the arboreal diversity, the Klamath region of California contains 33 species of coniferous trees and 20 broadleaved trees (Griffin and Critchfield 1976). There are about 60 coniferous trees native to western North America north of Mexico (Little 1971), and this corner of California has more than half of them! For comparison, other areas with varied conifer forests, such as the Olympic Mountains and the southern Sierra Nevada, have 16 to 18 species.

The Klamath conifer forests are perhaps more diverse than those found in any other small region in the world. The lower-elevation forests are characterized by Douglas-fir with mixed hardwoods—tanoak (*Lithocarpus densiflorus*), Pacific madrone, canyon live oak (*Quercus chrysolepis*), and others (Sawyer and Thornburgh 1977). On the lower eastern slope of these mountains, ponderosa pine and Oregon white oak dominate. At progressively higher elevations white fir, then Shasta red fir, and finally mountain hemlock become the climax dominant species on "normal" parent materials such as granitic rock.

The upper subalpine forest (mountain hemlock zone) and the timberline (whitebark pine zone) support at least a dozen tree species, all of which are conifers (Sawyer and Thornburgh 1977). In these zones, northern exposures and moist sites are occupied primarily by mountain hemlock with lesser amounts of Shasta red fir, Sierra lodgepole pine (*Pinus contorta* var. *murrayana*), western white pine, and Brewer spruce (*Picea brewerana*), which is an "endemic" (found only in this small region). Additionally, four timberline species from the North Pacific maritime forests reach their southern limits here on moist sites, forming relict populations that apparently are the remains of more extensive stands that occurred during cooler, wetter climates of the past. Residual stands

Foxtail pine and Shasta red fir atop 6900-foot Lake Mountain, in the Klamath Mountains south of Seiad Valley

of Pacific silver fir and Alaska-cedar occur in the northwestern portion of the Klamath region in the Siskiyous, while subalpine fir and Engelmann spruce occupy streamsides and cirque basins below 8183-foot Russian Peak in the Salmon Mountains. Unlike common regional trees, relicts such as Pacific silver fir, subalpine fir, Alaska-cedar, Engelmann spruce, and foxtail pine do not necessarily show predictable environmentally controlled patterns of distribution, but instead appear to be controlled primarily by chance events and by these species' inability to recolonize.

Although Brewer spruce is found in generally cool, moist areas and is restricted to the Klamath region, it differs from the other relicts in being rather abundant and in being able to grow on a broad range of sites (Sawyer and Thornburgh 1977). Brewer spruce is evidently drought resistant but has thin bark and is not fire resistant; this may be why it seems largely confined to north-facing slopes and rocky ridges where large fires were uncommon. It is a major component of the timberlines, reaching as high as 7500 feet on northern slopes in the Russian Peak area, but also extending down to 5000 feet. On favorable sites Brewer spruce forms large trees. Its other common name, weeping spruce, denotes its distinctive drooping appearance which is caused by the presence of thousands of long, hanging branchlets.

The mountain hemlock zone is characterized by heavily glaciated slopes with thin soils and abundant moisture. Consequently, forests are open and patchy with intervening bedrock slopes and wet meadows watered by melting snow. Mountain heaths (*Phyllodoce empetriformis* and *Cassiope mertensiana*), Labrador tea (*Ledum glandulosum*), bog laurel (*Kalmia polifolia*), Sitka alder shrubs, and huckleberry (*Vaccinium arbuscula*) are among the most abundant undergrowth plants in these moist timberline communities (Sawyer and Thornburgh 1977).

On ridge crests and upper southern or western slopes above 7200 feet, wind-deformed stands of whitebark pine occur with smaller amounts of mountain hemlock, Shasta red fir, Sierra lodgepole pine, and Jeffrey pine (*Pinus jeffreyi*). Foxtail pine (*Pinus balfouriana*) is dominant on some of these sites, but it differs from the other species in that it grows erect and develops a large single trunk, even under severely exposed conditions. Foxtail and the other timberline pines are prevalent on ultrabasic substrates, where they form open stands.

Foxtail pine is unique in being confined to two widely separated timberline areas in California. It occurs atop several peaks in the central and eastern Klamath Mountains (from Lake Mountain in the north to South Yolla Bolly Mountain) and on the southern Sierra Nevada over 300 miles away. This distinctive timberline dweller is closely related to the Great Basin bristlecone pine and is estimated to attain ages in excess of 1000 years in the Klamath Mountains. The Klamath and Sierra Nevada populations of foxtail pine have been isolated from each other so long that they have evolved different characteristics (R. and J. Mastrogiuseppe 1980). For example, Klamath foxtails have significantly larger cones. They also have downswept branches, while Sierra Nevada foxtails have upright branching. The bark of mature Klamath foxtails is gray and ridged, while mature Sierra foxtails have cinnamon-orange bark arranged in "alligator plates."

Even the deciduous shrubs forming undergrowth in the whitebark pine zone are typically wind-trained, and they are pruned to less than three feet tall. The California shrubs creamberry (*Holodiscus microphyllus*), goldenweed (*Haplopappus greenii*), chinquapin (*Chrysolepis sempervirens*), and manzanitas (*Arctostaphylos patula* and *A. nevadensis*) are among the most common undergrowth species (Sawyer and Thornburgh 1977).

The whitebark pine woodland is best developed on high, unglaciated southern exposures in the Trinity Alps (Ferlatte 1974). Here, the dwarfed tree groves grow *above* the pockets of alpine tundra that occupy the coldest microsites in glacial cirques on the highest peaks. The northern slope of 9002-foot Thompson Peak even harbors two ice remnants (covering five acres each) of a recent glacier. The alpine tundra microsites are inhabited by snowbed saxifrage (*Saxifraga tolmiei*), sibbaldia (*Sibbaldia procumbens*), Sierra primrose (*Primula suffrutescens*), and alpine sorrel (*Oxyria digyna*).

The alpine character of the Trinity Alps may be due to lack of soil development on the glacially scoured high-country, which provides tundralike habitats within the mountain hemlock and whitebark pine zones (Sawyer and Thornburgh 1977). Tremendous quantities of winter snowpack are undoubtedly important in creating this alpinelike environment at modest elevations. In the western Siskiyous, perhaps the heaviest snowfall area of the Klamath Mountains, pockets of alpine vegetation descend to slightly below the 6000-foot level on Preston Peak (7310 feet) (Major and Taylor 1977).

Ancient foxtail pine on Lake Mountain, high in the Klamath Mountains

Besides the exposed glacial bedrock, another factor that brings about the open woodlands at high elevations in the Klamath region is the presence of peridotite, dunite, and serpentine rock. The pattern of elevational change in the forest becomes subdued on these ultrabasic substrates because shade tolerance and competition are much less important. Success is guaranteed for any species that can tolerate dry soils, nutrient imbalances, and high levels of heavy metals (Sawyer and Thornburgh 1977). In Trinity and southern Siskiyou counties, ultrabasic parent materials are common in the subalpine and timberline zones on Scott Mountain, Eagle Peak, Red Rock Mountain, and others. These sites support open stands of foxtail pine, western white pine, and whitebark pine with a sparse herbland or dry-meadow undergrowth. Such woodlands extend to the summit of Mount Eddy (9038 feet), the highest peak in the Klamath region.

The picturesque groves of stout, windswept foxtail pines on the upper slopes of Mount Eddy can be reached in a day-hike via the trail up Deadfall Creek southwest of the town of Weed. Mount Eddy also provides a breathtaking view of massive Mount Shasta and its timberline, only 15 miles to the east across the low ridges that connect the Klamath Mountains to the Cascades.

The Russian Peak area, 20 miles west of Mount Eddy, harbors a remarkably rich assortment of subalpine conifers. A day-hike up Duck Creek to Little Duck Lake, north of Russian Peak, will take you through groves of subalpine fir, Engelmann spruce, and Brewer spruce, with foxtail and whitebark pines atop the 7500-foot ridge immediately south of the lake (Sawyer and Thornburgh 1977). Shasta red fir, mountain hemlock, western white pine, and Jeffrey pine also inhabit this rugged subalpine setting.

Sierra Nevada

The Sierra Nevada is a huge granitic fault-block mountain range that extends nearly 400 miles from the south end of the Cascade Range to southern California's Transverse ranges. Although the Sierra Nevada is 50 to 70 miles wide, its crest occurs near its eastern edge, above a massive fault scarp that drops off abruptly into the Great Basin deserts. The Sierra's western slope is a gradual incline, and the larger streams flow westward. The northern third of the Sierra rises to moderate elevations and has relatively few peaks exhibiting an alpine timberline, but in the central and southern portions of the range, timberline and alpine zones are extensive. This portion includes the "High Sierra," which is an almost unbroken stretch of timberline and alpine environment extending 170 miles along the Sierra crest from Sonora Pass (9626 feet, on State Highway 108) to Olancha Peak (12,136 feet, above the South Fork of the Kern River). Most of the High Sierra lies above 10,000 feet, and has several 14,000-foot peaks that tower 10,000 feet above the Owens Valley desert immediately to the east.

The long, gradual western slope of the Sierra starts only a few hundred feet above sea level on the eastern edge of California's Great

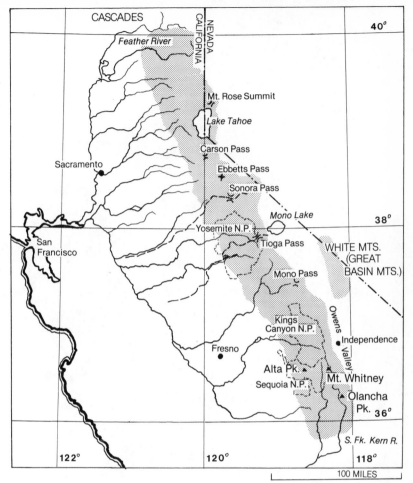

Sierra Nevada

Central Valley. Ascending the lower western slope, valley grasslands and agricultural areas give way to a broad belt of oak woodlands mixed with dense tall-shrub communities known as chaparral. Above this stand splendid conifer forests that extend up to the alpine timberline, which generally lies between 10,000 and 11,500 feet.

The west-slope Sierra forest receives ample precipitation from Pacific frontal systems in fall, winter, and spring; however, summers are quite dry. From Yosemite to Sequoia National Park annual precipitation averages 40 to 50 inches in the mid- and high-elevation forests, but it generally decreases southward in the Sierra. At higher elevations the greater part of the precipitation comes as snow, and it usually results in a generous

snowpack that lasts into July in most timberline areas.

Snowy but relatively mild winters and warm, dry summers on the western slope have allowed magnificent mixed-conifer forests to develop at middle elevations. In the past, frequent surface fires kept these stands open and occupied by the fire-resistant, shade-intolerant pines and sequoia. The giant sequoia (*Sequoiadendron giganteum*) groves occurring within this forest contain the world's largest trees. (The largest of all, the General Sherman Tree in Sequoia National Park, is 26¾ feet in d.b.h., 272 feet tall, and about 3000 years old.) Less widely known is the fact that several other species of conifers attain exceptionally large size on the Sierra's western slope. Sugar pine, ponderosa pine, Jeffrey pine, coastal Douglas-fir, and white fir all grow to 6 or more feet in d.b.h. and 200 feet in height in old-growth stands on good sites. At high elevations on this slope many timberline trees also reach large proportions. Following is a list of some record-size high-elevation trees from the Sierra Nevada compiled by the American Forestry Association (1982):

Tree	D.b.h. (feet)	Height (feet)	Location
mountain hemlock	7½	113	Alpine County
California red fir	8½	180	Sierra National Forest
foxtail pine	8⅓	71	Sequoia National Park
lodgepole pine	6¾	91	Stanislaus National Forest
Sierra juniper	13½	87	Stanislaus National Forest

Another characteristic common to both the mid-elevation big-tree forests and the timberline stands in the Sierra Nevada is their inviting openness. The high-country consists of patches of trees interspersed with moist meadows, lakes, and vast areas of glacially scoured bedrock as well as granite talus. These attributes of terrain and vegetation, along with the sunny summer climate, prompted naturalist John Muir to call the High Sierra the "Range of Light." Presumably because of droughty surface soils, undergrowth is sparse at Sierra timberlines, but deep-rooting trees are able to utilize the more abundant subsoil moisture.

The precipitous eastern slope or "escarpment" (face of the uplifted fault block) of the Sierra lies in a rain shadow and receives considerably less moisture than the western slope. The subalpine station at 9500-foot Ellery Lake, east of Yosemite National Park, records only 30 inches of annual precipitation. In addition to being drier, the east-slope climate is also colder in winter, due to frequent domination by continental air masses. Also, the eastern escarpment has much rockier, more broken topography. Hence, there is no big-tree forest zone, and Pacific Coast conifers are scarce. Instead, the Sierran species more tolerant of dry environments grow here, along with some Great Basin and Rocky Mountain trees—for example, singleleaf pinyon pine (*Pinus monophylla*), limber pine (*P. flexilis*), and Fremont cottonwood (*Populus fremontii*).

Thousand-year-old Sierra juniper at 8800 feet along the High Sierra Trail above Hamilton Lake, Sequoia National Park

Mountain hemlock is a common constituent of alpine timberlines as far south as Yosemite National Park, where it forms dense groves that have little undergrowth. John Muir called the mountain hemlock of the High Sierra, "the most singularly beautiful of all the California coniferae" (Muir 1894). He observed that mountain hemlock's rich blue-green foliage, ornate purple cones, and drooping branch tips give it a delicate grace, although it is in no way frail. Yet, at the same time, stout veteran hemlocks with wind-battered crowns and sturdy trunks covered with dark, furrowed bark have a rugged appearance. South of Yosemite, hemlock becomes restricted to shady and moist sites at high elevations. It may be significant that this species reaches its southern limit in the same general area as the southernmost glaciers in North America. Both mountain hemlock and glaciers seem dependent upon the snowy, cloudy, and cool climate that engulfs the North Pacific's coastal mountains.

The southernmost grove of mountain hemlock occupies a spring-riddled mountain slope near Silliman Lake in Sequoia National Park (Parsons 1972). It seems fitting that the stand of large conifers growing on the dry, sunny ridge several hundred feet directly above this site consists of foxtail pine, which is the characteristic timberline tree of the southern High Sierra. Whitebark pine and Sierra lodgepole pine are the principal timberline associates of mountain hemlock in the north and of foxtail pine in the south. However, foxtail pine stands out because it forms open groves of large trees, usually above the limits of Sierra lodgepole and where whitebark pine forms only stunted wind-timber or krummholz. In the Sierra, foxtail pine is largely confined to Sequoia and Kings Canyon National parks and the adjacent Inyo National Forest, and it is common only between 10,000 and 11,500 feet (R. and J. Mastrogiuseppe 1980). This, along with its scattered groves on the highest peaks of the Klamath Mountains, represents foxtail's entire distribution. Despite its restricted distribution, the species is abundant in the southern High Sierra, where it is evidently well adapted to the present-day climate and the stark granitic substrate. (Even the "soil" is primarily decomposed-granite sand.) Foxtail pines have deep and spreading root systems which probably occupy most of the openings between trees in the parklike groves.

The remarkably large size attained by foxtail pines in their exposed, rocky habitats is partially a function of longevity, since they often attain ages of 700 to 2000 years (R. and J. Mastrogiuseppe 1980). The stand at about 10,500 feet on the southern slope of Alta Peak in Sequoia National Park (accessible on a day-hike) contains some ancient foxtail pines 5 to 6½ feet in d.b.h. and about 60 feet tall (Arno 1973). Some of these trees have remained alive for centuries only because of a narrow strip of living cambium and bark clinging to the leeward side of the trunk. This cambium "lifeline" supports branches that survive on the leeward side of the crown.

Two of the foxtail pines on Alta Peak have "double piggyback" trunks that keep them alive in the same manner as the piggyback trunks of ancient bristlecone pines growing in the White Mountains 30 miles east of the Sierra keep them alive. This piggyback growth results when the main

Trees with "piggy-back" trunks: Bristlecone pine (left) from California's White Mountains, and foxtail pine in the Sierra Nevada

trunk of a large tree succumbs to ice-blasting blizzards. A large branch on the leeward side begins to grow erect and, after a century or two, may form a new trunk. This, too, may be killed by violent winds, but a branch on the leeward side of the second trunk then develops as a third trunk. The top of the third trunk of the largest Alta Peak tree is now dying, and a large branch on its sheltered side seems destined to become trunk number four!

On Alta Peak and elsewhere throughout the southern High Sierra, one often finds the charred remains of a single foxtail pine or of a small group of conifers that was struck by lightning and, with its abundance of dead pitchy wood, became a giant torch. However, fires seldom spread over large areas in these timberline stands because the trees grow 30 to 60 feet apart and the "forest floor" consists largely of mineral earth and rocks. In an effort to perpetuate fire as a natural ecological process, lightning fires have been allowed to burn without suppression in the high-country of Sequoia, Kings Canyon, and Yosemite National parks since 1973.

Another distinctive feature of High Sierra timberlines is the Sierra lodgepole pine (*Pinus contorta* var. *murrayana*). The Rocky Mountain form of lodgepole pine (var. *latifolia*) is a slender tree of modest size that grows in dense stands and seldom ascends to upper timberline; on moist sites it is relatively short-lived and is replaced by more shade-tolerant

Development of a gnarled foxtail pine over 1000 years of time

conifers. In contrast, the Sierra lodgepole pine is a major, long-lived component of timberline communities. It often develops a full, spreading crown and, on favorable sites, a trunk 3 or more feet in d.b.h. and 100 feet tall. Also, it seems to be a climax species, able to regenerate and remain a major stand component indefinitely. Sierra lodgepole pine is well adapted to wet sites such as meadows and lake basins. It is flood tolerant (Rundel and others 1977) and descends along streams and in frost-pocket meadows down as low as the ponderosa pine forest. It is also the most abundant species in the subalpine forest below the timberline zone. Perhaps because it is like eastern tamarack (*Larix laricina*) in being associated with wet sites, Sierra lodgepole was termed "tamarack pine" by John Muir. Local people often call it "tamarack," and the many "Tamarack lakes" and similar place names in the High Sierra attest to the abundance of lodgepole pine.

Whitebark pine is the most common wind-timber and krummholz species in the Sierra. Limber pine grows along the eastern side of the Sierra crest, and lodgepole pine is generally the fourth-highest-dwelling pine in the Sierra, reaching its upper limit a few hundred feet below whitebark, limber, and foxtail pine. Above Sphinx Lakes in Kings Canyon National Park, however, lodgepole reaches its upper limit as krummholz near 11,500 feet, while foxtail pine (erect) ascends only to about 11,000 feet and whitebark krummholz reaches 12,000 feet. Much of the timberline forest in the High Sierra is so patchy and isolated by alpine and barren rockland that groves may be individually composed of any combination of the pines or mountain hemlock.

In the western portion of the High Sierra, whitebark is less common as a well-formed tree, but groves of typical whitebark pine trees are well represented along the Sierra crest, especially outside the range of foxtail pine. The slopes above Tioga Pass (9941 feet) in Yosemite National Park support a sequence of whitebark pine growth forms, ranging from large

Flagged krummholz of whitebark pine above Bernice Lake, Yosemite National Park

single-trunk trees to smaller multi-stemmed trees, flagged krummholz, and cushion krummholz. Clark's nutcrackers harvest the whitebark pine seeds from these Sierra crest groves and often transport seeds down to wintering areas in the Jeffrey pine forests 3000 feet below to the east (Tomback 1978).

Limber pine is rather common, although seldom dominant, on steep, dry, rocky sites throughout the forest zone on the Sierra eastern escarpment from Mono Pass southward. It forms a relatively small, spreading tree and on less-severe sites seems unable to compete for growing room with the other conifers. Limber and foxtail pines grow together at upper timberline on the eastern slope of the southern Sierra, and the dramatic difference in their growth forms can be seen at elevations between 10,700 and 11,000 feet along the John Muir Trail above Whitney Portal. Here, on the steep bedrock slopes, limber pine forms huge, sprawling shrubs among the erect foxtail pine trees.

Western white pine sometimes ascends into the lower part of the timberline zone, especially in the northern part of the Sierra, and it forms a magnificent, large tree, overtopping associated lodgepole pines. A western white pine's trunk can be identified at quite a distance by its distinctive dark-brown, checkered bark. On Alta Peak in Sequoia National Park and at Sonora and Tioga passes individual white pines 5 feet in d.b.h. and 90 feet tall stand out among the other trees at the forest line.

Sierra juniper (*Juniperus occidentalis* var. *australis*) occasionally reaches the upper timberline, but more often it clings to nearly vertical

cliffs and occupies other sunny, exposed granite sites in the subalpine zone where other species cannot survive. It sometimes grows under these conditions at altitudes up to 10,000 feet, where it merges with foxtail pine that inhabits gentler slopes above the cliffs.

John Muir (1894) called the Sierra juniper "a thickset, sturdy, picturesque highlander, seemingly content to live for more than a score of centuries on sunshine and snow.... The burly Juniper, whose girth sometimes more than equals its height, is about as rigid as the rocks on which it grows." Sierra juniper is a close relative (geographical race) of the highly drought-tolerant western juniper (*J. occidentalis* var. *occidentalis* as described in Cronquist and others 1972) that grows at *lower* timberlines east of the Cascades. Unlike its relative, Sierra juniper finds a suitable unoccupied habitat, or "ecological niche," in the high-country on canyon walls and other severely rocky and dry sites, where its roots extend deep into cracks. It frequently survives 1000 years or more and becomes a craggy, weather-beaten, living snag. These stocky, bark-stripped, and weather-polished junipers with their tattered crowns look every bit their age. A western juniper estimated to be at least 3000 years old grows near Sonora Pass. This Methuselah tree, known as the Bennett juniper, is 13½ feet in d.b.h. and 87 feet tall and is apparently the largest juniper of any species in the world (American Forestry Association 1982).

Undergrowth vegetation is most notable by its sparseness on well-drained sites at Sierra timberlines; however, moist seepage slopes and meadows make up a major part of the timberline mosaic. Dwarf alpine willow (*Salix petrophila*) only two inches high, bog laurel (*Kalmia polifolia*), red mountain heath (*Phyllodoce breweri*), Labrador tea (*Ledum glandulosum*), and shorthair sedge (*Carex exserta*) are often abundant in these wet areas. In summer, both moist and dry sites of High Sierra timberlines are bedecked with dozens of species of colorful wildflowers.

The highways over Mount Rose Summit near Lake Tahoe and, southward, Carson, Ebbetts, and Sonora passes, as well as Tioga Pass in Yosemite National Park, ascend to within a short walk of upper timberline. Also, countless hiking trails lead into the timberline zone from numerous roadheads in the national forests and national parks along both the western and eastern slopes of the Sierra Nevada.

On the western slope, the lower limit of the coniferous forest zone is marked by the appearance of scattered ponderosa pine projecting out through the broadleaf woodland. Incense-cedar (*Calocedrus decurrens*) is also a component of many of these lower timberlines. East of Sacramento the ponderosa pine forest reaches down to the 2000-foot level, while southward at Sequoia National Park this ecotone is encountered at 4500 to 5000 feet. Downslope from the conifer forest lies an oak woodland or foothill woodland mixed intermittently with dense shrubby chaparral.

Blue oak (*Quercus douglasii*) and Digger pine (*Pinus sabiniana*) are the characteristic species of the Sierra oak woodland, although several other deciduous and evergreen oaks and the showy California buckeye are common associates. Both blue oak and Digger pine are deep rooted and can

Sierra junipers on a sun-exposed cliff in California's Sierra Nevada

occupy sites that have low water-holding capacity or that receive as little as 10 inches of precipitation annually (Neal 1980). They can endure very hot summers with almost no precipitation, partially because of their deep root systems. Blue oak was found to utilize water from depths of at least 69 feet during the summer (Griffin 1977)! This oak prospers on parched hillsides and does not even produce its full complement of leaves until summer has set in.

On a scorching summer afternoon, the oak's bluish foliage and dense form standing amidst the smoky haze tends to accentuate the traveler's feeling of oppressive heat. In extremely dry years, blue oaks become drought-deciduous and lose their leaves in late summer. Nevertheless, when irrigation ditches have been cut too near blue oaks, the trees are often killed, apparently by excessive water.

Digger pine is also exceedingly drought tolerant and is not a forest tree. John Muir observed that few people seeing a Digger pine for the first time would realize that it is a conifer. It has unusually sparse foliage and an open crown that branches like an elm. The foliage is so thin and gray that sunlight shines directly through it to the ground beneath. Below the blue oak-Digger pine zone lies an open oak savanna that gives way on the lowest, driest slopes to pure grassland, much of which has now become irrigated farmland.

On the eastern slope of the central and southern Sierra an elfin woodland of squatty singleleaf pinyon (*Pinus monophylla*), often with Sierra juniper, occurs below the main forest zone. This is a western extension of the pinyon-juniper woodlands that cover tens of millions of acres in the Great Basin and other desert regions to the east. Singleleaf pinyon is a small, gray-green tree with a rounded crown 15 to 30 feet tall that forms open stands below the Sierra's eastern escarpment at 5000 to 7500 feet. Pinyon grows in natural orchards in which the pine nuts are harvested intensively by jays, squirrels, and, in some areas, by Indians.

The Sierra's eastern slope also harbors a unique mixture of Great Basin species growing with California mountain conifers. In addition to the pinyon, juniper, and limber pine, this slope has mountain hemlock (north from Mammoth Lakes), red fir (*Abies magnifica*), lodgepole pine, Jeffrey pine, and California black oak. Rather than supporting well-developed forest zones, however, the eastern escarpment has patchy, mixed forests containing some unusual combinations of species. A remarkable example of this diversity is found at Onion Valley in the Inyo National Forest, west of the town of Independence. Here eight species of pine can be seen along the road or on slopes immediately above the roadhead at 9200 feet. Ponderosa pine and singleleaf pinyon grow at the lower elevations, and, with increasing elevation, Jeffrey, Sierra lodgepole, limber, western white, whitebark, and foxtail pine can be found (Little 1966).

Southern California Peaks

Three small but lofty mountain ranges bordering the San Bernardino Valley and the Los Angeles metropolitan area have alpine timberlines atop their highest peaks. These timberlines occur on (1) 10,064-foot Mount

San Antonio in the San Gabriel Mountains 10 miles north of the munici-
pality of Upland; (2) on 11,500-foot San Gorgonio and nearby peaks in the
San Bernardino Mountains 20 miles east of Redlands; and (3) on 10,805-
foot Mount San Jacinto in the San Jacinto Range 35 miles southeast of
Redlands and only 5 miles west of Palm Springs. The latter two mountain
masses lie within small wilderness areas in the San Bernardino National
Forest and are "islands of wilderness in a sea of civilization" because 7½
million people occupy the adjacent metropolitan area.

In addition to their intensely urban setting, these southern California
peaks have other unusual characteristics. They are steep fault-block
ranges, lying along the San Andreas geologic fault system. The peaks are
made up of granite and highly metamorphosed sedimentary and volcanic
rocks, and they rise approximately two vertical miles above the nearly
sea-level valleys. The mountain ranges are sandwiched between the hot
deserts of the interior and the subtropical lowlands along the coast. The
upper slopes of these mountains form the southern distributional limits
for much of the North Pacific and California mountain flora. There is a
10,126-foot peak (Cerro de la Encantada) about 200 miles farther south, in
Baja California, but its only high subalpine tree species is lodgepole pine,
and the mountain evidently has no alpine timberline.

Life zones on these southern California mountains range upwards
from the Mojave and Sonoran deserts on the inland side, and from coastal
grassland and chaparral on the seaward side, through oak woodlands and
montane and then subalpine conifer forests. A tiny area of alpine vegeta-

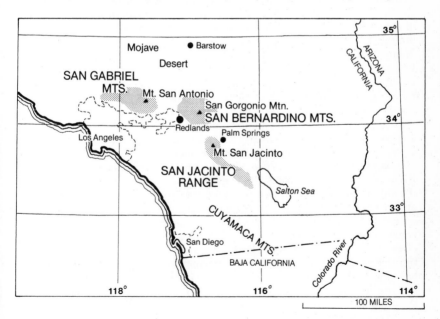

Southern California Peaks

tion also occurs atop the highest peak, San Gorgonio (Major and Taylor 1977). The regional climate is dry and subtropical, with frost rarely occurring at lower elevations even in mid-winter. In contrast, the timberline peaks have a cold, snowy winter and a cool, dry summer similar to that of the southern Sierra Nevada, but probably drier. A few snow patches persist into late summer near the summits of San Gorgonio and San Jacinto peaks.

The mountain forests of these southern California ranges are southern outliers of the Sierra Nevada floristic province. They contain about 18 broadleaved tree species, concentrated in the lower elevations, and 13 coniferous trees (Griffin and Critchfield 1976). Coulter pine (*Pinus coulteri*) and bigcone Douglas-fir (*Pseudotsuga macrocarpa*) are the only forest trees not found also in the Sierra Nevada. Coulter pine is, however, considered to be an ecological replacement for the Digger pine of the Sierra, and bigcone Douglas-fir is essentially a replacement for the Sierra's coastal Douglas-fir (Thorne 1977). Seven species of conifers and five species of broadleaved trees inhabiting the Sierra Nevada are absent from these southern California mountain ranges. Two of the four principal timberline species in the southern Sierra Nevada, lodgepole pine and limber pine, grow on the southern California peaks. Sierra juniper also joins the two pines, and these three species dominate the small areas of alpine timberline in southern California. Sierra lodgepole pine forms well-developed forests above 8000 feet on northern slopes and above 8500 feet on southern slopes, and this species extends nearly to the summits of the highest peaks (San Antonio, San Gorgonio, and San Jacinto) as scattered krummholz.

In the San Gabriel Mountains, limber pine is confined to the high (8500 to 9400 feet) ridge on the northern side of the range that rises directly above the Mojave Desert, and it does not occur southward on Mount San Antonio. Although limber pine forms bulky, gnarled trees undoubtedly of great age along this desert-facing ridge, the elevation is not high enough to produce an alpine timberline. The limber pines on this ridge and those atop the San Bernardino and San Jacinto mountains occupy exceedingly dry sites where the bare mineral soil is interrupted only by occasional drought-tolerant cushion plants such as the alpine buckwheat (*Eriogonum kennedyi* ssp. *alpigenum*), cinquefoil (*Potentilla wheeleri*), and dwarf fescue (*Festuca bracheophylla*).

San Gorgonio (Old Grayback) and its neighboring peaks in the San Bernardino Mountains support a band of limber pine-dominated forest at the highest elevations. The species is reduced to krummholz at 11,000 feet and extends almost to the windswept summit as scattered cushions. Moist microsites on the summit and lower in the timberline zone on San Gorgonio support red mountain heath (*Phyllodoce breweri*), a southern outlier of an important Sierra Nevada timberline plant; however, few other major timberline and alpine plants from the Pacific Coast ranges to the north can be found on the southern California peaks. Instead, plants from the desert mountain ranges are prominent, and several endemic species occur on these peaks (Hall 1902).

Sierra juniper forms a gnarled, picturesque tree on exposed rocky sites high up on the San Gabriel and San Bernardino mountains. In the

San Gabriels it extends nearly to the summit of 9661-foot Pine Mountain, two miles north of Mount San Antonio (Thorne 1977). The lowest-elevation juniper (at 7750 feet) in Icehouse Canyon is perhaps the largest tree in southern California. It is reported to be 15 feet in diameter, 73 feet tall, and possibly 3000 years old. In the San Gabriels, Sierra juniper usually grows scattered among other trees, often with stunted specimens of Jeffrey pine, lodgepole pine, and even white fir. It is much more abundant in the San Bernardino Mountains. Here it forms a high-elevation juniper woodland of trees 20 to 50 feet tall between about 6700 and 9000 feet on the northern or desert side of the range. Some large junipers ascend as high as 9800 feet on Sugarloaf Peak (Grinnell 1908). Surprisingly, Sierra juniper has not been reported on the San Jacinto Mountains, less than 20 miles to the south.

You can get to southern California timberline peaks on day-hikes. San Antonio's southern slope can be climbed from the Mount Baldy ski area. San Gorgonio and adjacent peaks are reached via trails that join State Highway 38 east of Redlands. An aerial tramway at Palm Springs hoists visitors to the high ridge east of Mount San Jacinto. Also, hiking trails lead up the peak from the mountain village of Idyllwild, east of the city of Hemet.

The lower timberlines on the seaward slopes of the San Gabriel, San Bernardino, and San Jacinto mountains are comprised largely of an open woodland of Coulter pine, California black oak, and canyon live oak mixed with chaparral, mostly between 4500 and 6000 feet elevation (Thorne 1977). Above this lies the ponderosa pine-Jeffrey pine forest. In contrast, the inland slopes of these mountain ranges generally support a woodland of California juniper (*Juniperus californica*) and singleleaf pinyon along with Joshua-tree (*Yucca brevifolia*), big sagebrush (*Artemisia tridentata*), rubber rabbitbrush (*Chrysothamnus nauseosus*), and various other species from the inland deserts (Vasek and Thorne 1977). Jeffrey pine and white fir form the very open montane forest immediately upslope.

The Pacific Coast form of ponderosa pine (var. *ponderosa*) is not tolerant of hot desert environments, and it reaches its southern limits as scattered groves on the Cuyamaca Mountains of San Diego County. Conversely, the somewhat similar Jeffrey pine does well adjacent to the hot deserts. It is evidently more tolerant of low temperature extremes (which can be severe in inland deserts), drought, and serpentine soils than ponderosa pine (Thorne 1977). Also, Jeffrey pine is less susceptible to smog damage than ponderosa pine. A 1970 report (Wert and others) found that air pollution in the Los Angeles metropolitan area had injured 1.3 million trees on 88,000 acres in the San Bernardino National Forest. Some ponderosa pine stands became so moribund that the trees were clearcut and, on better sites, less smog-susceptible species were planted.

6
Great Basin and Southwestern Mountains

The semi-arid region east of the Pacific Coast Mountains, west of the Rocky Mountains, and south of central Oregon's Blue Mountains is characterized by vast expanses of sagebrush-grassland in the north, shadscale (*Atriplex confertifolia*) cold desert in the middle, and creosote bush (*Larrea*) and desert-grassland types in the south (Billings 1951). This region also contains large plateaus covered with elfin woodlands of pinyon pine and juniper and smaller areas of scrub oak and other non-forest types. But because of the dry climate, coniferous forest covers only a minor portion of the landscape and is largely restricted to the high mountains, which are comparatively cool and moist. These mountain habitats are islands of forest rising above an ocean of desert or sagebrush-grass. Lower, drought-related timberlines are prevalent throughout this region, and the less-abundant alpine timberlines are themselves heavily influenced by drought, as well as by the cold growing seasons at very high elevations.

This vast semi-arid region encompasses the high, cold, sagebrush deserts of the Great Basin (Nevada and vicinity) and the Colorado River Plateau (southern Utah, northern Arizona, and northwestern New Mexico), as well as the hot deserts (Mojave, Sonora, and Chihuahua) stretching from southern California to west Texas. In the driest areas, including much of the Great Basin and the Mojave Desert, there is essentially no montane forest. In its place, a band of pinyon-juniper pygmy woodland extends up nearly to the patchy subalpine forest belt, which is composed of drought-resistant limber and bristlecone pines. Eastward, on the highest areas of the Colorado Plateau, montane and subalpine forests become well developed and diverse. These include most of the species characteristic of the Southern Rocky Mountains, still farther east, except for the notable absence of lodgepole pine. Southward, in the hot deserts of southern Arizona and New Mexico, forests are confined to the highest mountain ranges but are floristically rich, being composed of both Southern Rocky Mountain and Mexican tree species.

GREAT BASIN

The Great Basin is a region shaped like an upside-down triangle, covering most of Nevada, southeastern Oregon, western Utah, and much of southern and eastern California. Although it is surrounded by regions

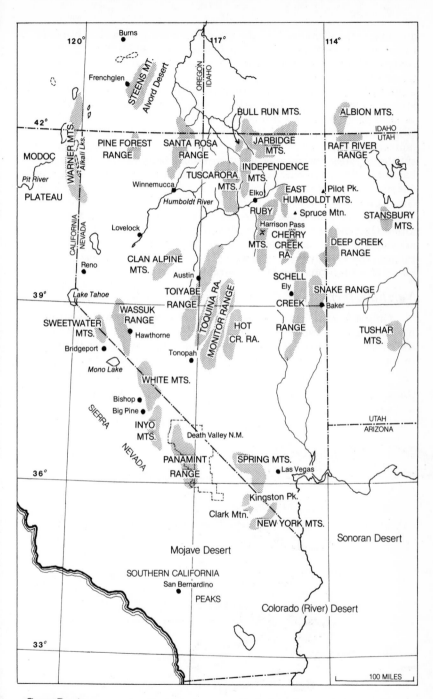

Great Basin

draining to the Pacific Ocean, the Great Basin has no external drainage. In fact, it consists of more than a hundred relatively small drainage basins separated from each other by fault-block mountain ranges, most of which are oriented in a north-south direction. All runoff water stays within each basin, and each has its own watercourse leading to a fresh-water lake, salt lake or marsh, playa (dry lake bed), or sink (underground drain) at the low point in the basin. About 200 isolated mountain ranges occur within the Great Basin, and many of these support a pygmy woodland of pinyon and juniper on their lower slopes. The taller ranges have a small zone of subalpine forest. Because of great distances between the small forest habitats, and contrasting rock substrates and local climates, subalpine forests and their timberline ecotones are remarkably varied across the Great Basin. Another major reason for differences in tree communities from one mountain range to the next is their individual long-term histories. Over the past tens of thousands of years, many chance factors have affected the migration of trees to suitable but small habitats on mountain ranges separated by great expanses of desert. Also, isolated groves were vulnerable to elimination by unfavorable changes in climate.

Northwestern Great Basin

Only a few mountain ranges in the northwestern Great Basin rise high enough to support an upper timberline, and none of these has a well-developed alpine zone. These subalpine ranges are Steens Mountain in southeastern Oregon, the Warner Mountains of northeastern Califor-

Quaking aspen and willow in a sea of sagebrush at Hart Mountain in south-central Oregon

nia, and the Pine Forest and Santa Rosa ranges of northwestern Nevada. Like the rest of the Great Basin, this area receives scant rainfall — 5 to 8 inches in the broad, 4000- to 5000-foot-high sagebrush-grass valleys. Most of the precipitation falls in winter, and the hot summer months are very dry.

This area is north of the distribution of pinyon and the southwestern junipers, and it is the only portion of the Great Basin inhabited by western juniper (*Juniperus occidentalis* var. *occidentalis*), which forms extensive, open elfin woodlands. These juniper woodlands occur on relatively moist and generally rocky sites receiving 8 to 10 inches of annual precipitation (Franklin and Dyrness 1973), and they are mostly confined to the western fringe of the region or to the lower west slopes of mountain ranges.

Old juniper trees are often restricted to especially rocky volcanic sites where fires spread with difficulty and have therefore failed to kill these fire-susceptible trees. Large stands of junipers less than 120 years old have now spread out from the original juniper woodlands (Caraher 1977, Young and Evans 1981), evidently as a result of heavy domestic grazing since the mid-1800s. Grazing greatly reduced the amount of grass and exposed a mineral-soil seedbed favorable for juniper seedlings. The depletion of grass fuels and the institution of fire suppression resulted in much longer intervals between wildfires, which allowed juniper to spread.

Steens Mountain is a 50-mile-long fault-block ridge rising more than a vertical mile above the high desert of southeastern Oregon. Its long, broad summit (9700 feet) has a timberline environment complete with alpine cushion plants, but there is no timberline as such simply because the mountain has no subalpine forest. While the mountain's western slope is a gradual incline, its east side is a spectacular escarpment with sheer cliffs dropping off thousands of feet to the Alvord Desert. Excluding patches of curl-leaf mountain mahogany shrubs (*Cercocarpus ledifolius*) 8 to 10 feet tall, there are no trees on the eastern slope.

The lower western slope of Steens Mountain has scattered western junipers amidst the sagebrush and bunchgrass. Higher up, a broken band of quaking aspen (*Populus tremuloides*) groves is sprinkled across the broad slopes between 6400 and 7800 feet. Some of these aspen groves occupy lake margins and meadow sites seemingly suitable for cold-tolerant conifers; but none is found here. The nearest stands of whitebark pine are 60 miles southward, and other cold-tolerant Great Basin conifers are much farther away.

The absence of coniferous forest on this subalpine mountain range makes it quite unusual, especially since this prominence lies within the Pacific Northwest region rather than in the southwestern deserts. Two factors likely to be responsible are the isolation of Steens Mountain from conifer seed sources and the cold-dry environment which is probably unsuitable for most northwestern forest trees.

There is, however, one grove of coniferous forest trees on Steens Mountain. A 40-acre patch of grand fir occupies the ravines at the junction of Big and Little Fir creeks, at the 6000-foot elevation. These trees are a

Curl-leaf mountain mahogany in the northern Great Basin

grand fir-white fir hybrid similar to that found in the Strawberry Mountains 75 miles to the north (Critchfield and Allenbaugh 1969). The presence of such timber trees in the sprawling high-desert was noted by geographers as early as 1896.

Ponderosa pine, the most drought-tolerant forest tree in eastern Oregon, is generally restricted to sites having 12 or more inches of annual precipitation (Franklin and Dyrness 1973). The Bureau of Land Management reports fair short-term survival of ponderosa pine when planted along the lower slopes of Steens Mountain. Nevertheless, it is likely that most of these lower slopes are marginally dry for ponderosa pine; and at the elevation where sites become moist enough for pine to grow and regenerate, the growing season may be too short. The Soil Conservation Service estimates that average annual precipitation on the mountain's lower slopes is about 10 inches, while the crest receives about 20 inches. In effect, the dry timberline for pine may occur so high up the mountain that it is above the species' cold limits. Still, it seems likely that some of the ravines and canyon sites at lower elevations would be moist and mild enough for ponderosa pine and inland Douglas-fir.

Steens Mountain rises majestically in a wide-open western landscape far from any population centers. The Bureau of Land Management maintains a gravel recreational loop road that ascends the mountain's broad western slope through glacial-carved gorges and aspen groves to the crest at above 9000 feet. This route heads east from Frenchglen, which is 57 miles by paved road south of the town of Burns, Oregon.

The Warner Mountains are a tall fault-block range arising in the northeastern corner of California, about 100 miles southwest of Steens Mountain. The crest of the north-south trending Warners forms about 60 miles of the boundary of the Great Basin, with the western slope of the mountains being drained by the Pit River, a tributary of the Sacramento. The eastern slope drains into three large alkali lakes at the foot of the mountains. Being on the western edge of the Great Basin rather than fully within it, the Warners have a forest that is an "impoverished" representation of the Cascade Range forests lying 70 miles farther west. However, this forest is much richer than those of mountains fully within the Great Basin.

The Warners rise above the 4500- to 5000-foot high Modoc Plateau, which is made up of volcanic rock and is covered with sagebrush and western juniper woodlands. The lower elevation montane forests consist of ponderosa pine, the Sierra form of white fir (*Abies concolor* var. *lowiana*), and Jeffrey pine, with shade-tolerant fir dominating mixed stands (Vale 1977). Whitebark pine is the primary subalpine and timberline tree from 8500 feet upward, and it grows as krummholz cushions on the highest summits—Eagle Peak (9892 feet) and Warren Peak (9710 feet). Sierra lodgepole pine is a secondary component of the rather dry, rocky timberline atop the Warners. The principal associates of the stunted pines are big sagebrush and drought-tolerant alpine cushion plants.

East of the Warner Mountains lie vast expanses of high desert-sagebrush country that typify the northern Great Basin. Several small, dry mountain ranges are scattered about the open landscape. About 80 and 135 miles east of the Warners, two tall ridges jut above the desert plateau. These are the Pine Forest and the Santa Rosa ranges. The adjacent desert receives an average of only five to six inches of precipitation annually, and these small subalpine mountain ranges are also quite dry. The Pine Forest Range, whose highest point is 9458-foot Duffer Peak, is apparently unique in that the small, open forest zone on its upper slopes is composed entirely of whitebark pine (Critchfield and Allenbaugh 1969). The Santa Rosa Range (maximum of 9701 feet), lying north of Winnemucca, is comparably dry, but its small, stunted forest is composed solely of limber pine, which is bordered below by sagebrush and patches of western juniper.

Northeastern Great Basin

Eastward across northern Nevada, a traveler passes through expansive high-desert valleys with prominent mountain ranges rising above them. Although still quite dry, the easternmost of these mountains intercept more moisture from Pacific storms in winter and receive more from summer convectional storms than the ranges of northwestern Nevada. The principal subalpine mountains in northeastern Nevada include the

Bull Run, Independence, and Jarbidge ranges, north of Elko on the Humboldt River, and the East Humboldt and Ruby ranges, southeast of the Humboldt River. Because of their larger and less-arid subalpine zones, the Jarbidge, East Humboldt, and northern Ruby ranges have larger stands of conifers, which are compositionally related to the Rocky Mountain forests farther east. By contrast, the Bull Run, Independence, and other ranges northwest or west of Elko support few trees. Southeast of the Humboldt River, patches of elfin woodland composed of singleleaf pinyon pine and Utah juniper (*Juniperus osteosperma*) cover the lower mountain slopes. North of the Humboldt River, only a few scattered groves of Rocky Mountain (*J. scopulorum*) and Utah junipers are found.

Subalpine fir is the dominant high-elevation tree on a wide variety of substrates in the Jarbidge, Independence, and Bull Run mountains north of the Humboldt River (Loope 1969). The Jarbidge Mountains (maximum 10,839 feet), lying near the Idaho border, have an impoverished Rocky Mountain subalpine forest, which is rather extensive between elevations of 7000 and 10,000 feet. Subalpine fir is the principal tree, with whitebark pine sharing dominance at upper timberline, while the scattered limber pine is confined to lower timberline. Because of the excessively drained, loose rock (rhyolite) substrate, even the highest peaks have very little alpine flora.

The Bull Run (maximum 9261 feet) and Independence mountains (10,349 feet) northwest of Elko have patchy subalpine forests dominated by subalpine fir confined to northern slopes and ravines at high elevations. The Bull Run forests also contain whitebark pine and limber pine along with groves of quaking aspen, while stands in the Independence Range are similar but without whitebark pine. The Tuscarora Mountains (8800 feet) and the other high mountains (maximum 9800 feet) scattered across the desert as far as 120 miles to the southwest, toward the Humboldt River's sink, apparently have no forest trees at all (Little 1971).

The massive northern Ruby and East Humboldt mountains, which have several 11,000-foot-high alpine peaks, arise southeast of the Humboldt River near Elko. The East Humboldt Range harbors groves of whitebark pine, limber pine, and quaking aspen, while the northern Ruby Range has a narrow forest zone consisting of those species along with isolated groves of white fir, bristlecone pine, and Engelmann spruce. These latter groves are apparently surviving relicts of a once richer and more extensive forest that included several species from the Rocky Mountains (Critchfield and Allenbaugh 1969, Loope 1969).

The high-country of the northern Ruby Range (north of 7200-foot Harrison Pass) is estimated to receive 40 to 45 inches of annual precipitation, which is considerably more than that of any other area in the Great Basin (Loope 1969). Consequently, the northern Ruby has the richest, best-developed alpine vegetation in the Great Basin. However, the subalpine forest is sparse and open, and it is dominated by whitebark pine from about 8800 feet to tree line, which occurs near 10,500 feet. Competition from shrubs and herbs may be part of the reason that whitebark pine is restricted to rocky sites and shallow soils. The vast areas of glacially scoured bedrock (mostly granite and crystalline metamorphic rocks) and talus at these elevations is largely responsible for the sparse, open forest. In fact, conifer forest is estimated to cover less than one percent of the area of the Ruby Mountains, while extensive stands of sagebrush occur even in the subalpine zone. As a result of glaciation and the scattered distribution of timber, the high-country of the northern Rubies is quite "open" and spectacular. Lovely aspen groves fill the valleys and basins between 7200 and 8000 feet. Small lakes and live streams abound, a condition which is unusual in the Great Basin.

Limber pine commonly grows with the lowest-elevation groves of whitebark pine in the northern Rubies, although it is clearly the dominant species in the adjacent East Humboldt Range, perhaps because of substrate differences. A northern population of Great Basin bristlecone pine (*Pinus longaeva*), uniquely mixed with whitebark pine, grows near the mouth of Thomas Canyon. The only stand of Engelmann spruce is situated in the main fork of Thorpe Canyon at about 9500 feet. The spruce's long-term residency is attested to by the presence of a tree 49 inches in d.b.h.; but this population seems to be neither expanding nor contracting (Loope 1969).

The southern section of the Ruby Range (south of Harrison Pass) contrasts ecologically with the northern Rubies. The southern Rubies are somewhat lower and are composed primarily of sedimentary rocks, much of it limestone and dolomite. In addition, the southern Rubies receive less precipitation. As a result of these environmental differences, their subalpine forests are made up solely of limber and bristlecone pine (Loope 1969). Pearl Peak, at 10,847 feet, is the highest point in this section of the range, and stunted limber pines reach almost to the very top. Pearl Peak's northeastern slope supports a fine stand of very old bristlecone pines. These trees attain 2000 years of age growing on white dolomite in much the same manner as the ancient bristlecones of the White Mountains described on page 41. A "fossil timberline" of bristlecone pine (standing snags, stumps, and remnants of forest trees that died long ago) stands ghostlike several hundred feet beyond the highest living trees on the ridge above Pearl Lake.

Several isolated mountain ridges rise out from the desert east of the Ruby Range and, like the southern Rubies, are capped with limestone. Still farther east, the Great Salt Lake Desert's salt flats stretch to the hazy horizon. The principal timberline peaks east of the Rubies are 10,262-foot Spruce Mountain, which supports a northern outpost of the Great Basin bristlecone pine, and 10,704-foot Pilot Peak. Both of these mountains have limber pine on their upper slopes, and Pilot Peak also has stands of Engelmann spruce (Loope 1969). The only other forest tree reported from these ranges east of the Rubies is the Rocky Mountain white fir (*Abies concolor* var. *concolor*), which sometimes extends nearly to upper timberline on northern slopes, as in the Cherry Creek Range. Travelers on U.S. Highway 93 south of Wells, Nevada, can readily view double timberlines on Spruce Mountain, east of the highway. These result from two separate bands of conifers — pinyon-juniper woodland on the lower slopes at about 6500 to 8000 feet, and limber pine-bristlecone pine above 9000 feet. Some very old bristlecone pines grow on a steep slope northwest of the summit. One tree was 2000 years old and had 1602 annual rings on an increment core only 16 inches long.

Immediately east of the northeastern corner of Nevada lie several small subalpine mountain ranges near the Idaho-Utah border. The most prominent of these are the Albion (10,335 feet maximum) and Raft River mountains (9898 feet). They have subalpine forests primarily of Engelmann spruce, subalpine fir, Rocky Mountain lodgepole pine (*Pinus contorta* var. *latifolia*), and limber pine, a mixture related to forests of the Middle Rocky Mountains farther east. And like the Wasatch and Bear River ranges of the Middle Rockies, the Albion and Raft River mountains are apparently without whitebark pine (Loope 1969). Rocky Mountain Douglas-fir and quaking aspen form the lower fringe of the montane forest, and at the base of these mountains some of the northernmost pinyons (singleleaf) form a woodland with Rocky Mountain juniper (Little 1971).

The sporadic and irregular distribution patterns of Rocky Mountain and Sierra Nevada-Cascade tree species in the northeastern Great Basin contrast with patterns in the middle and southern latitudes of the Great Basin (Loope 1969). In the middle latitudes, Sierran species are confined to the western fringe (Billings 1978). Rocky Mountain species occupy the eastern portion, disappearing westward in a rather predictable pattern related to increasingly dry conditions in the middle of Nevada. In the northeastern Great Basin, however, tree distributions from one mountain range to the next often appear unrelated to precipitation. Instead, they may reflect local extinction of species in the distant past, such as during Pleistocene glaciations when valley flooding created large glacial lakes (Thompson and Mead 1982, Wells 1983). Such glaciation was much more extensive in the northeastern Great Basin than farther south.

Middle Great Basin

The middle latitudes of the Great Basin, stretching from east-central California to western Utah, present a washboardlike succession of high, north-south trending mountain ranges. The entire area is open, cold desert country, with sagebrush and shadscale-greasewood (*Atriplex-Sarcobatus*) occupying the broad valley floors that lie between elevations of 4000 and 6000 feet. An extensive singleleaf pinyon-Utah juniper woodland covers the lower mountain slopes from about 6000 to 8500 feet. Above 9000 feet a sparse and varied representation of subalpine conifers is sprinkled along the ridges, giving way to alpine cushion plants above 11,000 feet on the loftiest peaks.

The westernmost ranges lie adjacent to the Sierra Nevada between Reno, Nevada, and Bishop, California, and they are essentially connected to the Sierra via 7000- to 8000-foot ridges. It is not surprising, then, that some of the Sierran forest species spill over into the most favorable habitats on these western Great Basin mountains. The Sierran species grow only in small numbers in isolated groves, and this results in some remarkable combinations of forest trees. The Sweetwater Mountains, near the Nevada border north of Bridgeport, California, rise to a maximum elevation of 11,700 feet, where they support dry alpine tundra communities. At the heads of east-facing canyons up to about 11,000 feet, the patchy coniferous forest of this range is made up of limber pine, with California white fir occurring at somewhat lower elevations. In contrast, the heads of canyons on the western slope of the Sweetwater Range support groves of whitebark pine and mountain hemlock, species from the Sierra Nevada (Vasek and Thorne 1977). Sierra lodgepole pine and quaking aspen are also members of the subalpine zone in the Sweetwaters.

Eastward across a desert valley rises the Wassuk Range. Walker Lake and the town of Hawthorne, Nevada, lie beneath the eastern slope of these mountains. The Wassuk Range is situated in the rain shadows of the Sierra Nevada and the Sweetwater Mountains and is therefore arid even by Great Basin standards. A storage rain gauge was maintained at the 9000-foot level on the range's highest peak, 11,245-foot Mount Grant, from March 1952 to May 1954, a period of slightly below normal precipitation in the surrounding area. It measured a total of only 19 inches of precipitation throughout that period, suggesting an adjusted annual rate of only about 9 inches.

Scattered limber pines are found in portions of the Wassuk Range, but only one small grove occurs on Mount Grant; consequently, botanists found it necessary to define the krummholz line, or lower boundary of the alpine zone, as the upper altitudinal limits of the shrubby species of sagebrush (*Artemisia tridentata* and *A. arbuscula*) (Bell and Johnson 1980). In the Great Basin where a krummholz line is present, this ecotone generally coincides with the upper limit of shrubby sagebrush. Based upon this standard, the alpine tundra zone begins at 11,000 feet on Mount Grant.

A few other similarly dry subalpine mountain ranges rise above the four-inch annual-precipitation desert between Hawthorne and Winnemucca, Nevada, a region stretching 170 miles northeast from the Wassuk Range. An example of these nonforested ranges is the Clan Alpine Mountains, which reach 9966 feet at its highest point, Mount Augusta; and although a pinyon-juniper woodland occupies the lower slopes, the subalpine upper slopes are devoid of trees.

East of these non-forested subalpine mountains, three major mountain ranges tower above the high, open valleys in the center of Nevada. These are (from west to east) the Toiyabe Range, with Toiyabe Dome reaching 11,788 feet; the Toquima Range, whose highest peak is 11,949-foot Mount Jefferson; and the Monitor Range, which has a broad, flat top 10,886 feet high. All these ranges have extensive pinyon-juniper woodlands on their lower slopes and sparse subalpine stands of limber pine on their upper slopes. The limber pine is reported to ascend to 11,000 feet on

Toiyabe Dome and to form krummholz that occasionally reaches 11,500 feet on Mount Jefferson. These peaks, particularly Toiyabe and Jefferson, have dry alpine tundra communities on their summits, which rise above glacial cirque basins that are sprinkled with timberline trees. Great Basin bristlecone pine is present in this area only on the highest peaks of the Monitor Range. This species is generally associated with limestone, dolomite, or other calcareous parent materials, and a lack of these rock types at high elevations in central Nevada may explain its scarcity here. An exception to this pattern occurs in the Hot Creek Range, immediately east of the Monitors, where bristlecone grows on volcanic rock above 9200 feet (Hart 1982). The only other trees found on these desert mountains are small groves of quaking aspen in comparatively moist basins. In spite of their impressive height, the ranges serve as the watershed for only one small year-round stream, Reese River, and for no permanent lakes.

About 100 miles east of the Monitor Range, in east-central Nevada and adjacent Utah, three especially tall and rugged mountain ranges loom above the cold desert. These are the highest mountains in the eastern Great Basin, and despite the fact that they are separated from the subalpine areas of the Colorado Plateau by more than 100 miles of sprawling desert-shrub communities, they contain forests related to those of the Plateau and the Rocky Mountains. These east-central Nevada ranges are the Schell Creeks (maximum elevation 11,890 feet) immediately east of Ely, the Snake Range (13,061 feet), and the Deep Creek Range (12,101 feet) just inside western Utah. Motorists on U.S. Highway 93 can readily observe the distinct double timberlines on the western slope of the Schell Creek Range north of McGill and on the western slope of the Snake Range from the valley 30 miles south of Ely. On these slopes the elfin woodland of singleleaf pinyon and Utah juniper and the subalpine conifer forest belt are separated by an intervening band of sagebrush that covers 1000 to 1500 feet of elevation (Billings 1951).

Upper timberlines on these three mountain ranges are composed primarily of Engelmann spruce and limber pine, with scattered stands of Great Basin bristlecone pine inhabiting limestone areas and other harsh sites (LaMarche and Mooney 1974). Additionally, subalpine fir grows in the Deep Creek Range. In contrast to the patchy stands in drier ranges to the west, the subalpine forest forms a nearly continuous zone in these ranges. Mean annual precipitation at timberline in the Snake and Schell Creek ranges has been estimated at 30 to 35 inches (Beasley and Klemmedson 1980, LaMarche and Mooney 1974). The less-arid climate of this area also seems largely responsible for the presence of the Rocky Mountain forms of white fir, Douglas-fir, and, locally, ponderosa pine at middle elevations. The snowy winter conditions are reflected by the presence of a tiny glacier in the deep cirque on the northeastern side of Wheeler Peak (13,061 feet), highest point in the Snake Range and in all of the eastern Great Basin.

A bristlecone pine known as "the Once-Oldest Living Thing" grew not far below the Wheeler Peak glacier on a boulder-strewn moraine at 10,750 feet. In 1964 a graduate student felled this ancient living snag, and

*"Double timberlines" in eastern Nevada: belts of pinyon-juniper
woodland, sagebrush-grass, and limber pine-bristlecone pine.*

examination revealed that it was somewhat over 5000 years old—older
even than the most venerable bristlecone in California's White Mountains
(Currey 1965, Hitch 1982). This decrepit bristlecone was only 17 feet tall at
its highest dead branch, while the uppermost living shoot stood merely 11
feet off the ground. It was very stout and gnarled, with a diameter of 6½
feet at a point 1½ feet above the ground. Most of the trunk was dead,
however, with a living strip of bark covering only 8 percent of the trunk's
original circumference. The bole was so deeply eroded that the pith was
missing along its lower 8 feet. Several investigators have concluded that
this ancient tree was a "living freak" and that similarly ancient specimens
will probably not be found in this vicinity (Trexler 1965). However, other
bristlecone pines older than 3000 years have been found in east-central
Nevada.

    The alpine timberline and glacier on Wheeler Peak can be reached in
short hikes from the Wheeler Peak Campground, Humboldt National
Forest, which is perched at the 10,000-foot level north of the peak and is
reached by a paved road from Baker, Nevada.

    Engelmann spruce and limber pine are co-dominant species in most of
the timberline stands in the Schell Creek, Snake, and Deep Creek ranges,
with spruce extending highest and forming krummholz. In local areas
where bristlecone pine grows, it and spruce occur predominantly in the
form of krummholz above 11,200 feet, and krummholz limit sometimes
reaches 12,000 feet (LaMarche 1966). A well-developed fossil timberline of
erect dead bristlecone pines occurs near the summit of 11,676-foot Mount
Washington in the southern Snake Range (LaMarche and Mooney 1972).
The few living trees above 11,500 feet are reduced to krummholz. This
provides clear evidence that the upper limit of tree growth has declined
within the past 2000 years.

    Eastward from the Snake and Deep Creek ranges stretch the sun-
baked salt-desert shrublands of the Sevier and Great Salt Lake deserts.
The nearest subalpine mountains to the east are the Tushars in southern

Utah and the Stansbury Mountains south of Great Salt Lake in northern Utah. The Tushars are near the Colorado River Plateau and have timberlines characteristic of that region, while the Stansbury Mountains are near the Middle Rocky Mountains and have subalpine forests resembling those of the driest parts of the Middle Rockies.

Southern Great Basin

Southward from 38°N (vicinity of Mono Lake, California, and Tonopah, Nevada) in the Great Basin, the valleys' elevations drop off rather rapidly. This area, the greater Mojave Desert region in southeastern California and southern Nevada, includes the driest region of North America. Most of the valleys receive three to five inches of annual precipitation, and California's Death Valley averages only one and one-half inches. The lowlands in the southern Great Basin also have the hottest summers found on our continent. Death Valley's mean July temperature (average of day and night) is 102°F. Yet, high mountain peaks adjacent to Death Valley and extending northward have subalpine timberlines where July mean temperatures are only 50 to 55°F. This dramatic range in temperatures reflects an extreme range in elevations from −282 feet in Death Valley to 14,242 feet at White Mountain Peak. At all elevations, however, the climate of this entire region is extremely dry.

The prevalent native vegetation in the lowlands is widely spaced creosote bush (*Larrea*), bur-sage (*Franseria*), and other hot-desert shrubs, often with scattered stands of the craggy arborescent yucca called Joshua-tree (*Yucca brevifolia*). Cacti and other succulents so prevalent in the Sonoran Desert are not abundant here because there is no summer monsoon. Only the northern part of this area—north of 35°N (the southern tip of Nevada)—has mountains sufficiently high to support an elfin woodland of pinyon and juniper and vestiges of coniferous forest. (The San Bernardino and San Jacinto mountains, whose crests form the southwestern boundary of the Great Basin, have been described in this book as part of the Pacific Coast Mountains.) Nevertheless, the broadest spectrum of desert vegetation zones in North America can be found in this region.

At the northern end, White Mountain Peak supports a large area of semi-arid alpine tundra above 12,000 feet. Subalpine bristlecone pine-limber pine and sagebrush communities occupy the White Mountains and other ranges as far south as Death Valley and Las Vegas. An upper montane strip of sagebrush, occasionally with small stands of white fir or aspen, lies between about 9000 and 10,000 feet. The pinyon-juniper woodland borders this and extends down to about 6000 feet. Downslope, this elfinwood gives way to a lower-elevation sagebrush or saltbush-greasewood zone. This in turn descends at about 3500 feet to the edge of the Mojave Desert creosote bush type. The region's various kinds of timberlines are most extensive in the White Mountains and taper off southward, as does the amount of tree growth.

The White Mountains are an exceptionally tall, but semi-arid and unglaciated range lying east of the Owens Valley in the rain shadow of the

Singleleaf pinyon and Utah juniper in the White Mountains

High Sierra Nevada. The crest of the White Mountains continues above 10,000 feet for almost 40 miles, and the range rises a maximum of 10,000 feet above desert valleys to the west and east. And yet, this range intercepts relatively little precipitation. For instance, a subalpine station at the Crooked Creek Laboratory at the 10,150-foot level in the bristlecone pine forest registers less than 14 inches per year (Pace 1968).

The elfin woodland of the White Mountains is composed primarily of singleleaf pinyon, with substantial amounts of Utah juniper occurring only in local areas, primarily along the ephemeral water courses (St. Andre and others 1965). The pinyon zone receives only 8 to 12 inches of annual precipitation, and its woodland is unique in occurring at the relatively high elevation of 6500 to 9500 feet. At its upper boundary the pinyons become wind-pruned and stunted, with scattered krummholz reaching as high as 10,000 feet. Despite the high elevations reached by pinyon, it seldom overlaps the subalpine woodland of bristlecone and limber pine. And, in the rare areas where overlap does occur, pinyon and juniper are reduced to krummholz while the subalpine pines attain normal stature (St. Andre and others 1965). Many of the small, rounded pinyon pines growing at 8000 to 9000 feet live for 400 years, but this is only one-tenth the antiquity of the bristlecone pines found higher up the mountainsides.

State Highway 168 climbs east from the town of Big Pine, California, in the Owens Valley, up a dry desert canyon to 7271-foot Westgard Pass at the southern end of the White Mountains. From this point a paved national forest road ascends northward to the crest of the range and into the Schulman Grove of bristlecone pines, above 10,000 feet. A gravel road climbs into the thin atmosphere of the alpine zone above 12,000 feet.

The late Dr. Edmund Schulman's 1958 feature article in *National Geographic* on the "Bristlecone Pine, Oldest Known Living Thing" made this subalpine forest famous. Schulman, for whom the ancient grove is named, and his colleagues from the University of Arizona's Laboratory of Tree-Ring Research had discovered 17 bristlecone pines over 4000 years old in this area. The known number of 4000+-year-old trees has been enlarged by subsequent discoveries, but the 4600+-year-old called "Methuselah" that Schulman dated is still the oldest known living tree.

In addition to the ancient living trees, standing snags that died hundreds of years ago and trunks of fallen bristlecones that died thousands of years ago are still partially intact and have provided overlapping tree-ring chronologies extending back 9000 years. From examination of the weathered remains of bristlecone pines once growing above present timberlines in the White Mountains, it has been determined that timberline has retreated downward about 330 feet in the past 1000 years (Schmid and Schmid 1975).

In 1958 the Inyo National Forest set aside a 29,500-acre botanical area called the Ancient Bristlecone Pine Forest to be managed for scientific study and public enjoyment. The collecting of pieces of bristlecone pine wood is strictly prohibited because of the priceless scientific value of these remnants for dendrochronology.

Bristlecone and limber pine make up the open subalpine forests above 9500 feet in the White Mountains. There is little undergrowth beneath these spreading, often gnarled, subalpine trees, and no year-round streams flow off these desert mountains. Limber pine extends up to about 11,000 feet, where it is reduced to krummholz, while bristlecone pine forms tree line at about 11,500 feet. Bristlecone grows erect even at its extreme upper limit of nearly 12,000 feet. Unlike populations in eastern Nevada's Snake Range, bristlecone does not form krummholz in the White Mountains (LaMarche and Mooney 1972).

The three major geologic substrates that are represented in the White Mountains subalpine zone—dolomite, quartz sandstone, and granite—have pronounced effects upon the distribution of trees (Billings and Thompson 1957, Wright and Mooney 1965). Limber pine is most abundant on relatively moist granitic soils, while bristlecone pine is much more prevalent on dolomite sites and prefers northern aspects. (Bristlecone pine does become abundant on granite at the north end of the White Mountains near Boundary Peak. Here, above 11,000 feet, it spreads out like a giant shrub but is 25 feet tall [W. D. Billings, personal communication].)

Dolomite, a calcareous rock, yields soils poor in nutrients, but it makes a nearly white surface, which reflects the intense sunlight and thus has a cool temperature that allows bristlecone seedlings to survive. Sagebrush (*Artemisia tridentata*) is bristlecone pine's principal competitor in the subalpine zone and is more drought tolerant than pine. However, the sagebrush appears to have higher nutrient requirements than the pine. As a result, sagebrush communities complement those of bristlecone pine. Sagebrush tends to dominate on most of the better-developed sandstone and granitic soils, especially on dry southern slopes, but does poorly on dolomite.

The ancient trees in the Schulman Grove and along the Methuselah Walk are growing on white dolomite with scant undergrowth of any kind (Wright and Mooney 1965). Even the younger bristlecone pines here are stunted and slow-growing. A curious dwarf bristlecone pictured in Schulman's *National Geographic* article is 3 inches thick, 3 feet tall, and 700 years old! The old trees are usually more dead than alive, since only a narrow band of living, bark-covered tissue continues to grow on the otherwise barren, weather-polished trunk. Also, just a small part of the crown of an ancient tree continues to live. Such growth occurs on the driest of sites, usually near the bristlecone's lower limit, between 9500 and 10,000 feet.

Under more moderate conditions, which paradoxically occur near the upper limit of trees, comparatively fast-growing bristlecones have their bark intact and support a full crown; but they tend to develop heart rot after attaining about 18 inches in d.b.h. (Wright and Mooney 1965). In contrast, trees in the "ancient area" do not become uniformly diseased in such a manner. Instead, most of their tissue dies outright. Virtually all trees in the ancient area remain sound to the center even when most of the

Bristlecone pine "living driftwood" in the Patriarch Grove, White Mountains

bark has died and the trunk wood has been exposed to erosion for more than a thousand years.

Bristlecone pines grow as low as 9300 feet on southern aspects along the Methuselah Walk. Some of these trees require 200 to 250 years to expand one inch in radial growth, and this production occurs only in the narrow band where there is living bark. But the woody cells that do develop are so highly lignified and decay resistant that some trees are still standing 2000 years after their death. These observations by C. W. Ferguson of the University of Arizona's tree-ring laboratory support Schulman's statement that longevity requires adversity for these ancients of the desert timberlines (Wright and Mooney 1965).

Intriguing examples of gnarled and picturesque growth-forms line the Methuselah Walk. One writer called these trees "living driftwood!" Many of the ancient trees have double piggy-back trunks like those of the foxtail pine in the southern Sierra Nevada. And like the closely related foxtail pine, bristlecone pines grow tall, straight, and spirelike on a productive, sheltered site such as a protected subalpine basin. Nevertheless, in much of the bristlecone's range such sites are controlled by more competitive (shade-tolerant) trees like Engelmann spruce.

At higher elevations in the White Mountains, bristlecone pines develop into large, spreading trees, although portions of their main trunks are often dead. The most remarkable example of such a tree is the "Patriarch," which grows at the 11,300-foot level along the road above Schulman Grove. This multi-stemmed giant of the alpine timberline is the largest known bristlecone pine; it is 12½ feet in d.b.h., although only 47 feet tall and merely 1500 years old. Ecologist Ronald Lanner (1984) concludes that the Patriarch consists of seven or more individual trees that grew together after arising from a seed cache, probably made by a Clark's nutcracker.

Other groves of subalpine trees in the White Mountains consist of Sierra lodgepole pine and quaking aspen (Vasek and Thorne 1977). Lodgepole pine occurs sporadically in some of the northern canyons between 9000 and 10,500 feet. Aspen forms widely scattered groves on moist sites on the eastern slope of the range and ascends in dwarfed form to 11,000 feet.

The Inyo Range extends southward, as a continuation of the White Mountains, along the eastern side of the Owens Valley. From the top of Mount Whitney on the crest of the Sierra Nevada the Inyos appear as a hazy purplish desert range, rising high across the arid Owens Valley. The highest Inyo peaks are just over 11,000 feet and support stands of bristlecone and limber pine. Other subalpine trees such as Sierra lodgepole and aspen are not reported from the Inyos, suggesting that conditions here are even drier than in the White Mountains. The lower slopes of the Inyos are clothed with an elfin woodland of singleleaf pinyon and Utah juniper.

Southeast of the Inyos lies the Panamint Range, which forms the western edge of Death Valley. Telescope Peak (11,049 feet) is its highest point, and this summit supports a subalpine woodland only 10 air miles from the torrid depths of Death Valley. A zone of singleleaf pinyon and Utah juniper extends up to 9000 feet, where pinyon forms krummholz.

Broken and twisted bristlecone pine in the White Mountains

Then a narrow treeless zone occurs. This is superseded above 9600 feet by groves of limber pine, joined by bristlecone pine at about 10,300 feet. The two subalpine trees form a patchy, open woodland, and then erect bristlecone pine and krummholz limber pine inhabit the summit. They are joined by a few Sierra juniper and the ever-present big sagebrush (Vasek and Thorne 1977). Some of the bristlecone pine on this mountain are reported to be over 3000 years old (Kirk 1965).

A seven-mile-long trail leads up Telescope Peak from Mahogany Flat (8100 feet) in the pinyon, juniper, and mountain-mahogany zone. The view from the summit is so awesome that W. T. Henderson, the first person to climb it (in 1860) reputedly exclaimed, "You can see so far it's just like looking through a telescope!" (Kirk 1965). The Sierra Nevada appears as a snow-capped mountain wall far to the west; Death Valley sprawls 11,000 feet directly below to the east; and the lofty Spring Mountains rise in the far distance, 90 miles to the east. The Panamint and the Spring mountains harbor the southernmost subalpine habitats in the Great Basin.

The Spring Mountains occupy a small area west of Las Vegas, Nevada, but their highest point, 11,912-foot Charleston Peak, towers nearly two vertical miles above that desert metropolis. Charleston Peak and its adjacent ridges support an upper timberline of bristlecone and limber pine. Above 10,500 feet, the open-growing bristlecones are scattered across pink-brown limestone slopes, with scarcely any undergrowth—a scene reminiscent of California's White Mountains (Hart 1982). Limber pine reaches the 11,000-foot level, and nearly pure stands of bristlecone extend to 11,500 feet, where some of the gnarled trees are still 20 to 30 feet tall. Bristlecone pine also forms krummholz here (V. C. LaMarche, personal correspondence).

The top of Charleston Peak is a largely barren rockland above tree line and does not support an alpine community as such. None of the alpine flora of either the Sierra Nevada or the Rockies is present (Clokey 1951). Instead, the extreme isolation of this high-mountain area has resulted in many endemic plants.

A western extension of Rocky Mountain white fir (*Abies concolor* var. *concolor*) inhabits the montane and lower part of the subalpine zone, between 7500 and 10,800 feet, especially on cool exposures. Also, ponderosa pine, probably related to stands in northern Arizona and southern Utah, contributes to a montane forest here (Griffin and Critchfield 1976). An elfin woodland of singleleaf pinyon and Utah juniper covers the middle elevations, still high above the searing heat of the creosote bush desert.

The Spring Mountains are a popular year-round recreation area within the Toiyabe National Forest. A paved road heads west from the Las Vegas area and ascends Kyle Canyon, a gorge beneath the eastern wall of Charleston Peak. The roadhead lies above 7500 feet in the canyon, in the shadow of the mountain, and from here a loop trail climbs to the crescent-shaped timberline ridge that encircles the head of the canyon. For 13 miles the trail threads through stands of bristlecone pine, subalpine meadows, and colorful rocklands on top of this ridge that juts so high above the purplish desert (Hart 1982).

Directly south of the Spring Mountains lie three small ranges whose highest peaks harbor relict stands of a Rocky Mountain white fir forest that represent the westernmost extension of the white fir, Douglas-fir, and blue spruce (*Picea pungens*) zone of the Colorado Plateau (Vasek and Thorne 1977). This Rocky Mountain white fir occurs amidst the singleleaf pinyon-Utah juniper woodland on the relatively moist and shady north-facing slopes of the Kingston (maximum elevation, 7323 feet), Clark (7929 feet), and New York mountains (7445 feet). During the last Pleistocene ice age the white fir forest was evidently confined to the *lower skirts* of these small mountain ranges, and a bristlecone pine-limber pine forest covered the upper slopes. Two ancient woodrat middens from the 6200-foot level, dating back 24,000 and 29,000 years, contained foliage of these two subalpine conifers (Mehringer and Ferguson 1969); but this timberline forest disappeared with the warming climate since the Pleistocene.

The relict white fir groves are small indeed, with only about 150 trees in the Kingston Mountains and just 30 trees on two acres in the New York Mountains. A warmer, drier climatic period could easily eliminate these vestiges of coniferous forest in the eastern Mojave Desert. The white fir stand on Clark Mountain is larger (about 1000 trees on 140 acres) and is located only about four miles north of the 4700-foot mountain pass on Interstate 15, about 17 miles west of the Nevada state line.

COLORADO PLATEAU

The Colorado Plateau Province (Fenneman 1931) lies east of the southern Great Basin. It covers central and eastern Utah (south of the Wasatch and Uinta mountains), the western edge of Colorado, northwestern New Mexico, and northern Arizona. This vast area is made up of many elevated tablelands or individual plateaus, ranging in height from 5000 to 11,000 feet. This province is distinguished by having large expanses of nearly horizontal sedimentary rock formations that are dissected by countless streams into steep and colorful canyons, including the Colorado River's Grand Canyon. There is also an abundance of igneous (such as granite and basalt) rock structures, including high lava-capped plateaus and mesas, and dome-shaped mountain ranges caused by local intrusions of igneous rock. The Colorado River drains the central core of the province. Rivers that drain sizeable areas of the periphery include the Sevier (a Great Basin drainage) in south-central Utah, the upper Gila in east-central Arizona, and the San Jose in adjacent New Mexico.

The region's topography and geologic structure is like a stack of saucers (layers of sedimentary rock) tilted toward the northeast, where the plateaus adjoin the Rocky Mountains—in northern Utah, western Colorado, and northern New Mexico (Hunt 1967). Thus, the highest elevations are generally near the western and southern edges of the region, and the interior (including Canyon Lands and the Navaho Section) is comparatively low in elevation and climatically hotter and drier. Although much of the region is quite arid, the higher rims receive more moisture than do the isolated mountain ranges of the Great Basin. This is largely a result of

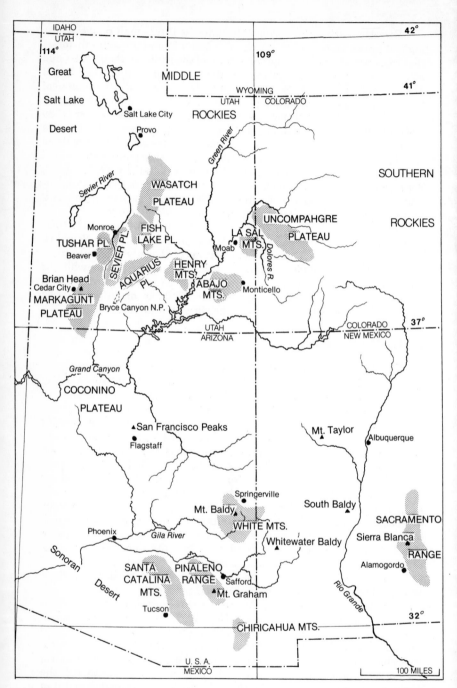

Colorado Plateau

Colorado pinyon-Utah juniper woodland at Desert View on the South Rim of the Grand Canyon

subtropical air masses bringing moisture from the Gulf of Mexico and the Gulf of California during the summer; whereas the Great Basin and southern Pacific Coast mountains have very dry summers.

In general, the Colorado Plateau is characterized by a semi-arid climate, sparse vegetation, and an abundance of exposed, often brilliantly colored rock. Forest vegetation is restricted to the higher elevations and moist areas. Upper timberlines develop at elevations of 11,000 to 12,000 feet and are confined to the very highest peaks and plateau prominences. Lower timberlines are widespread and will be discussed in conjunction with the scattered areas having upper timberlines. Timberlines related to those of the Colorado Plateau occur immediately southward in the mountains of the Sonoran and Chihuahuan deserts, and they are also described in this chapter.

The Colorado Plateau forests are most closely related to those of the Rocky Mountains and are less comparable to Great Basin forests. They bear very little resemblance to forests of the southern Pacific Coast mountains. The uppermost forest zone is primarily Engelmann spruce and subalpine fir, as in the Rockies, but it also contains groves of Great Basin bristlecone pine (*Pinus longaeva*), which contrasts with the Colorado bristlecone (*P. aristata*) of the Rockies. Below the subalpine zone lies a mixed conifer forest of Rocky Mountain Douglas-fir, white fir, and blue spruce. As in the adjacent Middle and Southern Rockies, quaking aspen is a prevalent component of both these forest zones, but the abundant lodgepole pine of the Rockies does *not* appear in the Colorado Plateau.

The lowest forest zone (about 6000 to 8000 feet) is dominated by the Rocky Mountain form of ponderosa pine mixed with stands of inland chaparral (composed of scrubby Gambel oak (*Quercus gambelii*), maples, and mountain-mahogany). Below this ponderosa pine zone, or in drier areas at comparable elevations, lies an extensive elfin woodland made up primarily of Colorado pinyon (*Pinus edulis*) and Utah and one-seed (*Juniperus monosperma*) junipers. The driest and lowest-elevation vegetation zone found throughout the Colorado Plateau is composed of sagebrush, shadscale (*Atriplex*), blackbrush (*Coleogyne*), and related desert shrubs.

Utah High Plateaus

This section stretches northeast from the vicinity of Zion and Bryce Canyon national parks to the center of Utah. It is made up of nine individual plateaus lined up in three rows (extending southwest to northeast) separated by deep, flat-bottomed valleys. Together, these undulating tablelands cover an area larger than the State of Maryland. They have been lifted to elevations of 9000 to 11,000 feet. The southernmost is the Markagunt Plateau, which includes the towering rosy cliffs and subalpine forests of Cedar Breaks National Monument and reaches its highest elevation in a timberline environment at 11,315-foot Brian Head. The Markagunt Plateau rises 5000 feet above Cedar City (to the west) via the prominent Hurricane Fault scarp. Northward along the east side of this fault (east of Beaver, Utah) looms the Tushar Plateau, which is mountainous in its northern portion and climaxes in two 12,000-foot peaks that support the only alpine tundra in the High Plateau country.

Immediately east of the Tushar Plateau, across the Sevier River Valley, lies the Sevier Plateau, which is capped with lava and forms an upper timberline at its highest elevations—such as 11,226-foot Monroe Peak, southeast of the town of Monroe. Immediately northeast of this tableland in the center of Utah lie the narrow Fish Lake Plateau (maximum elevation, 11,600-foot Mount Marvine) and the 75-mile-long Wasatch Plateau (maximum, 11,300-foot West Tent Mountain) which adjoins the Wasatch Range of the Middle Rocky Mountains about 30 miles south of Provo.

Apparently the most extensive and diverse upper timberline environment is found on the Aquarius Plateau, east of the Sevier Plateau in south-central Utah (Fenneman 1931). The northeastern portion of the Aquarius Plateau, known as Boulder Top, is a glaciated tableland above 11,000 feet that is 6 miles wide and 10 miles long. (Its highest point is 11,328-foot Bluebell Knoll.) The Aquarius Plateau is a lava-covered highland bounded by lofty cliffs throughout most of its circumference, and the drop from its east rim into the arid Canyon Lands is nearly 6000 feet. From any side, this plateau's towering rim looks "like the threshold of another world" (Fenneman 1931). Unlike the area's other plateaus, this one was

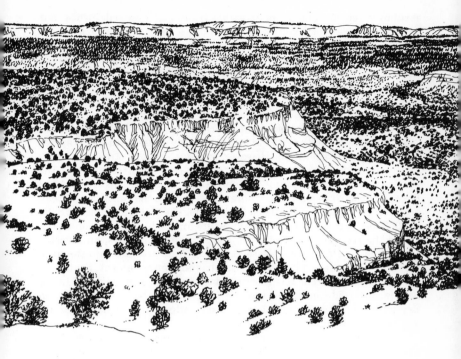

Pinyon-juniper woodland, Circle Cliffs, southeastern Utah

high enough to support extensive glaciers during the Pleistocene. The testimony of glaciation lies in the numerous lakes still being fed from melting snows. Abundant precipitation supports dense Engelmann spruce forests that open into subalpine grasslands and wet meadows.

The vegetation zones of Utah's high plateaus are similar to those described for the Colorado Plateau as a whole. Big sagebrush communities inhabit dry areas in the low valleys, giving way to the Colorado pinyon-Utah juniper woodland about where average annual precipitation reaches 10 inches (Daniel 1980).

Patches of chaparral, composed primarily of Gambel oak and big-tooth maple (*Acer grandidentatum*), together with ponderosa pine forest make up the next zone. Ponderosa pine generally develops where annual precipitation averages 15 inches or more and where distribution of rainfall during the year is favorable. The species must be able to effectively use the moisture before it is lost to evaporation or runoff (Daniel 1980). In sheltered canyons and other favorable sites in southern Utah, old-growth ponderosa pines attain large sizes—3 to 4 feet in d.b.h. and 100 feet in height. At the lowest elevations, where rainfall is least and evaporative stress is great, ponderosa pine is restricted to sandy or gravelly soils. The low fertility of such rocky, sandy soils puts competing herbaceous and shrubby vegetation at a competitive disadvantage. These soils also permit more rapid tree-root penetration and allow a light rain to soak in and become available to pine roots. As rainfall increases, soil texture and depth become less restrictive. Ponderosa pine is able to form the lowest forest zone because it can survive after the soil's moisture has been lowered to the permanent wilting point (as measured by sunflowers). Ponderosa survives by reducing transpiration losses to a minute fraction of what they are with a normal water supply (Daniel 1980).

Above the ponderosa pine zone, precipitation is much more abundant (25 to 35 inches) and the climate is considerably cooler, with less evaporative demand on vegetation. However, extreme drought stress can occur locally in rocky, wind-exposed sites at the edges of the plateaus where the gentle terrain breaks off into "badland" amphitheaters. This is evident at Bryce Canyon National Park, where viewpoints on the rim of the plateau overlook the fantastically eroded Pink Cliffs. The plateau rim lies at 8200 to 9000 feet in the moist Douglas-fir, white fir, and blue spruce forest; but where the rim breaks off into the badland amphitheaters, an inverted timberline develops. Trees descend only a short distance into the arid, unstable, infertile, and wind-exposed badland environment. Scattered, severely stunted Great Basin bristlecone pines can even be found in the narrow inverted-timberline ecotone immediately beneath the rim in Bryce Canyon. This is much lower than bristlecone pine's usual habitat and far below a climatic timberline.

In the vicinity of Cedar Breaks National Monument, east of Cedar City, the Markagunt Plateau rim rises above 10,000 feet and supports a subalpine forest of Engelmann spruce, subalpine fir, and clones of quaking aspen. At the very edge of the rim an inverted timberline develops with krummholz descending a short distance into the dry limestone amphitheaters. Limber and bristlecone pines are the most common inhabitants of the harsh rim environment. Bristlecone is largely, perhaps entirely, restricted to limestone substrates. These same five species make up the subalpine forest and, without aspen, the upper timberlines on all the high plateaus. However, bristlecone pine is evidently absent from the Tushar and Sevier plateaus (Little 1971). The Aquarius and Markagunt plateaus do support some fine stands of bristlecone pine, including individual trees 1000 to 2000 years old. Still, the bristlecone pine of the Utah plateaus are rarely as gnarled and ancient as those in the Great Basin, and neither limber nor bristlecone pine forms forests resembling the subalpine woodlands of the Great Basin. One and a half miles north of Cedar Breaks National Monument, a national forest road leads to Brian Head (11,315 feet), which rises slightly above tree line and has a grassy parkland at the top.

Forests seem to develop at higher elevations on the plateaus than on steep mountain slopes, perhaps because the gentle topography reduces wind exposure and holds moisture. Engelmann spruce sometimes forms thick stands of comparatively large trees — up to 3 feet in d.b.h. and 100 feet tall — near the 11,000-foot level on the plateaus. At this elevation, spruce stands surpass the upper limits of subalpine fir, and some are so dense and shady that virtually no undergrowth occurs.

In some areas, high-elevation stands have been clearcut (clear-felled). Tree regeneration has been difficult in these areas because of the greatly altered microclimate. In high-elevation clearcuts, spruce saplings can be exposed to lethal intensities of solar radiation as well as to frost damage during the short growing season; beneath an overstory canopy seedlings are protected. Another problem with managing the highest elevation spruce stands for maximum timber production is that 300 or more years may be necessary for a timber rotation.

Above tree line on the highest points, Engelmann spruce and limber pine grow as patches of krummholz among windswept subalpine grasslands that become rather dry by midsummer (Cronquist and others 1972). In glaciated areas like Boulder Top the subalpine parkland also contains numerous wet meadows and small lakes. The plateau parklands serve as summer range for livestock and are traversed by several national forest roads. The Skyline Drive is a recreational road that follows the crest of the Wasatch Plateau in subalpine and timberline habitats.

The only true alpine tundra in the Utah plateaus occurs on Delano Peak and Mount Belknap, both of which rise from the Tushar Plateau and exceed 12,000 feet (Cronquist and others 1972). Engelmann spruce and limber pine form tree limit slightly above 11,000 feet, and alpine cushion plants are scattered across these two rocky peaks.

Krummholz Engelmann spruce and limber pine atop central Utah's Wasatch Plateau

Mountains of Southeastern Utah

Three small clusters of subalpine mountains rise from the Colorado River plateau in southeastern Utah—the Abajo Mountains (maximum elevation, 11,360-foot Abajo Peak), Henry Mountains (11,605-foot Mount Ellen), and La Sal Mountains (12,721-foot Mount Peale). These are laccolithic mountains consisting of domes that were produced by volcanic injections of molten igneous rock between layers of sedimentary rock (Cronquist and others 1972). Since the injections occurred, erosion has exposed some of the granitic core of these mountains, so their present surfaces are mixtures of sedimentary and granitic rock.

The Henry Mountains rise out of the middle of the arid Canyon Lands section and have a very limited amount of subalpine forest (Engelmann spruce, subalpine fir, and limber pine) on protected northern slopes of the highest peaks (Little 1971). Great Basin bristlecone pine reaches eastward only to the Henry Mountains. Farther east, near Monticello, Utah, stand the Abajo Mountains, which the early botanical explorer P. A. Rydberg (1913) described as having "...no timber line at all on the southern and western sides, for no timber is growing between the semi-arid cedar [juniper]-pinyon belt and the top of the mountains." In contrast, the northern and eastern slopes have a complete series of zones from pinyon-juniper to Engelmann spruce-subalpine fir. Rydberg attributed the lack of forest on the bunchgrass-covered southern and western slopes to desiccating winds that blow across the arid Canyon Lands area, immediately to the south and west.

The La Sals, east of Moab, are the only mountains of these three groups that are tall and massive enough to have harbored Pleistocene glaciers, and only the La Sals have an alpine tundra. They are considered to be floristically similar to the nearby Southern Rockies in Colorado. Indeed, forests of the La Sal Mountains are separated from the extensive subalpine stands on western Colorado's Uncompahgre Plateau by only about 10 miles of the intervening Dolores River Valley. The La Sals rise from a 6000-foot-high plateau covered with pinyon and juniper, and only the eastern skirts of this mountain mass are moist enough to support a ponderosa pine forest (Richmond 1962). A Gambel oak-mountain mahogany association occupies the same elevational zone as ponderosa pine but extends entirely around the La Sals. Above this zone, between about 8500 and 10,000 feet, is a rather unique band of quaking aspen groves and grass-forb meadows which seems to represent the climax vegetation in the virtual absence of a Douglas-fir, white fir, and blue spruce zone. Perhaps the climate is too dry to support the mixed-conifer forest. Between the aspen zone and the alpine tundra lies an Engelmann spruce-subalpine fir forest, with the upper tree line averaging 11,000 feet on northern exposures and 11,500 feet on south-facing slopes. Timberline appears to be advancing up some of the rocky slopes, with vigorous young spruce trees developing in the lower part of the tundra (Richmond 1962). However, the remains of an earlier, higher timberline that appears to have been killed by climatic conditions can also be found. Rock glaciers, rubble streams, solifluction mantles, and other slowly creeping geologic masses interrupt the timberline and subalpine forest stands throughout the La Sal Mountains.

San Francisco Peaks

Nearly 200 miles south of Utah's High plateaus and the Henry Mountains, across the Grand Canyon, sprawls the Coconino Plateau of north-central Arizona. This 7000-foot-high tableland is covered with sagebrush-grass, pinyon-juniper woodland, and, to the south, with a magnificent parklike ponderosa pine forest. Out of this ponderosa timberland immediately north of Flagstaff, an extinct volcano looms up an additional mile in height. This eroded volcano is known as the San Francisco Peaks (12,670 feet), and it harbors the only alpine tundra in Arizona. At 35°N, it also constitutes the southernmost climatic alpine area north of central Mexico. This snow-capped landmark can be sighted even from the Sonoran Desert north of Phoenix.

In 1889, long before Arizona became a state, the eminent biologist C. Hart Merriam investigated the diverse environmental zones found between the desert and the summit of San Francisco Peaks, and as a result of his studies, proposed a series of seven life zones for classifying all the earth's habitats. Until the mid-1900s, Merriam's temperature-based life zones were widely used as a rudimentary ecological classification of the landscape. The notable feature of the San Francisco Peaks vicinity is that six of the seven life zones are visible from the desert view of this mountain mass: lower Sonoran zone (Sonoran Desert); upper Sonoran zone (pinyon-juniper and scrub oak); transition zone (ponderosa pine forest); Canadian zone (Douglas-fir, white fir forest); Hudsonian zone (subalpine forest and timberline); and the arctic-alpine zone. Only Merriam's tropical zone was missing from the transection up San Francisco Peaks.

Lower (ponderosa pine) and upper timberlines at San Francisco Peaks, as seen from the northwest

Today this transection from Sonoran Desert to alpine tundra can be traveled in a few hours by driving north from Phoenix (elevation 1080 feet) to Flagstaff and then to the Arizona Snow Bowl (about 9000 feet). From here, a chair-lift ride can be taken, summer or winter, to the lower edge of the alpine tundra at 11,600 feet. San Francisco Peaks are four distinct volcanic cones in one mountain mass, and the area above timberline is nearly two square miles (Lowe 1964). This alpine area supports 51 species of tundra plants, most of them species from the Southern Rocky Mountains (Moore 1965). However, today the nearest areas of alpine tundra are over 250 miles away in southwestern Colorado. San Francisco Peaks was one of the southernmost areas in North America to have been glaciated during the Pleistocene, and undoubtedly during the ice ages, alpine and subalpine plants were distributed along some of the highest terrain between these peaks and the Southern Rockies (Billings 1978).

Considering the Rocky Mountain affinities of the alpine flora on San Francisco Peaks, it is not surprising that the forest zones are also closely allied to those of the Southern Rockies. For instance, the subalpine forest is composed of Engelmann spruce, limber pine, the Colorado bristlecone pine (*Pinus aristata*), and corkbark fir (*Abies lasiocarpa* var. *arizonica*). The latter two species occur also in the Southern Rockies but are not found in the Great Basin or in Utah.

On the San Francisco Peaks, forest line occurs near 11,000 feet but varies with exposure. Krummholz extends to about 11,500 feet on the average. Engelmann spruce and corkbark fir form the upper subalpine forest and timberline on cool exposures, but groves of bristlecone and limber pines accompany the other species on southern slopes. Stunted spruce and bristlecone pine generally extend highest but are surpassed in this regard by the subalpine forest shrubs common juniper (*Juniperus communis*) and mountain gooseberry (*Ribes montigenum*).

Between 1917 and 1919 the U.S. Forest Service maintained several weather stations in different forest zones on San Francisco Peaks (Pearson 1931). By comparing the three years of record with long-term normals for nearby weather stations, scientists were able to estimate long-term averages of annual precipitation and monthly temperatures for each zone. Some of these precipitation and temperature values are shown below.

Location	Annual Precip. (inches)	Mean July Temperature (°F)
11,500 feet, tree line	36	49
10,500 feet, Engelmann spruce forest	33	53
8700 feet, Douglas-fir forest	31	58
7000 feet, ponderosa pine forest	23	65
5100 feet, pinyon-juniper woodland	14	73
Sonoran Desert	10	88

The cool temperatures and plentiful moisture in the subalpine zone on San Francisco Peaks help produce dense stands of Engelmann spruce.

The dominant trees in the 250- to 300-year-old stands attain 30 inches in d.b.h. and 100 feet in height. Corkbark fir is smaller and shorter lived, and as a result it dies out in such venerable subalpine forests. As indicated by the weather data for the 8700-foot station, the middle elevations of the forest zone are nearly as moist, and yet they have a warmer growing season than the subalpine forest. As a result, a rich mixed-conifer and aspen forest develops at mid-elevations here and at comparable levels on other high mountains in Arizona. On San Francisco Peaks this zone includes the lowermost Engelmann spruce and corkbark fir, the uppermost ponderosa pine, and Douglas-fir, white fir, and aspen.

The majestic ponderosa pine forest covering the 7000-foot plateau beneath the peaks is the northwestern portion of the famous yellow pine type of central Arizona. This vast forest of essentially pure ponderosa pine 20 to 35 miles wide extends 200 miles southeast along the Mogollon Plateau (atop the scenic Mogollon Rim) and into the White Mountains of east-central Arizona.

Southern Arizona and New Mexico

The White Mountains, whose highest peak is 11,590-foot Mount Baldy southwest of Springerville, are the second highest range in Arizona. The summit of Mount Baldy and the adjacent ridge tops are severely windswept and, as a result, support a subalpine grassland or "bald." However, tall Engelmann spruce grow immediately below the crest, suggesting that it barely rises above a climatic forest line. Also, no alpine tundra vegetation is present. The subalpine forest is composed entirely of spruce and corkbark fir, and in a few places the spruce forms krummholz atop the ridge crests. Similar subalpine grassy balds are found atop the highest peaks (for example, 10,892-foot Whitewater Baldy and 10,987-foot South Baldy) in western New Mexico (Brown and Lowe 1980). These may be partially the result of an absence of limber and bristlecone pines in this southern region, since if those drought-resistant subalpine species were present, they would presumably occupy much of the ridgetop "bald" environment. A good place to test this hypothesis might be 11,300-foot Mount Taylor, west of Albuquerque. This subalpine peak has a small area of bald but also is reported to support some of the southernmost limber pine (Little 1971).

The southernmost patch of alpine timberline north of subtropical Mexico is probably that on the summit of 12,003-foot Sierra Blanca at 33°N in south-central New Mexico. Sierra Blanca is the high point of the Sacramento Range, northwest of the town of Alamogordo. However, this peak, too, has erect Engelmann spruce trees ascending to within about 100 feet of the summit on the sheltered northern slope. Ridgetops and southern slopes near the summit are windswept and treeless. These sites have thin, stony soils and they support only sparse cushion plants and lichens (Moir and Smith 1970, Dye and Moir 1977). These fellfield communities have a very impoverished representation of the alpine tundra flora found in northern New Mexico and Colorado, including the following widespread tundra herbs — arctic sandwort (*Arenaria obtusiloba*), Ross' avens (*Geum rossii*), alpine lily (*Lloydia serotina*), and alpine fescue (*Festuca brachyphylla*). Sierra Blanca's summit might well support timberline trees were it not for severe wind exposure.

The mountain's highest point lies just inside the Mescalero Apache Indian Reservation, but the Sierra Blanca Ski Area in the adjacent Lincoln National Forest has its upper terminal in the corkbark fir-Engelmann spruce forest at 10,400 feet. The dominance of large, old corkbark fir on this mountain contrasts with the spruce-dominated subalpine forests in northern New Mexico, Arizona, and Colorado.

An analysis of mountain climates of the western United States suggests that if a much taller mountain were found in southern New Mexico, it would have a climatic timberline zone extending to 13,000 feet (Baker 1944). It is interesting to note, however, that southward from southern Colorado (at about 38°N) decreasing latitude has little effect on the altitude of upper timberlines. For example, timberlines on the giant volcanoes near Mexico City at 19°N are formed just above 13,000 feet. Evidently the summer climate does not get much warmer at a given elevation south of about 38°. (Death Valley, which has the hottest summers in North America, lies north of 36°.)

The highest mountains of southeastern Arizona have small areas of Engelmann spruce-corkbark fir forest on their summits. The southernmost well-developed subalpine spruce-fir forest on this continent appears to be the one covering the gentle upper slopes of 10,721-foot Mount Graham in the Pinaleno Range. This range rises high above its Sonoran Desert surroundings, south of Safford, Arizona. Nevertheless, the most interesting feature of the conifer forests on the Pinaleno Range — and on the Santa Catalina, Chiricahua, and other high mountains of southeastern Arizona — is the mixed conifer forest below the spruce-fir zone. This mixed conifer forest is replete with Mexican species including a five-needle variety of ponderosa pine (*P. ponderosa* var. *arizonica*) called Arizona pine. The other large forest trees of southern Arizonan and Mexican origin found in these ranges are Chihuahua pine (*P. leiophylla* var. *chihuahuana*), Apache pine (*P. engelmannii*), southwestern white pine (*P. strobiformis*), and Arizona cypress (*Cupressus arizonica*). These southern species accompany Rocky Mountain Douglas-fir, white fir, and quaking aspen, and the large Arizona alder (*Alnus oblongifolia*) in the mixed-conifer mountain forests. At the lower boundary of the montane forest in southeastern Arizona (about 6000 feet), the pines give way to oak and pinyon-juniper woodlands enriched with numerous Mexican species (Lowe 1964, Whittaker and Niering 1965).

Recreational roads in the Coronado National Forest lead up Mount Graham as well as the Santa Catalina and Chiricahua mountains, allowing easy inspection of the Mexican-influenced forest and woodlands.

7
Rocky Mountains

The Rocky Mountains of North America form a complex chain of lofty ranges extending northwesterly from the vicinity of Santa Fe, New Mexico, at about 35°N and 105°W. This mountain system stretches 2700 miles to within sight of the Arctic Ocean in Alaska and the Yukon Territory, at 69°N and 142°W. It forms the backbone of the North American continent, and its high peaks consistently rise above the alpine limit of trees. The Rockies have a complex and diverse geologic structure, and their upper-timberline terrain has been sculptured by glaciers during the Pleistocene. Throughout the prodigious length of this high mountain chain, it is well clothed in coniferous forests. Only at the far northern end, on the Arctic Slope of the Brooks Range in northern Alaska, do the Rockies extend past the Arctic timberline.

Near their northern end, the Rockies have only a narrow band of subarctic forest-tundra or northern timberline that occurs where forests give way to arctic-alpine tundra. Southward from about 65°N to about 53°—the latitude of Edmonton, Alberta—the vast boreal forest covers essentially all of the lowlands and extends with minor changes in composition up the lower slopes of the Rockies, forming an alpine timberline at moderate elevations. Southward from about 53°N, however, the lowlands bordering the Rockies become increasingly warm and dry. Thus, drought-resistant forests form on the lower skirts of the mountain ranges, while at higher elevations boreal (subarctic) tree species are replaced by subalpine species. These latter species—especially Engelmann spruce, subalpine fir, and Rocky Mountain lodgepole pine—dominate the subalpine forest southward to Colorado.

In southern Canada and in the northwestern United States several high mountain ranges stand between the main Rocky Mountains and the Pacific Coast mountains. These Northwest inland ranges include the Blue and Wallowa mountains of Oregon, the Bitterroot Mountains of Idaho and western Montana, and the Selkirks and Purcells, which lie mostly in southern British Columbia. These ranges have vegetation related to that of the main Rocky Mountains and are described in this section. It is in these latitudes, the inland portion of the Pacific Northwest, that a strong climatic influence extends eastward from the Pacific to the crest of the Rockies. This inland-maritime climate allows many of the Pacific Coast trees to spread into the Selkirks, Bitterroots, and other ranges almost to the Rocky Mountain divide. Both lower and upper timberlines of the inland Pacific Northwest contain trees not found elsewhere in the Rocky Mountain system.

From southern Montana southward in the Rockies the climate generally becomes drier and more continental, and the forests are very different from those of Pacific Coast mountains. Increasingly warm and dry conditions occur at lower elevations, and forests become confined to higher elevations that are comparatively cool and moist—much more moist than high-elevation sites in the Great Basin. In Utah, Colorado, and New Mexico, the forests and timberlines include a pinyon-juniper zone and several other tree elements characteristic of the American Southwest. Nevertheless, the distinctive Rocky Mountain Engelmann spruce-subalpine fir forest is dominant at high elevations.

SOUTHERN ROCKIES

The Southern Rockies form a continuous high-mountain barrier stretching north from Santa Fe, New Mexico, to slightly beyond Laramie, Wyoming, a distance of 450 miles. These mountains can only be crossed through high passes, all of which are above 9000 feet, and several passes on major roads lie in the upper timberline zone above 11,000 feet. The Southern Rockies are a complex of several major and numerous small mountain ranges, reaching a maximum width of 180 miles in southern Colorado. The principal alpine timberline ranges are the Sangre de Cristo, Wet Mountains, Front, and Medicine Bow ranges, which combined form the eastern wall of mountains rising directly above the upper Great Plains. Colorado's Sawatch and Park ranges form a second mountain barrier farther west, and the San Juan Mountains extend westward through southwestern Colorado. All of these ranges have alpine peaks jutting above 12,000 feet, and they contain 55 mountains above 14,000 feet. The San Juan, Sawatch, and Front ranges have many broad ridges lying wholly above the krummholz line, supporting the most extensive areas of alpine tundra south of Canada.

However, only a short distance eastward from this expansive mountaintop tundra sprawls the semi-arid Great Plains prairie. Also, desert shrub communities occupy the lowest intermountain valleys to the west. A broad array of forest and stunted woodland types spans the intermediate elevations. The diversity of natural vegetation is enhanced by the varied geology of the Southern Rockies—which include extensive areas of igneous, metamorphic, and sedimentary rocks. Limestone areas often support distinctive vegetation. The variation in moisture across these mountain environments also produces interesting patterns of vegetation. Some high-elevation sites are comparable in aridity to those in the Great Basin, but large areas have an abundance of moisture resulting from heavy winter snowfalls and ample summer rains.

Another source of diversity in forest and woodland types, and thus in timberlines, is the mingling of vegetation from the Southwest and the north, and of species that are endemic to the Southern and Middle Rockies.

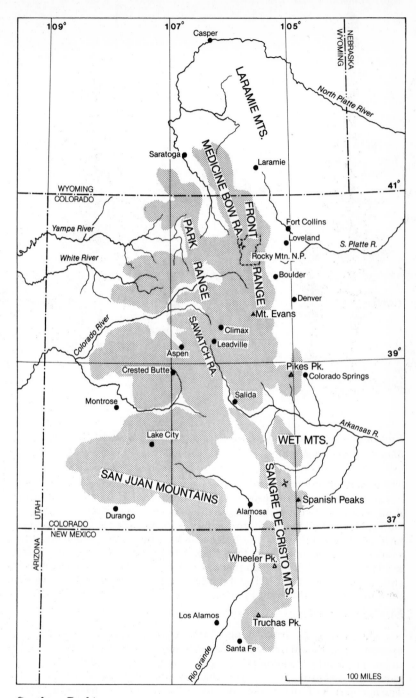

Southern Rockies

Engelmann spruce and subalpine fir at 10,650-foot Thunder Lake, Rocky Mountain National Park

The climate of the Southern Rockies also strongly reflects southern and northern influences. Two peak periods of precipitation are characteristic: a summer monsoon of cool, rainy weather comes into this region from the Gulf of Mexico and the southern Pacific Ocean; winter precipitation in the form of snow enters from the North Pacific. The southern and western ranges tend to be more moist than the eastern ranges, which lie in a rain shadow. Also, the Front and other eastern ranges are exposed to drying chinook winds as well as to frigid continental polar air masses that sweep in from the northern Great Plains.

Eastern Ranges

The Sangre de Cristo Range forms a crescent of lofty mountains extending northward from Santa Fe to Salida, Colorado, a distance of 200 miles. The southern half of this range includes several 12,000- to 13,000-foot ridges and peaks that support the only alpine tundra in New Mexico. The northern half, in Colorado, has numerous 14,000-foot peaks that rise 7000 feet above semi-arid valleys lying immediately to the west and east. In the southern Sangre de Cristo near Santa Fe, the upper subalpine forest is composed of Engelmann spruce, corkbark fir, and some bristlecone pine (Bailey 1913). Forest line varies from 11,000 feet on northeastern exposures to nearly 12,000 feet on southwestern slopes, with krummholz line reaching 12,500 feet on warm exposures. Spruce grows in extensive pure stands at the highest elevations (Peet 1978).

The highest spruce stands have grouse whortleberry (*Vaccinium scoparium*) as the principal undergrowth. This dwarf shrub, closely related to mountain huckleberries, spreads northward through the Rockies well into Canada, forming a yellow-green carpet beneath subalpine forests. Its tiny leaves and tasty little red berries serve as food for portly blue grouse and other fauna. The New Mexican spruce-whortleberry timberlines also provide some of the habitat for the southernmost populations of the arctic grouse known as white-tailed ptarmigan. These groves also provide shelter for the tundra-dwelling bighorn sheep (Moir and Ludwig 1979). Some of the spruce trees are over 500 years old.

Access to the New Mexican timberlines is primarily via hiking trails, although a ski lift at Santa Fe Ski Basin ascends to 12,200 feet. Much of the alpine timberline and tundra lies within the Pecos and Wheeler Peak wildernesses, which include New Mexico's two highest peaks—13,110-foot Truchas and 13,160-foot Wheeler Peak.

Bristlecone pine is confined to the exceptionally dry, rocky, wind-exposed sites, mostly above 10,000 feet, while limber pine occurs primarily on comparable locations at middle elevations (Peet 1978). A mixed-conifer blue spruce, white fir, Douglas-fir forest is confined to canyons and other moist sites at mid-elevations, although quaking aspen and Douglas-fir forests also spread across most of the middle slopes of the Sangre de Cristo. The lower forest zone is made up of ponderosa pine with an understory of

White-tailed ptarmigan

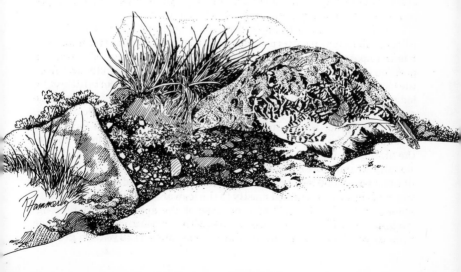

Gambel oak occurring between elevations of 7000 and 9000 feet. The broad, lower skirts of the Sangre de Cristo, including the townsite of Santa Fe (6954 feet), lie within an elfin woodland of Colorado pinyon and one-seed juniper. Evidently, this woodland type has expanded within the last two centuries in response to heavy domestic grazing that depleted former mountain grasslands and thereby prevented surface fires from spreading across the foothill slopes.

The Spanish Peaks are an eastern, volcanic outlier of the Sangre de Cristo, extending into the Great Plains northwest of Trinidad, Colorado, about 100 miles north of Santa Fe. (A secondary road climbs to 11,005-foot Apishapa Pass in the subalpine forest on the Spanish Peaks.) The Spanish Peaks especially, and even the nearby main portion of the Sangre de Cristo, are drier than the mountains above Santa Fe (Peet 1978). Evidently in response to the drying influence of the Great Plains, Colorado bristlecone pine dominates the drier two-thirds of the subalpine forest on the Spanish Peaks. Bristlecone forms tree line slightly above 12,000 feet without much krummholz. On moist sites Engelmann spruce is the principal timberline tree, and below forest line it is joined by corkbark fir. Interestingly, bristlecone pine also extends down to middle elevations on dry exposures, where it is joined by limber pine and, near its lower limits (about 9100 feet), by the ponderosa pine-Gambel oak forest in an unusual mixture. Despite the relative dryness of this portion of the Sangre de Cristo, the sheltered north-facing slopes of the main range harbor the southernmost stands of Rocky Mountain lodgepole pine.

Besides the increasing abundance northward of lodgepole pine in Colorado, another noticeable pattern is the decrease in pinyon-juniper and scrub oak northward along the eastern ranges. This may be partially explained by the high elevations of valleys in south-central Colorado. Semi-arid grassland extends upward to 8000 feet in much of this area, and evidently the growing, or frost-free, season is too short for the southwestern woodland types. The northern end of pinyon-juniper and scrub oak zones lies at the headwaters of the Arkansas River.

In this area, immediately southwest of Colorado Springs, 14,110-foot Pikes Peak forms an eastern extension of the Front Range. This mountain has an unpaved road to its alpine summit. Evidently because of its isolated position east of the Front Range and its exposure to drying influences from the Great Plains, Pikes Peak is comparatively dry and supports little or no lodgepole pine or subalpine fir (Whitfield 1933, Little 1971). Instead, the characteristic subalpine trees are Engelmann spruce, bristlecone pine, and limber pine, which are about equally abundant above forest line (about 11,000 feet). Spruce forms krummholz islands at the lower edge of the alpine tundra. Limber pine also takes on a prostrate form, and occasionally krummholz cushions of quaking aspen are found. At its upper limits, near 12,000 feet, bristlecone pine forms a gnarled, twisted, stunted tree with branches confined mostly to the leeward side. Bristlecone is also known locally as "foxtail" pine because of the appearance of its long, whiplike branchlets, which are covered with a dense growth of short pine needles, representing the accumulation of as much as 20 years of growth.

About 50 miles farther north, west of Denver, stands 14,264-foot Mount Evans in the main Front Range. This alpine peak, which has a paved road to its summit, supports a timberline typical of the Front Range, with the exception that it also harbors some of the northernmost stands of Colorado bristlecone pine. Bristlecone pine is most abundant on open, south-facing slopes—dry sites with some soil development (Peet 1978). In contrast, limber pine dominates rocky, exposed sites from middle elevations to the krummholz line. Some of the stout, wind-battered bristlecone pines on Mount Evans are more than 1500 years old.

Except for the disappearance of bristlecone pine north of James Peak, the forest zonation is relatively similar along the eastern slope of the Front Range north to the Wyoming border. The forest zones are traversed by three highways that lead to upper timberline—at Loveland Pass (11,992 feet) and Berthoud Pass (11,314 feet) west of Denver, and Trail Ridge (12,183 feet) in Rocky Mountain National Park. Engelmann spruce, subalpine fir, and limber pine form timberline in the northern Front Range.

Krummholz limber pine, Engelmann spruce, and subalpine fir above 11,000 feet on Trail Ridge, Rocky Mountain National Park

Spruce is the dominant tree at forest line, which averages about 10,800 feet, and the high-elevation spruce stands contain the largest timber in these mountains. In fact, high-elevation Engelmann spruce represents Colorado's primary timber resource. Together, spruce and the smaller subalpine fir form timberline communities on moist sites, with a rich, meadowy parkland developing between the groves and tree islands. Grouse whortleberry and mountain gooseberry (*Ribes montigenum*) are the principal shrubs within tree islands. The timberline parkland is well developed and quite handsome because of the relatively broad, moderate slopes found on the high ridges. Large krummholz islands are common as high as 11,500 feet.

Above 9000 feet on south-facing slopes and rocky ridges, limber pine becomes abundant. It forms a low, spreading tree and exhibits a continuum of stunted growth forms ranging down to cushion krummholz. In the absence of bristlecone pine, which reaches its northern limits here, and whitebark pine, which does not extend south of west-central Wyoming, limber pine becomes somewhat of a forest tree in the rather dry and extremely windy Front Range (Peet 1978). It even spreads as a seral species into sites where the spruce-fir forest has been killed by wildfire or avalanche. Interesting mixed krummholz communities of limber pine, spruce, and subalpine fir often occupy sites having intermediate moisture. The combination of dense krummholz, dwarf willows (*Salix brachycarpa* and *S. planifolia*), meadow and tundra herbs, and rocky outcrops covers large expanses in the gently rolling uplands of the Front Range. This is especially good habitat for white-tailed ptarmigan who live in and near the krummholz belt the year around.

Another interesting feature of the windy alpine country of the Front Range is the presence of numerous tiny glaciers in what is seemingly too dry an environment for them. These are "aeolian glaciers," created by immense wind-deposited snowdrifts. The Arapahoe Glacier in the city watershed of Boulder, Colorado, is the largest (about 70 acres); others can be seen just above the krummholz line in Rocky Mountain National Park.

In and below the lower part of the spruce-fir zone in the Front Range lies an extensive lodgepole pine forest composed of densely packed small trees. Downslope, this gives way to scattered aspen groves, a rather stunted Douglas-fir forest on northern slopes, and a broad zone of ponderosa pine that reaches down from 8500 feet to the foot of the Front Range near 5500 feet. The lower half of the ponderosa pine zone has been termed a "woodland" in recognition of its openness and the stunted form of the trees. These woodland ponderosas are often only 18 to 30 feet tall at maturity and almost resemble pinyon pines! Perhaps significantly, this stunted ponderosa woodland is a replacement for the pinyon-juniper zone, which does not extend north of Colorado Springs. However, much farther north there is an interesting isolated stand of Colorado pinyons at Owl Creek, 20 miles north of Fort Collins, that may have been "planted" inadvertently by Indians (Lanner 1981).

The stunted, "weedy" growth form of ponderosa pine in this area evidently is the result of severely dry atmospheric and soil conditions in the chinook wind belt at the base of the Front Range. In contrast, near the species' upper limits in moist, wind-sheltered valleys, ponderosa pines often develop into well-formed trees as much as 3 feet in d.b.h. and 80 feet tall. The transition from a stunted woodland form to the regular form of ponderosa pine can be seen along the highways leading from Loveland in the Great Plains to the headquarters area of Rocky Mountain National Park. In addition to the warm, dry, windy atmospheric conditions at the foot of the Front Range, annual precipitation in the stunted ponderosa woodland is only 11 to 14 inches. In fact, the entire forest zone on upland slopes on the eastern side of the Front Range has a somewhat stunted appearance, probably related to drought stress. A notable contrast to this stunted forest is the magnificent blue spruce, Engelmann spruce, Douglas-fir, and quaking aspen mixture inhabiting mountain valleys at elevations of 7500 to 8500 feet.

Similar ponderosa forest zones occur northward along the eastern ranges of the Rockies, except that in southeastern Wyoming the valleys are 7000 feet high and thus are cold as well as dry. As a result, here in the Medicine Bow Range ponderosa pine becomes confined to a few relatively warm, rocky slopes in the lower foothills. Douglas-fir also has a rather limited occurrence, on the lower north-facing slopes. Instead of these forest types forming lower timberline, limber pine and quaking aspen communities adjoin the high-valley sagebrush-grass zone, near 7500 feet.

The Medicine Bow forests include a broad band dominated by lodgepole pine. At higher elevations, lodgepole gives way to dense stands of Engelmann spruce and subalpine fir. At 10,500 feet on the wide,

windswept ridges, spruce and fir develop ribbon forest-snowglade formations, and at 11,000 to 11,500 feet, vast stands of krummholz subalpine fir
can be seen (Billings 1969, Peet 1978). The bulky subalpine ridges are so
severely wind-lashed that a timberline spruce stand (at 10,500-foot Libby
Flats) that burned repeatedly in wildfires more than a century ago has not
regenerated to trees. Instead, this fossil timberline area is covered with
moist-site tundra (Billings 1969). Wind speeds on an open tundra site here
averaged 19 times those in an unburned ribbon forest, and gusts over 75
mph were frequent in winter at the open site. The howling winter wind
blows nearly all snow off non-forested sites, leaving tree seedlings without
protection from desiccation or cold. Also, the lack of snowpack brings
about a soil-moisture deficit early in the summer.

The rather narrow forest zone of the Medicine Bow Range—primarily
of aspen, lodgepole pine, and spruce-fir—is characteristic also of northwestern Colorado and western Wyoming. In all of these areas no elfin
woodland or ponderosa pine forest occurs, and the montane Douglas-fir
zone is quite limited because of the high elevations and dry site conditions
at the base of the mountains. Adequate moisture for tree growth occurs
only near the subalpine zone. A beautiful transection can be made through
the forest zones to upper timberline in the Medicine Bow Range by driving
State Highway 130 west from Laramie over 10,800-foot Snowy Range Pass
and down the west side of the mountains toward Saratoga.

Western and Central Ranges

The San Juan Mountains of southwestern Colorado form a rugged
upland 120 miles wide, where the average elevation is 10,000 feet. These
mountains are of volcanic origin, mostly lavas, but include other geologic
types also, and they have been carved by Pleistocene glaciers into sharp
ridges and deep cirques. "Rock glaciers" (large masses of talus and other
rock debris with an ice core) flow within many of the highest cirques. The
San Juans have several 14,000-foot peaks and large expanses of alpine
tundra, above 12,000 feet. They also support a rather diverse forest and
woodland zone with moist Engelmann spruce stands at high elevations
watered by a copious winter snowpack and ample summer rains from
subtropical air masses. A long-term weather record at 10,000 feet near
Wolf Creek Pass averages 40 inches of annual precipitation. However, the
desert plateaus lying immediately south and west, near the Four Corners
area, contribute arid southwestern vegetation to the mixture found in the
San Juans.

Upper timberline is almost entirely spruce and subalpine fir, although in the northeastern portion of the San Juans (north of Creede)
groves of bristlecone pine occupy some of the south-facing slopes. Both
spruce and fir form krummholz in some areas at about 12,000 feet; but the
amount of such wind-dwarfed conifer growth seems notably less than in
Colorado's eastern ranges, suggesting a less windy, or at least a less
desiccating winter environment. Groves of tall Engelmann spruce are
interspersed with meadows at forest line on sheltered slopes and in high
basins.

A few of the timberline spruce stands are situated on excessively watered, unstable geologic material and, as a result, they are creeping downslope. Recent mud flows and rock glaciers can be seen at the Lake Fork Recreation Area near Lake City. A major attraction here is two-mile-long Lake San Cristobal, which was impounded by the giant Slumgullion Mud Flow originating at timberline. This flow is covered with a living spruce forest!

The subalpine forest proper extends from forest line (about 11,000 feet) down to the 10,000-foot level and is composed of Engelmann spruce, subalpine fir, quaking aspen groves, and subalpine meadows (Petersen 1981). Below this, generally reaching down to about 8200 feet, lies a handsome southwestern mixed-conifer forest composed of Douglas-fir, ponderosa pine, aspen, white fir, Engelmann spruce, limber pine, blue spruce, and subalpine fir. A ponderosa pine forest extends downslope to perhaps 6800 feet on the average. Below the lower timberline lie elfin woodlands of Colorado pinyon, Utah juniper, and Rocky Mountain juniper as well as scrubby Gambel oak thickets and, on the driest sites, sagebrush-grass.

Although these mountains are directly connected to the Sawatch and other ranges to the north, where lodgepole pine becomes a major forest component, most of the San Juan region has no lodgepole. This absence is another southwestern characteristic of the region. The highway from Durango to Montrose, Colorado, makes an up-and-down transection of the San Juans from the sagebrush through woodlands and forests to upper forest line at 11,000 feet.

The Sawatch Range forms the continental divide in central Colorado and includes a large amount of alpine timberline and tundra as well as numerous 14,000-foot peaks and a small city (Leadville) perched at the 10,200-foot level! Upper timberlines are primarily of Engelmann spruce, with lesser amounts of subalpine fir, although bristlecone pine occasionally forms tree line on south-facing slopes. Some of the highest-dwelling erect trees in Colorado are thought to be a stand of wind-battered bristlecones on a southwestern slope at 12,300 feet near Saint Elmo, northwest of Salida (Cary 1911). Groups of erect spruce trees and tree islands often reach the 12,000-foot level on sheltered slopes.

Copious quantities of summer rain, sleet, hail, and wet snow fall on these upper timberlines; thus, luxuriant meadows spring up wherever soil development permits. Today this glacially sculptured terrain is without residual icefields; however, permafrost, extending as deep as 100 feet, remains as a probable relict of the Pleistocene. Permafrost has been encountered in several locations where mine or exploration shafts were dug (Curry 1962, Langenheim 1962).

Because of the high elevations of the major valleys in central Colorado and because of the more northern latitude of this area, there are fewer forest zones than in the San Juan Mountains or on the eastern slope of the Front Range. For instance, in the Crested Butte area, south of the city of Aspen, sagebrush generally predominates up to 9500 feet (Langenheim 1962), and quaking aspen forms the lowermost band of forest, extending

Timberline parkland on the west slope of the Continental Divide in Colorado

up to about 10,500 feet. The spruce-fir subalpine forest spreads from there to nearly 11,500 feet, with the timberline belt immediately above. Spruce krummholz reaches 12,500 feet.

The pinyon-juniper and ponderosa pine zones are absent, presumably because of the high elevations of the valleys. Occasional frosts can be expected in mid-summer even at the lower timberline. Douglas-fir and limber pine are restricted to small patches on steep south-facing slopes on limestone substrates. Annual precipitation in the subalpine forest averages 40 inches or more, and even the townsite of Crested Butte in the sagebrush zone records 28 inches! This should be amply moist for Douglas-fir, but perhaps the growing season is too frosty and short. Presumably because of the relatively moist conditions, bristlecone pine is rare in the Crested Butte area.

The steep topography and heavy snowfall of the central Colorado Rockies give rise to spectacular snow avalanches. Massive flows thunder down from the alpine ridges and flatten large swathes of subalpine forest. At Crested Butte, tree trunks up to 42 inches in d.b.h. (no doubt Engelmann spruce) have been snapped off in avalanches (Langenheim 1962).

Farther north, the Park Range and other high-mountain areas of northwestern Colorado have a similar sequence of vegetation zones, although only a few peaks rise high enough (above 11,500 feet) to support alpine tundra. Also, the topography is much less rugged than in central Colorado and this allows extensive ribbon forest and snow glade formations to develop at timberline. In northwestern Colorado, an elfin forest of Colorado pinyon and Utah juniper occupies the lowest-elevation country along the Yampa, White, and Colorado rivers. However, this gives way upslope, near the mountainous uplands, to an extensive sagebrush steppe (Küchler 1964). Ponderosa pine is rare and Douglas-fir occurs only in patches on warm topographic sites. Evidently these species are excluded from the more moderate elevations by drought and from the higher elevations by low temperatures (Hoffman and Alexander 1980). The lower timberlines are generally marked by aspen woodlands beginning near 7400 feet. Large stands of "oak-brush"—scrubby Gambel oak with tall shrubs of chokecherry (*Prunus virginiana*) and serviceberry (*Amelanchier alnifolia*)—often form between the sagebrush and aspen types. Annual precipitation increases rapidly with elevation in northwestern Colorado, averaging about 20 inches at the 8600-foot level in the aspen zone and 40 inches at 10,000 feet in the Engelmann spruce-subalpine fir forest. Perhaps because of the moist conditions in the subalpine zone, limber pine is confined to middle elevations on especially dry ridges, unlike its widespread occurrence eastward in the Front Range.

MIDDLE ROCKIES

The Middle Rocky Mountains lie west and north of the Southern Rockies and are completely separated from them by the sprawling Wyoming Basin desert. The Middle Rockies stretch 425 miles northward from Nephi in north-central Utah to Livingston in south-central Montana. Unlike the essentially continuous chain of the Southern Rockies, the Middle Rocky Mountains are an assemblage of well-separated ranges that have contrasting geologic structure and rock types. The vegetation is also diverse and in several respects represents a transition between the Southern and Northern Rockies.

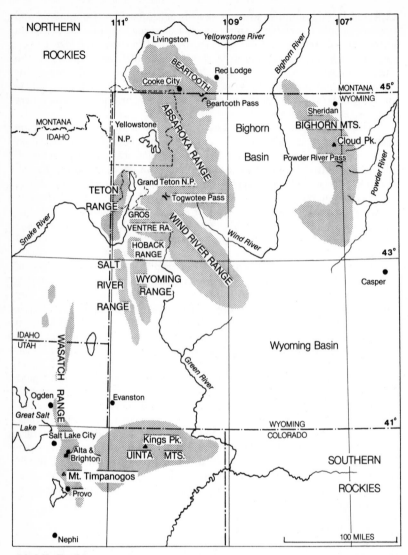

Middle Rockies

    The principal high mountain ranges having upper timberlines are the Wasatch and Uinta ranges of northern Utah, the Wind River, Gros Ventre, and Teton ranges of western Wyoming, the Absaroka Range of northwestern Wyoming and adjacent Montana, and the Bighorn Range of north-central Wyoming. All of these ranges have alpine peaks above 11,000 feet, and several summits exceed 13,000 feet. Sizeable plateaulike alpine areas occur atop the Uinta, Wind River, Absaroka-Beartooth, and Bighorn ranges. The bases of the mountains lie at elevations between 4300 and 7000 feet and are covered primarily with sagebrush-grass communities.

The southern part of this province, in Utah, has some vegetation characteristic of the Great Basin and Southwest—for example, pinyon-juniper, oak-maple chaparral, and Rocky Mountain white fir. Northward in Wyoming, however, the vegetation is without these elements and is generally similar to that of the drier, eastern portion of the Northern Rocky Mountains. The Wyoming portion of the Middle Rockies, like the Northern Rockies, has whitebark pine at most of its upper timberlines.

The climate of the Middle Rockies also reflects a south to north transition, with summer precipitation generally less abundant than in the Southern Rockies but more than in the Northern Rockies. Winter snowpack that saturates the soil when it melts in spring is the primary source of growing-season moisture. Overall, the climate is continental, and lower elevations are distinctly semi-arid.

Wasatch and Uinta Ranges

The Wasatch and the Uintas of northern Utah are two large mountain ranges that make up the southern portion of the Middle Rockies. Despite the fact that they are separated by only 10 miles, these mountain ranges differ from each other in several respects—including topography, geologic structure, climate, and vegetation.

The Wasatch Range is an exceptionally steep and rugged complex fault-block that consists of various sedimentary, metamorphic, and igneous rocks, having a great range in ages (Precambrian to Quaternary). The Wasatch trends north-south and forms the eastern side of the Salt Lake

Limber pine and Engelmann spruce on a high ridge in the Wasatch Range

Basin. It represents the western edge of the Rocky Mountains, and the Wasatch Front, or western escarpment, towers above the sprawling Ogden-Salt Lake City-Provo metropolitan area. High peaks in the Salt Lake City to Provo area (the southern Wasatch) reach elevations above 10,000 feet and have upper timberlines as well as a few patches of alpine tundra. The loftiest peak is jagged, 12,008-foot Mount Timpanogos, 10 miles north of Provo. Mount Nebo (11,928 feet) is an imposing, isolated alpine summit at the south end of the range, 30 miles south of Provo.

Because of the limited area and extremely steep and rocky conditions above 10,000 feet, the Wasatch Range has a rather poorly developed upper timberline, consisting of Engelmann spruce, subalpine fir, and some limber pine. Krummholz spruce can be found as low as 9500 feet on steep, wind-exposed ridges of Mount Timpanogos, while normal-sized trees grow much higher on sheltered slopes (Hayward 1952). Access to the rugged upper-timberline country of the Wasatch Range can be had via ski lift or hiking trail at the Alta and Brighton areas southeast of Salt Lake City.

This steep terrain receives heavy winter and spring snowfalls from Pacific storms, resulting in frequent avalanches. These snowslides hinder the development of subalpine and middle-elevation forests and result in patchy, broken stands and vertical stringers of timber between avalanche swathes. Where terrain permits, a mixed-conifer forest develops at middle elevations (near 9000 feet) in the southern Wasatch. This is dominated by Douglas-fir and includes white fir, blue spruce, limber pine, and quaking aspen. Like southwestern mixed-conifer forests, its forests are without lodgepole pine (Cronquist and others 1972). Unlike southwestern forests, however, the Wasatch and other ranges to the north in the Middle Rockies are essentially without ponderosa pine. Lynn Hayward (1948) reported that ponderosa planted on the Wasatch Front appeared to grow well, lending support to the suggestion that this species may have been eliminated during a colder Pleistocene climate when vegetation zones were forced to lower elevations. At that time, the waters of Glacial Lake Bonneville covered the lowest slopes, flooding the site where ponderosa pine might have otherwise survived.

In addition to the lack of ponderosa pine, the southwestern pinyon-juniper woodland is absent (as a vegetation zone) from the Wasatch and other ranges to the north. Instead of pinyon-juniper or ponderosa pine, a well-developed chaparral zone covers the lower slopes from about 5000 to 7500 feet. The Wasatch chaparral consists of Gambel oak, mountain-mahogany, and other tall shrubs, along with bigtooth maple (*Acer grandidentatum*), and it makes up a colorful skirt on the slopes of this desert-fronting range. In spring and summer the chaparral is deep green in contrast to the desert below. By early September, patches of crimson maple become conspicuous, and, later, variegated reds, yellows, and browns appear (Hayward 1948). The chaparral becomes dull gray in winter, when it serves as prime habitat for a large population of mule deer.

The Uinta Range lies immediately east of the Wasatch in the latitude of Salt Lake City. The Uinta is the largest mountain range in the western hemisphere that extends in an east-west direction (Fenneman 1931). This range is a massive, uplifted dome or anticline, 150 miles long and 35 miles wide, and its crest is a gently sloping tableland ranging in elevation from 11,000 to 13,498 feet (at Kings Peak). The upper portions of the range were heavily glaciated, and much of the crest is deeply incised with scooped-out cirque basins. The cirques open into glacial canyons that are separated by flat-topped or knife-edged ridges (Cronquist and others 1972). The high elevations are composed primarily of very old (Precambrian) but resistant quartzite and have little soil development.

The Uintas support an extensive and floristically rich alpine tundra above 11,000 feet, which spreads along the crest for 60 miles without a break and covers more than 300 square miles (Cronquist and others 1972). The Uintas also have a sequence of forest and woodland zones similar to those of the Colorado Front Range but different from the other ranges of the Middle Rockies. Engelmann spruce and subalpine fir form the subalpine forest (above 10,000 feet) and, with limber pine, they make up the tree line (averaging 11,000 feet) and krummholz line (near 11,500 feet). Grouse whortleberry forms a carpet beneath most of the spruce-fir stands, as it does elsewhere in the Rockies except in the southern Wasatch Range.

The next lower zone is dense lodgepole pine forest extending down to about 9000 feet. This is the only extensive lodgepole pine forest in Utah. Below this lies a band of quaking aspen groves and then, on the southern slope of the range, a patchy belt of ponderosa pine. Ponderosas are best developed in the mountain valleys or "parks," down to about 7000 feet. The northern slope of the Uintas has a more extensive ponderosa forest. The Uintas have the only appreciable occurrence of this tree in northern Utah or in the Middle Rocky Mountains, except for stands east of Wyoming's Bighorn Range. Douglas-fir is widespread at middle elevations in the Uintas, and blue spruce occurs on moist valley sites.

Below the conifer and aspen forests, the southern slope of the Uintas has mixtures of sagebrush, serviceberry, and mountain-mahogany but none of the Wasatch oak-maple chaparral (Graham 1937). In further contrast to the nearby Wasatch Range, a Colorado pinyon-Utah juniper woodland forms at 5500 to 7000 feet on the southern slope of the Uintas. Pinyon-juniper also occupies exposed sites below lower timberline on the northern slope of the range, and this is the northernmost pinyon-juniper woodland of any extent in the Rocky Mountains (Little 1971). The lowest elevations and driest areas, with less than 10 inches of annual precipitation, have sagebrush or desert shrub communities.

Like the Southern Rockies, the high Uintas evidently receive more summer rain than the frequently summer-dry Wasatch Range. This factor, coupled with the differences in rock types and topography, and the effect of the Wasatch Front as a barrier to plant migration, seem largely responsible for the differing vegetation on the Wasatch and Uinta ranges.

A popular vacation highway between Kamas, Utah, and Evanston, Wyoming, climbs above 10,000 feet into the western end of the Uinta Range in the Mirror Lake area. Campgrounds and resorts are located in the spruce-fir forest along this road, and upper timberline is a short hike's distance from here.

Western Wyoming Ranges

One hundred twenty-five miles north of the Uintas, across the 6500-foot-high Wyoming Basin desert, stands another major alpine mountain mass—the Wind River Range. West of the Wind Rivers, across the broad Green River Valley, several smaller mountain ranges have high peaks in the timberline and alpine zones. These are the Gros Ventre (pronounced "Gro Vont"), Hoback, Wyoming, and Salt River ranges, near the Idaho border. They are connected to the Wasatch Range via a chain of lower mountains. Northwest of the Gros Ventre, across Jackson Hole, jut the jagged Tetons, and north of the Gros Ventre and Wind Rivers stretches a broad mass of high mountains called the Absaroka ("Ab-sar-ka") Range. The Absarokas reach 150 miles northward into southern Montana where to the east they merge with the magnificent alpine tableland known as the Beartooth Plateau.

These ranges of western Wyoming and south-central Montana have similar timberlines and a rather narrow forested belt. Whitebark pine is a major component of the subalpine forest and timberline throughout these mountains, and on warm exposures it often becomes a large, spreading tree, reaching three to four feet in d.b.h. after several centuries of growth. Engelmann spruce and subalpine fir accompany the pine, and all three species form krummholz on windswept sites above 10,000 feet.

Most of the forest zone in this large mountain area, however, is dominated by lodgepole pine. (The exception is limestone substrates, where this species is quite limited.) The lodgepole forest begins near the lower timberline (averaging perhaps 7000 feet) and stretches to 9000 or 9500 feet, nearly to the upper forest line. Near the lower timberline, large, colorful groves of quaking aspen separate the lodgepole pine forest from the broad sagebrush-covered valleys below. Patches of Douglas-fir and limber pine occupy rocky, warm exposures but, except on limestone, there is no continuous belt of Douglas-fir in this high, cold country. In fact, all the subalpine conifers are occasionally found at *lower* timberlines in western Wyoming. Engelmann spruce, blue spruce, and subalpine fir grow along some of the major mountain streams at lower timberline, and the fir would doubtless be more abundant except for the fact that its saplings and low branches are a favorite winter food of the plentiful moose. At some locations in northwestern Wyoming, elk also heavily browse the Douglas-fir at lower timberline.

While the high intermountain valleys and southwestern slopes are often covered by sagebrush communities (*Artemisia tridentata* spp. *vaseyana*), these sites are not nearly as hot or dry as sagebrush (other subspecies) country below ponderosa pine timberlines in the Southern Rockies or the inland Pacific Northwest. Thus, the lower timberline is formed by the less drought-tolerant quaking aspen and lodgepole pine. In much of western Wyoming even Douglas-fir is restricted to favorably warm slopes and certain geologic types (limestone, andesite, and basalt) (Steele and others 1983). Similarly, pinyon-juniper and mountain chaparral are absent from this cold mountain region.

*Douglas-fir at lower timberline in the northern part of Yellowstone Park.
Trees are high-lined by browsing elk.*

Annual precipitation exceeds 40 inches in some of the upper timberline basins in the Teton and Absaroka ranges, while the southern and eastern portion of the Wind River Range, extending into the Wyoming Basin, is semi-arid even at high elevations. This area receives 20 inches or less precipitation on the average and supports dense, stunted, extremely slow-growing stands of climax lodgepole pine that give way near forest line to whitebark pine (Steele and others 1983). The coarse granite substrate in this area supports little undergrowth. In contrast, the northwestern portion of the Wind River Range is relatively moist and harbors the largest glaciers in the Rocky Mountains south of Canada. However, the glaciers are perched in the alpine tundra zone above 11,000 feet (Arno 1969).

Hiking trails provide the only access to the heavily glaciated and strikingly rugged timberline and alpine country in the Wind River and Teton ranges. In the southern Absaroka Range, however, a highway climbs over 9658-foot Togwotee Pass, east of Grand Teton National Park. This route leads through stands of large whitebark pine, Engelmann spruce, and subalpine fir, interspersed with lush meadows near forest line. Farther north in the Absaroka Range in Yellowstone National Park a highway crosses 8859-foot Dunraven Pass and a limited-access road ascends nearby 10,243-foot Mount Washburn. Whitebark pine groves and

Whitebark pine and Engelmann spruce above forest line (10,200 feet) on the west slope of the Wind River Range

meadows cover the pass and the slopes of Mount Washburn, giving way to krummholz atop the peak. In late summer the raucous calls of Clarks nutcrackers, along with the chatter of red squirrels, fill this forest. Large caches of whitebark pine cones made by squirrels are a principal food of grizzly and black bears in this area (Kendall 1981). Timberline parklands in western Wyoming are also summer habitat for thousands of elk, and in the northeastern portion of Yellowstone Park, bands of native mountain bison also summer in the timberline meadows.

The northern Absaroka Range, east of Yellowstone Park's volcanic plateau, has many alpine peaks, and its northeastern extremity is a rolling, tundra-covered tableland 30 miles long. This is the Beartooth Plateau, perched above 10,000 feet on the Montana-Wyoming border. The scenic highway from Cooke City to Red Lodge, Montana, travels through a timberline parkland sprinkled with glacial lakes and groves of whitebark pine, Engelmann spruce, and subalpine fir. The road also climbs for a few miles across a dense low carpet of alpine tundra, reaching 10,940 feet at Beartooth Pass. The descent on the Montana slope of the Beartooth highway leads into the huge, U-shaped glacial canyon of Rock Creek. At the

9200-foot level above this gorge, a viewpoint is set amidst subalpine firs that are clinging to the canyon wall and that have great circular mats of lower branches and wind-battered flags protruding from them.

A maintained dirt road climbs north from Cooke City to tree line at 9800-foot Daisy Pass, immediately west of the Beartooth Plateau. This rugged area is highly mineralized and the timberline environment has been heavily disturbed by prospecting and mining activity. Revegetation studies have been conducted on mine spoils and stripped sites here, and recovery has been exceedingly slow (Brown and others 1978a). Large mining developments have recently intruded into the timberline and alpine areas around Picket Pin and Iron mountains, 30 miles north of Cooke City.

In the mountains a few miles northeast of Daisy Pass lies the Grasshopper Glacier, where hordes of migrating grasshoppers have been caught repeatedly by snowstorms and rest entombed in the ice. The Beartooth has a total of about 40 glaciers that lie entirely above timberline.

Bighorn Range

The Bighorn Range of north-central Wyoming rises out of the northern Great Plains about 70 miles east of the main Rocky Mountains. It is separated from the Absarokas by the arid Bighorn Basin. The Bighorn Range is a large, uplifted dome, or anticline, that has a granitic core exposed along its broad, plateaulike crest. The Bighorns extend high above timberline, to a maximum elevation of 13,175 feet atop Cloud Peak. These mountains are relatively dry, with only about 25 inches of annual precipitation falling at the 9000-foot level in the subalpine forest (Hoffman and Alexander 1976).

Throughout the drier ranges of the Rockies, east of the continental divide from Colorado to Alberta, geologic substrate has a profound influence on vegetation. In the Bighorns three prominent rock types support contrasting vegetation. Granite yields coarse, sandy soils poor in nutrients and covered by forest, predominantly of lodgepole pine. At the other extreme, shale produces fine-textured soils high in nutrients which are largely occupied by grasslands. Limestone and dolomite soils are intermediate in texture and nutrients and support forest on moist sites and grass or shrubland on dry sites. Often, an abrupt forest line coincides with the boundary between different rock types. The flanks of the Bighorn Range are composed of sedimentary rocks, including large areas of shale, limestone, and dolomite (Despain 1973).

The upper subalpine forest and timberlines in the Bighorn Range consist solely of Engelmann spruce and subalpine fir. This is the only major mountain range north of the Wyoming Basin and south of the Boreal Rockies in Canada that does not harbor whitebark pine. Presumably whitebark's absence is related to the Bighorns' isolated location in the Great Plains. Forest line averages about 9600 to 9800 feet and is reached by U.S. Highway 16 at 9666-foot Powder River Pass west of Buffalo. Engelmann spruce and subalpine fir are joined by lodgepole pine at timberline on warm exposures on the dry granite substrate. On granitic sites, the subalpine and mid-elevation forests are dominated by nearly pure stands of lodgepole pine extending down to about 7000 feet (Despain 1973). In contrast, lodgepole is seldom found on shale and limestone. Where these substrates are forested, spruce and fir give way downslope to Douglas-fir and aspen groves. Douglas-fir seldom grows on the granitic substrates.

On the desert, western slope of the Bighorns, Douglas-fir forms the lower timberline at about 6200 feet (Hoffman and Alexander 1976). A broken band of Utah juniper woodlands lies downslope from the Douglas-fir. Although this is without pinyon, the squatty limber pines growing among the uppermost junipers appear similar to pinyons and also provide large seeds (Despain 1973). Annual precipitation in the Bighorn Basin, below the western slope, averages as little as five inches, and the basin has the northernmost saltbush-greasewood desert type in North America (Küchler 1964).

On the eastern slope of the Bighorns, adjacent to the Great Plains, ponderosa pine forms a narrow forest belt below the Douglas-fir and lodgepole pine, at elevations of 5000 to 6000 feet. Similar ponderosa pine stands, composed of rather small trees compared to those west of the continental divide, extend northeast from the Bighorns across the hilly Great Plains of southeastern Montana. An arm of this ponderosa pine distribution even reaches eastward 90 miles from the Bighorns to the western edge of the Black Hills. The Black Hills of western South Dakota and northeastern Wyoming are the easternmost outlier of the Rocky Mountains and are largely covered by ponderosa pine forest, while Douglas-fir, Engelmann spruce, subalpine fir, and most other Rocky Mountain species are absent.

NORTHERN ROCKIES

The Northern Rockies are a conglomeration of rugged, mountainous uplands and distinct ranges that stretches 400 miles north from Idaho's Snake River plains to the Canadian border. (The same structural complex of mountains also extends several hundred miles northward in British Columbia and Alberta, but for convenience that portion is treated as the "Southern Canadian Rockies.") The Northern Rocky Mountains average 300 miles in width, reaching from the northwestern tip of Yellowstone National Park to Hells Canyon on the Snake River, which forms the boundary between Idaho and Oregon. The sprawling Blue Mountains of northeastern Oregon lie west of this mile-deep gorge. They have vegetation similar to that of the Northern Rockies and will be included in this discussion. The Northern Rockies also stretch from central Montana westward across northern and central Idaho and northeastern Washington to the Okanogan Valley, which separates them from the Cascades.

Generally, the western and northern portions of the Northern Rockies are more moist as a result of the strong oceanic influence on their climate. A nearly continuous mantle of dense forest, containing several Pacific maritime trees, covers this mountain landscape, with only the highest peaks (above 7000 feet) developing an alpine timberline. Conversely, the southern and eastern portions of the Northern Rockies have drier, more continental climates. Forests are without the Pacific tree and under-growth species and are similar to those of the Middle Rockies. They are often confined to cool, moist aspects and higher elevations, while sage-brush and grasslands are extensive. Thus, lower or drought-caused tim-berlines are prevalent. Peaks tend to be higher than in the western and northern area, generally 9000 to 11,000 feet, and they support alpine timberlines as well as small areas of tundra.

In Montana alone, at least 25 separate mountain ranges rise above the alpine limit of trees. Most of these alpine areas are quite small, but the timberline zones are more extensive, and they are isolated from those in other ranges, often by large grassland valleys. This isolation, coupled with the regional variation in mountain climates and diverse geologic types in the Northern Rockies, gives rise to many kinds of timberline communities (Pfister and others 1977). To facilitate study of timberlines, the Northern Rockies can be divided into four climatic regions: southern continental, northern continental, intermountain, and inland-maritime.

Southern Continental Ranges

This climatic region includes east-central Idaho (east from U.S. Highway 93) and southwestern Montana (the Butte, Bozeman, and Dillon areas). It is a cool, dry country where sagebrush-grass communities cover the valleys and forest is confined to the higher mountains (Arno 1979). Since it lies in a rain shadow downwind from Oregon's Blue Mountains and central Idaho's high mountain mass, this region receives little of the moisture from Pacific storm systems. Average annual precipitation in the high valleys is only 8 to 14 inches. Lower timberlines are usually formed at 6000 to 7500 feet and consist of Douglas-fir or occasionally limber pine. Ponderosa pine is absent, evidently because the climate is too cold. The forest belt is rather narrow with upper tree line developing near 9300 feet. In fact, in some of the driest mountain ranges south of Dillon, sagebrush-grass communities extend up entirely through the subalpine zone, and timber is confined to small groves in north-facing ravines.

Douglas-fir is the principal tree in the lower portion of the forest belt. During the last few decades, Douglas-fir has vigorously invaded down-slope in the sagebrush-grass and also thickened the formerly open forest stands. This invasion and thickening of Douglas-fir at the lower timber-line is evidently a result of livestock grazing (which removed competing grass) coupled with a dramatic reduction in wildfires. Prior to settlement in the late 1800s, fires swept along the lower timberlines at average intervals of 25 to 40 years (Houston 1973, Arno and Gruell 1983).

On these dry sites it takes about 40 years for Douglas-fir seedlings to grow large enough to survive surface fires. Thus, in the past, Douglas-firs were confined to rocky or moist sites where fires were less frequent or burned in a patchy manner. Once well established, the thick-barked vet-eran trees survived numerous surface fires, some attaining d.b.h. of 3 to 5 feet and ages of 500 to 700 years. They seldom reach 100 feet in height,

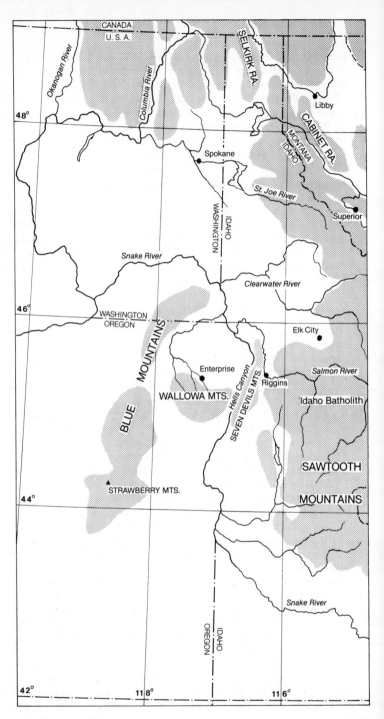

Northern Rockies

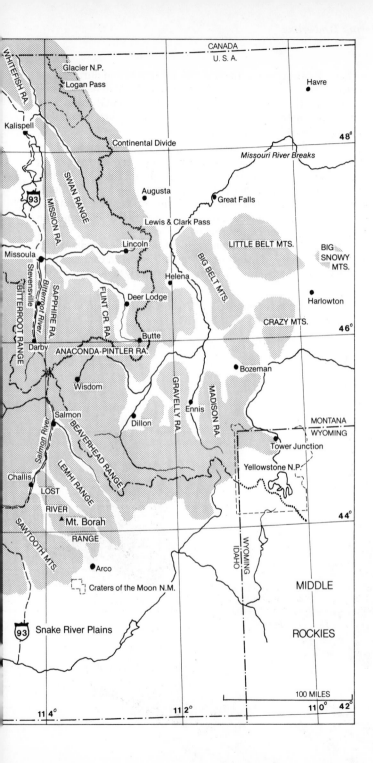

however, in these dry continental forests. The thickness and durability of the old-growth Douglas-fir bark can be verified in a visit to Roosevelt Lodge at Tower Junction in northern Yellowstone National Park. This large building was constructed near the turn of the century from stout, bark-covered Douglas-fir logs that are still intact.

Limber pine is largely restricted to dry timberlines in the Northern Rockies. It becomes most abundant on limestone and certain other geologic types. Perhaps the most remarkable stands are those inhabiting the stark, black volcanic lava (basalt) at Craters of the Moon National Monument near Arco, Idaho. Short, spreading limber pines are essentially the only tree occupying this inhospitable rock substrate that lies considerably below the general lower timberline for the area.

On some of the limestone ranges, arid conditions extend upward throughout the forest belt, and thus limber pine becomes a component of upper as well as lower timberline. The limestone-derived soils are often

Engelmann spruce and limber pine at 9500 feet on Mount Borah in the Lost River Range

excessively drained. This is the case on the southwestern slope of 12,655-foot Mount Borah in Idaho's Lost River Range, where the band of arid forest is plainly visible from U.S. Highway 93A northwest of Arco. Limber pine and Douglas-fir form the lower timberline at about 7500 feet, while limber pine and Engelmann spruce constitute upper tree line, directly above, at about 9600 feet. Spruce and limber pine take on a variety of stunted and krummholz forms on this steep limestone mountainside.

In contrast, moist timberline sites can be found in cirque basins beneath alpine peaks in the southern continental ranges. Here, tree islands of Engelmann spruce, subalpine fir, and whitebark pine are sprinkled amidst meadows and talus slopes. These timberline mosaics are well developed in Idaho's Sawtooth Range, the Beaverhead Range southwest of Wisdom, Montana, and the Madison Range southwest of Bozeman.

The high, rounded ridges in this region commonly support stands of large, spreading whitebark pines with an undergrowth of grouse whortleberry, elk sedge (*Carex geyeri*), or dry-site herbs. Often these stands give way abruptly to subalpine grassland if there is a slight change to a drier (more southerly) aspect or to a less favorable substrate for tree growth. This pattern can be seen along the crest of the Gravelly Range south of Ennis, Montana, where a dirt road maintained by the Beaverhead National Forest travels near the 9000-foot level for several miles. The change from dense subalpine timber to grassland is often sudden and follows a straight line, sometimes without apparent differences in aspect or soils. This latter situation can also be witnessed by looking west from Deer Lodge, Montana, to the sharp, natural boundaries between mountain grasslands and dense lodgepole pine stands on the broad slopes of the Flint Creek Range. Patterns of wind-deposited snow may be partly responsible for these abrupt forest edges.

Northern Continental Ranges

This climatic region extends from the Helena and Harlowton areas of central Montana north along the eastern slope of the Rockies to the Alberta border (Arno 1979). The valleys here are lower and the climate somewhat less arid than in the southern continental ranges. This combination results in lower timberlines at 4000 to 5000 feet. The Rocky Mountain form of ponderosa pine makes up the lower timberline in much of central Montana, but it is absent farther north—north of Augusta, Great Falls, and Havre. In this latter area (north-central Montana) lower timberline is formed at 4500 to 5000 feet by combinations of quaking aspen, Douglas-fir, limber pine, and occasionally lodgepole pine. Here, and northward along the eastern slope of the Rockies in Alberta, ponderosa pine is unable to grow because of severe red belt conditions resulting from extreme fluctuations of temperature in winter accompanied by high winds. This is the northern "chinook belt" where the tongue of the continental polar air mass from northern Canada interacts with invasions of mild Pacific air much of the winter.

The principal high mountains lie east of Helena in central Montana and along the eastern slope of the continental divide northward to Glacier National Park and the Canadian border. These mountains are covered with Douglas-fir and lodgepole pine forests, giving way at high elevations to stands of subalpine fir, Engelmann spruce, and whitebark pine. Tree line occurs near 8500 feet in the latitude of Helena and lowers to about 7500 feet on the eastern slope at Glacier National Park.

The Rocky Mountain variety of ponderosa pine forms lower timberline in the Helena Valley and along much of the Missouri River, including the eroded badlands of the Missouri River Breaks. This tree is distinguished from the Pacific ponderosa pine, growing west of the continental divide, by its short growth form and frequent two-needle clusters, or fascicles. (The Pacific variety consistently bears three-needle fascicles.) The driest ponderosa pine timberlines in central Montana receive only about 10 inches of annual precipitation, and old-growth trees reach heights of only 40 feet. Undergrowth includes such dry-site Great Plains species as prickly pear cactus (*Opuntia* spp.), yucca (*Yucca glauca*), and blue gramma (*Bouteloua gracilis*).

Northward, in the chinook belt west of Great Falls, interesting elfin woodlands develop on the high plains at the foot of the Rocky Mountain Front ranges. These appear similar to pinyon-juniper woodlands but are actually made up of limber pine and Douglas-fir reaching only about 20 feet in height. Westward, inside the mountain canyons, both species attain a more normal size, evidently as a result of the modicum of shelter from relentless winds that is provided by the mountain topography. Quaking aspen grovelands are well developed at lower timberline along the Rocky Mountain Front. Aspen is occasionally wind-dwarfed here, even though its deciduous nature spares it from the full effects of winter winds. Severe wildfires swept over much of the Rocky Mountain Front during the late 1800s and early 1900s, no doubt fanned by stiff breezes, and even today much of the burned area remains treeless.

The highway from East Glacier Park north to Saint Mary winds through aspen groves and climbs ridges where stunted limber pine, Douglas-fir, and aspen survive on severely exposed sites. Prevailing winds of 30 mph or more are very common in this area. An even more vivid example of wind-timber at moderate elevations can be seen at 6400-foot Lewis and Clark Pass, accessible via a short hike from the graded road up Alice Creek northeast of Lincoln, Montana. This little-known pass on the continental divide is the route that explorer Meriwether Lewis's party used on its return trip across the continent in 1806. (The other half of the expedition, under William Clark, took a more southerly route across what is now Montana, and the two parties re-assembled at the mouth of the Yellowstone River.) This pass is a spectacular wind funnel, and although it lies 2000 feet below their usual lower limits, it harbors numerous alpine tundra species. These cushion plants grow in patches between krummholz forms of both mid-elevation trees (Douglas-fir, aspen, and limber pine) and subalpine trees (lodgepole pine, whitebark pine, subalpine fir, and Engelmann spruce).

Large areas of forest and timberline in central Montana are underlain by limestone, and the boundary between limestone and acidic rocks (such as granite or quartzite) often corresponds with a dramatic shift in tree and

Sharp boundary is apparent between this grassland on limestone (foreground) and the subalpine fir/grouse whortleberry forest on acidic rock (rear) at 8000 feet in the Little Belt Mountains.

undergrowth vegetation. Such changes are readily seen while following the dirt roads along the crest of the Little Belt Mountains east from 7389-foot Kings Hill Pass on U.S. Highway 89. These roads wind along broad 8000-foot ridges through dense forests of subalpine fir, Engelmann spruce, and whitebark pine with grouse whortleberry undergrowth on acidic rock types. Suddenly the substrate changes to limestone (which yields an excessively drained soil), and a parklike stand of whitebark pine or even limber pine with a grass-forb undergrowth appears. Or, the limestone may support a subalpine grassland with scattered tree islands. A truck trail in this area leads up 9100-foot Yogo Peak, which is covered with a mat of alpine tundra above the tree line at about 8400 feet.

Along the high ridges of the Rocky Mountain Front, small patches of stunted alpine larch inhabit northern slopes and cirques at upper tree line, but this species is absent on the dry, limestone sites.

Intermountain Ranges

This could also be called the "intermediate" region, because although its climate is strongly influenced by Pacific air masses, it does not receive the deluge of rain, snow, and cloudiness associated with the inland-maritime mountains of northern Idaho and vicinity. This climatic region includes west-central Montana (west of the continental divide), most of central Idaho (west of U.S. Highway 93), and the Blue Mountains of northeastern Oregon. It differs from the continental or "east-side" mountains in having a milder, modified-maritime climate without the severe chinook winds, the cold-dry winter conditions, or the drastic temperature changes.

Diverse forests cover most of the rugged landscape, but sagebrush or bunchgrass communities occupy the driest valleys and lower southern slopes. The lower-elevation forests are characterized by large Pacific ponderosa pines that form lower timberline. Much of the original montane forest was a mixture of ponderosa pine, Douglas-fir, and western larch (*Larix occidentalis*) attaining 3 to 4 feet in d.b.h. and 150 feet in height on favorable sites. Prior to settlement, in the late 1800s, these stands were kept open by surface fires ignited by lightning and Indians (Barrett and Arno 1982). Many areas had fires at intervals averaging 10 to 20 years, adequate time to allow regeneration of the fire-resistant ponderosa pine and larch (Arno 1980). Since the advent of fire suppression in the early 1900s, dense growths of the more shade-tolerant Douglas-fir and grand fir have developed.

The forests extend from 3000 or 4000 feet up to tree line at about 9000 feet. Lodgepole pine, perpetuated by occasional severe fires, covers much of the middle elevations, but the upper subalpine forests and timberlines are dominated by whitebark pine and subalpine fir with lesser amounts of Engelmann spruce. Additionally, alpine larch becomes the principal timberline tree on northern slopes in some parts of western Montana and adjacent areas in Idaho.

Alpine timberlines are extensive in several of the intermountain ranges, such as the southern Swan (Bob Marshall Wilderness), Bitterroot, and Anaconda-Pintler ranges in Montana, the vast Salmon River Mountains of central Idaho, and the Wallowa Mountains of northeastern Oregon. Picturesque, open stands of large whitebark pine with spreading branch-trunks often form forest line on ridgetops and gentle southern slopes in these areas. Moist northern slopes and the numerous cirque basins have a timberline parkland of subalpine fir, whitebark pine, Engelmann spruce, or locally alpine larch, with luxuriant heath undergrowth—grouse whortleberry, red mountain-heath (*Phyllodoce empetriformis*), and smooth woodrush (*Luzula hitchcockii*)—interspersed with moist meadows. Most of these timberline areas were heavily glaciated and thus also have large amounts of exposed bedrock, cliffs, and talus.

The Bitterroot Range is a fault block forming the eastern edge of the huge granitic uplift known as the Idaho Batholith. The Bitterroot Range divide forms the Idaho-Montana border west of Montana's Bitterroot Valley, and this range was deeply carved and scoured by glaciers. The Montana slope, which contains the highest terrain, consists of parallel,

Alpine larch and mountain heath at tree line on a north slope in the Montana Bitterroot Range

east-west trending, knife-edge ridges separated by U-shaped glacial canyons whose sides are massive bedrock and talus. Cool exposures support alpine larch, whitebark pine, and other timberline vegetation down to relatively low elevations, presumably because of moist conditions and stark granite substrate where competition from mid-elevation species is minimized. Thus, on north slopes, alpine larch reaches its limit as an erect tree at about 8800 feet, but this species and other timberline vegetation often dominate down to 7000 feet (Arno and Habeck 1972). The larch and accompanying heath and woodrush seem to have, in effect, inherited these rockland sites by default, since a normal subalpine fir-dominated forest does not develop.

Alpine larch extends lowest on north-facing talus slopes, but even where talus spreads down to the canyon bottoms (4500 to 5000 feet), larch rarely occupies it below 6500 feet. Whitebark pine occasionally grows into mature trees as low as the canyon bottoms on open, rocky sites. In contrast, the other timberline dwellers, subalpine fir and Engelmann spruce, fill the rocky canyon bottoms and even grow vigorously along stream courses threading through bouldery glacial moraines as low as 3800 feet in the Bitterroot Valley. Occasional large plants of red mountain heath also grow along these low-elevation moraines. On less rocky terrain, however, these species are absent, presumably because they cannot compete in the vigorous lower-elevation forests.

Essentially pure, open stands of alpine larch cover many north-facing talus slopes in the Bitterroot, Sapphire, Anaconda-Pintler, and Flint Creek ranges; whereas in most mountain regions (without alpine larch) such sites are treeless. These stands can be recognized from the valleys far below when they turn golden at the end of September. Alpine larch is also the principal tree inhabiting fresh glacial moraines and avalanche chutes in the highest cirques. The species is evidently unable to compete for growing room with other conifers; it does not extend down into the subalpine forest except on extremely rocky or avalanche sites.

Southern slopes at upper timberline in the Bitterroot and other intermountain ranges are dominated by whitebark pine. Many of these stands have turned into "ghost forests" of sun-bleached snags as a result of epidemics of mountain pine beetle in the early 1900s. The beetle did not kill smaller trees, however, and whitebark continues to dominate most of

Whitebark pine with severe spiral grain on a harsh site in central Idaho

these ridgetop and south-slope sites even in the presence of the shade-tolerant subalpine fir. The fir is less vigorous in these inherently open, cold-dry sites.

Thousands of miles of hiking trails lead into the upper timberline country of the intermountain ranges. A few timberline areas can also be reached by national forest roads to fire lookouts atop high peaks. For instance, single-lane dirt roads lead up 10,340-foot Twin Peak and nearly to the summit of 9882-foot Sleeping Deer Mountain northwest of Challis, Idaho. Occasionally, in some of the drier sites, cushions of Douglas-fir can be found scattered among the whitebark pine krummholz up to 9650 feet on Sleeping Deer Mountain. Whitebark pine is prevalent in these relatively dry mountains, and undergrowth is sparse, but one area along the road just across Twin Peak Pass is truly exceptional. This site is a sheet-erosion desert of loose, white rhyolite sprinkled with grotesquely contorted trees and no undergrowth. Root systems of the severely stunted and twisted (but not krummholz) whitebark pine, subalpine fir, and Engelmann spruce have been exposed by the natural sheet erosion of at least a foot of surface material in the past few hundred years. Animal caches of whitebark pine and fir seeds that have germinated represent virtually the only small green plants growing on the white surface.

Another narrow, winding mountain road leads to the summit of 9942-foot Pinyon Peak, just above krummholz limit, 35 air miles west of Challis. This rather dry timberline area is dominated by whitebark pine that has been called "pinyon" locally, perhaps in recognition of its short, spreading form and its pine-nut crops.

About 80 miles northward, across the rugged Salmon River Canyon, another road reaches timberline on the shoulder of 8950-foot Salmon Mountain. This road is best approached from the east, out of Darby, Montana. Although it is a through road across the Salmon River Mountains to Elk City, Idaho, the route is very long and exceedingly narrow, steep, and sinuous. The Salmon Mountain road, however, provides about the only automobile access to an alpine larch-whitebark pine timberline in the Northern Rockies. This area lies west of the southern portion of the Bitterroot Range and is more moist than mountains south of the Salmon River Canyon. Northern slopes support fine stands of alpine larch, subalpine fir, and Engelmann spruce with mountain-heath, whortleberry, and woodrush undergrowth. Pure larch groves occupy the cirques on Salmon Mountain, while whitebark pine covers the ridgetops.

About 45 miles to the east of Salmon Mountain, at the head of the Bitterroot Valley, another road leads directly to a dramatic timberline formation. This is the "ridgetop ribbon-forest" of whitebark pine and subalpine fir described on page 55. One of these strip forests is about 30 feet wide and nearly half a mile long and stretches precisely along the Montana-Idaho boundary (crest of the Bitterroot-Salmon River divide), one mile south of 8482-foot Saddle Mountain. This ribbon-forest can be reached via the narrow dirt road leading to Saddle Mountain from the Lost Trail Pass Ski Area on U.S. Highway 93. Like other ribbon-forests on subalpine ridges in western Montana, this one is bordered on the south-

Sheep grazing at timberline in the Wallowa Mountains, 1907.

western or windward side by a dry mountain grassland and on the northeastern or lee side by a moist snowdrift community.

Westward across the Salmon River Mountains distinctive subalpine grasslands dominated by green fescue (*Festuca viridula*) become increasingly common. Small amounts of green fescue are found on Salmon Mountain, and this bunchgrass also grows atop the Seven Devils Mountains rising high above Hells Canyon in west-central Idaho. A national forest road ascends more than 6500 feet from the Salmon River Canyon at Riggins, Idaho, to reach timberline stands of whitebark pine and grass-lands atop 8400-foot Heavens Gate Peak in the Seven Devils area. This ridge point overlooks Hells Canyon and the lofty Wallowa Mountains to the west in northeastern Oregon.

The Wallowas are the only part of the Blue Mountain region having a sizeable area of alpine timberline. And, although the tree and under-growth flora here is related to that of the Rockies, the Wallowas are unique in having extensive timberline grasslands dominated by green fescue. That is, green fescue *was* the dominant grass in the Wallowa high-country prior to the early 1900s; then overgrazing by tens of thousands of sheep severely damaged these ranges (Strickler 1961). With controlled grazing in the past 40 years, however, green fescue is slowly recovering.

The Wallowas are an isolated cluster of high mountains including 40 peaks that rise above 9000 feet—which is near the krummholz line for whitebark pine on warm exposures. The Wallowas were heavily glaciated and have about three dozen lakes lying in cirques at or above the forest line, which is depressed to about 7500 feet in cool basins. Whitebark pine is the most conspicuous timberline tree in the Wallowas and is accom-panied by subalpine fir and Engelmann spruce. Great, spreading whitebark pine trees rise out of the grassy parklands, and dense stands of whitebark krummholz cover some of the south-facing ridges, such as along the trail up 9600-foot Eagle Cap.

The Wallowas are geologically complex and contain some outcrops of limestone, dolomite, and marble that are, remarkably, inhabited by limber pine (Eliot 1938, Cole 1982). Sprawling limber pines can be found on these substrates at middle elevations on the walls of Hurricane and Lostine canyons. This is one of very few occurrences of limber pine in the Pacific Northwest, except for eastern Idaho. However, here, as is the usual case eastward in the Northern Rockies, limber pine does not ascend to upper timberline.

Inland-Maritime Ranges

This portion of the Northern Rockies includes the northwestern corner of Montana, northern Idaho, and the northeastern corner of Wash-ington (Arno 1979). It has a relatively moist climate, with annual precipi-tation even at low elevations generally exceeding 20 inches. (However, like other parts of the Northern Rockies, this region often has a mid-summer dry period.) This moisture enables lower elevations to have a rather limited ponderosa pine type and a broad area dominated by grand fir, western redcedar, and western hemlock. These latter, inland-maritime forests are similar to forests on the western slope of the Cascade Moun-tains except for the addition of inland species such as seral western larch, lodgepole pine, and ponderosa pine. Higher elevations receive copious amounts of precipitation and snowfall, and subalpine fir, Engelmann spruce, and sometimes mountain hemlock are the principal components of upper timberlines. Whitebark pine is often abundant on moisture-stressed sites such as rocky ridgetops and steep southern slopes. However, it suffers considerable damage from white pine blister rust in this region, presumably because the high frequency of wet, cloudy conditions favor the survival of the wind-transported blister rust spores (Arno and Hoff 1984).

Pacific air masses predominate in winter and produce inland mountain climates that cause little winter desiccation and that are not extremely cold. Although subzero continental-polar air occasionally settles over the mountains of northern Idaho and vicinity, tree crowns are usually well insulated by a heavy cloak of rime ice and packed snow. The trees at high elevations are firmly encased in a snowy "cocoon" most of the winter, producing bizarre forms called "snow ghosts." These moist mountains are climatically similar to the Cascades, and many of the Cascade trees and undergrowth plants occur inland only in this small region of the Rockies, including southeastern British Columbia. Some of the maritime species extend almost to the continental divide in the Lake McDonald area of Glacier National Park.

Other characteristics of the inland-maritime region include the denseness of its forest growth, the prevalence of impenetrable swathes of Sitka alder on steep mountainsides (especially in avalanche chutes), and the presence of small glaciers at comparatively low elevations in the loftiest mountains.

The best-known upper timberline area in this inland-maritime zone is the western slope and continental divide in Glacier National Park, in northwestern Montana. (British Columbia's Glacier National Park, in the Selkirk Range, is also in the inland-maritime region, as discussed later in this chapter.) Other inland-maritime ranges that have upper timberlines include the Whitefish, Mission, northern Swan, and Cabinet of northwestern Montana, the Idaho-Montana divide west of Superior, and the Selkirks of northern Idaho.

Upper timberlines throughout the inland-maritime ranges probably receive an average of 60 to 70 inches of precipitation annually, and in certain cirque basins in Glacier National Park annual precipitation exceeds 100 inches. Perhaps the mildest subalpine climate is experienced along the Idaho-Montana divide west of Superior. This is the eastern portion of a large, undifferentiated mass of mountains drained mostly by the North Fork of the Clearwater and Saint Joe rivers. Only near this interstate divide do some of the peaks rise into the timberline zone above 6000 feet. This is the only timberline country in the Rockies south of British Columbia where mountain hemlock is a major species. Apparently this is a reflection of especially humid conditions and relatively mild winter temperatures. Timberline is a mosaic of luxuriant heathlands, meadows, and groves containing hemlock, subalpine fir, Engelmann spruce, and whitebark pine—reminiscent of the Cascades.

A two-lane logging road ascends into the extensive subalpine meadows at 6000-foot Hoodoo Pass on the Idaho-Montana Divide southwest of

Superior. Much of this open ridgetop country that appears to be near timberline was actually burned off in the 1910 and other early fires and is slowly regenerating to subalpine forest. Even the highest peaks (the highest is 7690-foot Illinois Peak) have, or had before the early 1900s fires, large timberline trees on their summits. The prodigious snowpack seems to be largely responsible for the lush meadow growth.

Farther east, more climatically severe inland-maritime timberlines occur in the Mission Range and in Glacier National Park. Annual precipitation continues to be great in these areas, but invasions of subzero continental-polar air occur commonly in winter. Although western hemlock, western redcedar, and, in the Missions, mountain hemlock inhabit these areas, they are largely restricted to protected "cove" sites (mid-slope ravines), and on most other sites they sustain frost damage to their growing tips. The environmental severity of upper timberlines in Glacier Park is easily witnessed at spectacular Logan Pass (6664 feet) on the Going-to-the-Sun Highway. Tree line occurs at only 7000 feet, and extensive ribbon-forest and snow-glade formations (primarily of subalpine fir) can be seen at Logan Pass on the walk to Hidden Lake Overlook. Large snowfields usually remain until early August, and even in mid-summer, storms often dump several inches of wet snow. Severe blizzards with hurricane-force winds often detonate when Pacific and continental air masses collide and jostle each other along this jagged spine of the continental divide. The summer dry season is brief or absent, and the stunted subalpine fir, Engelmann spruce, and whitebark pine are spread among lush meadows filled with yellow glacier lilies (Habeck 1969).

Storm-battered subalpine fir at Logan Pass, Glacier National Park

Glacier Park's awesomely precipitous topography is coupled with a climate that reflects the harshest elements of both maritime and continental regimes. It has heavy snowfall, cold rain, and cloudy coolness in summer from the maritime air, and it has extreme cold, fluctuating temperatures, and desiccating winds from the continental climate. The result of this severe climate and accompanying avalanche conditions is a marked lowering of forest belts and a broad timberline zone that starts as low as 5500 feet along the Going-to-the-Sun Highway. This is comparable to the elevation of some *lower* timberlines 150 miles southward.

Small groves of alpine larch can be found in some areas of Glacier Park, but this species does not seem as well adapted to Glacier's sedimentary rock types as it is to the granite and quartzite talus of other ranges. Where gentle topography occurs on southwestern exposures, krummholz line extends locally to 8000 feet. But much of the terrain above 6000 feet is composed of sheer mountain walls and sites released from glacial ice only during the last century or two. The small glaciers here receded rapidly during the late 1800s and early 1900s, as has been confirmed by measuring ages of trees invading the moraines beneath glacial snouts (Carrara and McGimsey 1981).

In summer, Glacier Park's timberlines have a plethora of wildlife along with an army of hikers. Grizzly bears spend considerable time in this habitat and can occasionally be seen grazing on succulent herbs or digging out bulbs of glacier lilies. Evidence of their efforts to unearth ground squirrels or the large gray hoary marmots abounds, although they seem more successful in frightening humans! Mountain goats and bighorn sheep are summer residents at timberline, and white-tailed ptarmigan are often seen feeding in the timberline parkland.

Whitebark pine is generally less abundant than subalpine fir in the moist high-country along and west of the continental divide in Glacier Park, but in less-rugged terrain in the northern Mission and the Whitefish ranges it sometimes becomes a major forest component and reaches great size. The whitebark pine on productive sites probably became established after a severe wildfire—a rare occurrence in the moist high-country of these ranges. (Without fire, the subalpine forests are monopolized by a heavy growth of subalpine fir and Engelmann spruce with a layer of four-foot-tall menziesia shrubs beneath.) Once established, with some room to grow, whitebark pines just below forest line often will exceed 100 feet in height and can produce a clear, straight bole 3 feet in d.b.h. However, these trees require 300 or more years to attain large sizes, and they are easily surpassed by the associated 130- to 150-foot-tall Engelmann spruce.

The Cabinet Range, southwest of Libby, Montana, supports some interesting maritime timberlines. Alpine larch is often the dominant tree in the high basins and on northern slopes. It is also invading fresh moraines below the Blackwell and Elephant Peak glaciers and is mixed with mountain hemlock at the latter site.

In the northern part of the Idaho Panhandle, about 60 miles northwest of the Cabinets, stands the glacially scoured granite backbone of the Selkirk Range, with several timberline peaks rising to between 7000 and 7900 feet. The open granite terrain on the Selkirk divide is populated with small groves of subalpine fir, Engelmann spruce, and whitebark pine, but it is strangely without mountain hemlock and alpine larch, both of which occur northward in the contiguous British Columbia Selkirks.

The absence of alpine larch in the Idaho Selkirks is not complete, however, since this species does inhabit the northern slopes and cirques of 7264-foot Roman Nose. This is an isolated peak on an arm extending southeasterly from the main Selkirk divide. Evidently alpine larch survived Pleistocene mountain glaciation on Roman Nose as it did 40 miles northward along the Selkirks in Canada but was extirpated on the intervening high backbone. The stands on Roman Nose can be visited via a forest road to Lower Roman Nose Lake (5900 feet). This road leads through the massive, 56,000-acre Sundance burn of 1967 that swept the ridges of Roman Nose, killing most of the whitebark pine. But most of the alpine larch, which grows in moist, rocky cirques, survived. One alpine larch growing at the toe of a boulder pile near the trail to Upper Roman Nose Lake is 50 inches in d.b.h., 95 feet tall, and 600 to 650 years old. A typical larch "patriarch," it shelters smaller subalpine firs that ascend into its lower crown.

SOUTHERN CANADIAN ROCKIES

The Southern Canadian Rockies comprise a broad swathe of spectacularly high and rugged glacially sculptured mountains extending more than 400 miles northwest from the international boundary at 49°N. The principal ranges of the Canadian Rockies consistently rise into the alpine tundra zone above 8000 feet, with many peaks exceeding 10,000 feet. This high-mountain province is roughly triangular in shape, being widest in the south, along the international boundary, and, at its northern end, culminating in the narrow Rocky Mountain backbone east of Prince George, British Columbia, at 54°N. Northeast of Prince George and the great bow of the Fraser River, the Rockies drop off in elevation and no longer form a continuous barrier. This more northerly and less rugged section is treated in this book as the Boreal Rockies.

The Southern Canadian Rockies form the backbone of the North American continent, and their crest, known as the Great Divide, constitutes the border between British Columbia and Alberta northward nearly to the 54° parallel. A few subalpine mountain ranges, known as Front ranges, extend parallel to the Great Divide on the Alberta side. The British Columbia side has a series of deep valleys or geologic trenches, and major mountain ranges—the Purcell, Selkirk, and Monashee ranges—paralleling the main Rocky Mountain backbone.

The climate of the Alberta mountains is decidedly continental, with prolonged periods of domination by polar air masses in winter and drying chinook winds and fluctuating temperatures brought about by surges of descending ("dried out") Pacific air. Conversely, the British Columbia

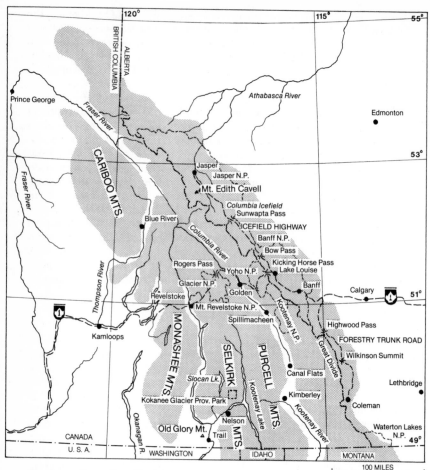

Southern Canadian Rockies

Rockies are sheltered from the brunt of polar air invasions and experience warmer but wetter and snowier winters as a result of Pacific storm systems.

The lowest-elevation valleys in south-central British Columbia are semi-arid and support sagebrush-grass types below a ponderosa pine timberline. Montane forests (representative of a temperate climate) are extensive in British Columbia and are dominated by various species, depending upon relative moisture. In Alberta, only a narrow band of the more cold-tolerant montane trees, including Douglas-fir and limber pine, adjoins the upper Great Plains grassland. (Northward, in the Boreal Rockies, the strictly montane tree species are entirely absent.) Alpine timberlines are extensive throughout the Southern Canadian Rockies,

Timberline depressed by snow and ice at the head of Marvel Creek, below Mount Assiniboine, south of Banff

as are alpine tundra communities. To facilitate discussion of this large province, it will be convenient to split it into two sections at the Great Divide.

British Columbia Mountains

The southern Rockies of British Columbia are similar environmentally to the portion of the United States Northern Rockies lying west of the continental divide, since only the political boundary at the 49° parallel separates these regions. The low-elevation interior valleys of south-central British Columbia are the warmest-driest areas in all of Canada, largely because they lie in the rain shadow of the Cascades and Coast ranges. The lower Okanagan and Thompson river valleys (about 1000 feet in elevation) receive only about 10 inches of annual precipitation. Here, sagebrush and bunchgrass communities give way to ponderosa pine at the 2000-foot level or higher on south- and west-facing slopes. Despite the hot, dry climate, these valleys are occupied by large rivers and lakes and by irrigated apple and peach orchards. Yet, even the highest mountains in these vicinities receive only 20 to 30 inches of annual precipitation.

Eastward in the mountainous interior of southern British Columbia, the valleys become slightly higher and are hemmed in by taller mountain ranges that milk increasing quantities of precipitation out of the eastward-traveling Pacific storm systems. Some low-elevation sites along the major valleys in the Selkirk Range, such as the towns of Revelstoke and Blue River, receive 40 inches or more of annual precipitation. The nearby subalpine forests are drenched with 60 to 100 inches of precipitation, including annual snowfalls of 400 inches or more.

In the wet major valleys of southeastern British Columbia, dense forests dominated by inland-maritime species (western hemlock and western redcedar potential climax) are prevalent. Northward, in the vicinity of Prince George, these species give way to lowland boreal forests (white spruce [*Picea glauca*] and black spruce [*P. mariana*] potential climax). At higher elevations in the wet mountain ranges, subalpine fir, Engelmann spruce, and, locally, mountain hemlock form the forest, and upper timberline often develops primarily as a result of late-lingering snowfields. The highest peaks (near 10,000 feet) in these heavy-snowfall areas support glaciers and "mountain icecaps" that flow down in several glacial tongues. The automobile-accessible Columbia Icefield, on the Great Divide along the Banff-Jasper Highway, covers several dozen square miles. This is the best known of the icecaps, which are much larger than glaciers elsewhere in the Rocky Mountain system.

Whitebark pine and even alpine larch seem to be restricted in the snowiest regions of the Canadian Rockies, but they become abundant in the somewhat drier ranges southward from the Trans-Canada Highway. Alpine larch forms extensive, pure stands in some of the areas that receive medium amounts of annual precipitation (probably 40 to 60 inches), such as the southern Purcell Range. Whitebark pine becomes a major component of upper timberlines in the dry ranges, such as the one at Old Glory Mountain near Trail, British Columbia, where the long-term average annual precipitation was slightly less than 30 inches at the krummholz line (7700 feet). Virtually everywhere in the Southern Canadian Rockies, however, subalpine fir and Engelmann spruce are major components of the upper timberlines.

In south-central British Columbia's sunny Okanagan Valley, a band of very open ponderosa pine forest, superimposed on a community of bluebunch wheatgrass (*Agropyron spicatum*), Idaho fescue (*Festuca idahoensis*), and big sagebrush typically forms the lower timberline at 1500 to 2000 feet (McLean 1970). This belt gives way to a broader band of dry montane forest in which Douglas-fir is the potential climax-dominant species. Above 4500 feet, subalpine fir becomes the potential climax species, but as a result of past wildfires, lodgepole pine covers much of this high-country. Upper timberlines develop only on the highest peaks, with forest line near 6800 feet and krummholz line at or above 7500 feet. Subalpine fir, whitebark pine, and Engelmann spruce are underlain by a carpet of grouse whortleberry, along with red mountain heath and mountain arnica (*Arnica latifolia*).

Eastward, in the much wetter northern Monashee Range and the Selkirk Range, there is no lower timberline, and the ponderosa pine as well as much of the Douglas-fir zone is replaced by western hemlock-western redcedar (potential climax species) forests. This area has a strong maritime climatic influence and is the only part of the Canadian Rockies supporting mountain hemlock. It is also the only portion of the entire Rocky Mountain system supporting relict stands of Alaska-cedar. This Pacific maritime species grows in the subalpine forest at Hird and Evans lakes near Slocan Lake, northwest of the city of Nelson. Alpine larch is a major timberline species in the southern Selkirks west of Kootenay Lake, but in Kokanee Glacier Provincial Park in this area, the subalpine forests and timberline are largely missing. They were destroyed by large wildfires in the early 1900s, and regeneration is proceeding very slowly, probably because of the lack of a seed source.

Farther north in the Selkirks, both annual and summer precipitation increases. Annual precipitation exceeds 80 inches in the high-country of British Columbia's Glacier National Park, which is traversed by the Trans-Canada Highway between Revelstoke and Golden. Despite the modest elevation of this route (4354 feet at Rogers Pass) through the Selkirks, both the highway and the Canadian Pacific Railway are protected by giant snowsheds at the foot of large avalanche swathes, thus attesting to the tremendous winter snowfall.

In the early 1900s, pioneer ecologist C. H. Shaw studied this area and concluded that late-lingering snow is the primary factor causing the

Trees on humps and persistent snow in low areas at Numa Pass, Kootenay National Park

formation of upper timberlines. Ascending the mountain valleys, Shaw (1909b) found that the subalpine fir and Engelmann spruce forest gives way to tree islands somewhat above the 5500-foot level. The conifers are set in a parkland with mountain-heath (*Phyllodoce* and *Cassiope*) and moist-meadow communities. Near the 6500-foot level in the basins, Shaw found open heathlands and meadows with widely scattered clumps of spire-shaped trees that showed no evidence of wind-caused deformation. At still higher elevations in the basins, tree clumps are confined to mounds and spots where the snowpack melts earliest; however, exposed ridges support wind-shaped trees above 7000 feet.

Several miles west of Glacier National Park, also in the Selkirks, lies Mount Revelstoke National Park. Here a major road ascends to the timberline parkland atop 6200-foot Mount Revelstoke. Mountain hemlock grows above the 5000-foot mark, but the tall, slender spires of subalpine fir and intervening meadows are the outstanding features of the summit area, along with a splendid view of the 10,000-foot glacier-draped peaks of the Selkirk Range.

East of the southern Selkirks and Kootenay Lake (1745 feet in elevation) juts the massive Purcell Range, containing many rugged 10,000-foot peaks. One of the most spectacular and popular areas lies at the head of Bugaboo Creek, reached by logging roads west of Spillimacheen. In this

Spirelike subalpine fir amid meadows on Mount Revelstoke

heavily glaciated area, upper timberline is interrupted by bare rock and ice and consists of small groves of alpine larch with subalpine fir and Engelmann spruce. The area is so wet that luxuriant pocket meadows and larch groves often develop on steep southern slopes. Alpine larch is the primary tree colonizing freshly exposed moraines and barren rocky slopes (above 6500 feet) that have recently been released from glaciation. It is also invading the gravel outwash apron beneath the snout of Bugaboo Glacier to elevations as low as 5200 feet.

Southward in the Purcells, between the town of Kimberley and Findlay Creek, west of Canal Flats, a series of broad, 8000-foot ridges are covered with essentially pure forests of alpine larch. These stands sweep along the ridges and spill over into the cirques, covering most of the terrain between about 6800 and 7800 feet. These appear to be the largest pure stands of alpine larch anywhere (Arno and Habeck 1972).

The Rocky Mountain Trench is the deep valley (2000 to 3000 feet in elevation) extending several hundred miles along the western slope of the main Rocky Mountain backbone, from western Montana to Prince George, British Columbia. This valley is occupied by the Kootenay, Columbia, and Fraser rivers, and is covered with an inland-maritime forest, largely western redcedar and western hemlock (potential climax species). Immediately east of the Rocky Mountain Trench looms the main Rocky Mountain backbone, with the Great Divide only 20 to 40 miles from the valley bottom. The western slope of the Great Divide supports an inland-maritime forest, whereas the eastern slope, in Alberta, has none of the Pacific tree species.

However, both slopes have similar subalpine forests. They are largely dominated by seral lodgepole pine, which gives way near forest line to stands of subalpine fir, Engelmann spruce, alpine larch, and a limited amount of whitebark pine on exposed ridges. Mountain hemlock is absent on the western slope of the Great Divide ranges, but in other respects this very moist and snowy environment seems comparable to the Selkirks. Ascending through the forest line, tall huckleberry (*Vaccinium globulare*), menziesia (*Menziesia ferruginea*), and white azalea (*Rhododendron albiflorum*) shrubs give way to a rambling heath-dominated parkland, with scattered tree islands and abundant rivulets fed by summer snowfields and glaciers.

Strangely, some isolated stands of the Great Plains species limber pine are found on the western slope, along with bushy Rocky Mountain junipers. These drought-tolerant trees occupy south-facing scree slopes, possibly limestone, above the Kicking Horse River a few miles east of Golden at about 3000 feet in elevation. They lie along the route of the Trans-Canada Highway.

Alberta Rockies

The Alberta portion of the Southern Canadian Rockies includes the eastern slope of the Great Divide Range and, eastward, a few very prominent Front ranges that run parallel to the main divide. The entire area is dominated by a continental climate, where winter brings severely cold polar air masses tempered periodically by Pacific systems and warm-dry chinook winds. This climatic condition precludes the occurrence of inland-maritime trees and of ponderosa pine in Alberta. Pacific storms dump a copious winter snowfall on the main-divide range; but eastward across the Front ranges conditions become increasingly dry. Also, the effects of continental-polar air, chinooks, and desiccation become more prominent eastward. Dry site conditions are pronounced on the limestone areas in the geologically complex, folded-and-faulted Front ranges. At high elevations average annual precipitation ranges from about 60 inches along the Great Divide north of Lake Louise to a low of perhaps 25 inches on the eastern Front ranges. It is reduced to 17 inches at Calgary and other sites in the Great Plains grassland (now largely wheat fields) east of the mountains.

The lower timberline at the western edge of the southern Alberta prairie is made up primarily of aspen groveland mixed with interior Douglas-fir. Occasional patches of short limber pines occur along with the Douglas-fir on windswept ridges of the lower foothills. The Alberta lower timberline is a chinook-belt area, like north-central Montana, where conifers are subjected to severe winter desiccation. Were it not for the rapid and extreme temperature fluctuations and drying in winter, it seems likely that ponderosa pine forest would extend north into Alberta. Annual precipitation is adequate for that species, and growing-season duration does not appear to be the limiting factor. The lower timberlines are formed at elevations of 3500 to 4000 feet.

North of Calgary, aspen groves become abundant even far out into the Great Plains, and the boreal forest covers the lowlands north from Edmonton (about 53°N). An arm of the boreal forest—dominated by white spruce, black spruce, lodgepole pine, and quaking aspen—extends south along the foothill slope opposite Calgary. Interestingly, one of the driest areas in Alberta is at Jasper, in the large intermountain valley of the Athabasca River, west of Edmonton. Jasper (3470 feet) receives an average annual precipitation of only 16 inches, and some of the surrounding dry valley flats and southwestern slopes support montane grassland dominated by June grass (*Koeleria cristata*) and plains reed grass (*Calamagrostis montanensis*) or by savanna (Tande 1977). Pure stands of Douglas-fir grow near Jasper, although this area marks the species' northern limits east of the Great Divide.

The most extensive forest type in the Alberta Rockies is seral stands of lodgepole pine. As a result of major stand-replacing wildfires that have burned at 50-to-150-year intervals, lodgepole pine dominates most well-drained sites from just above the lower timberline nearly to the alpine forest line. In the long-term absence of fire, lodgepole is replaced by subalpine fir and spruce—white spruce at lower elevations and Engelmann spruce in the subalpine forest.

Waterton Lakes National Park lies at the southern end of the Alberta Rockies, adjacent to Montana's Glacier National Park. The timberline environments are similar to those described for the eastern slope at

Glacier Park, except that at Waterton alpine larch becomes more abundant. This species is widespread on cool, moist northeastern exposures at 6700 to 7500 feet, and mixed stands of larch, subalpine fir, Engelmann spruce, and whitebark pine occupy ridgetops and west- or east-facing slopes (Arno 1970). No alpine larch stands have been found on southern aspects in Waterton Park, although they are fairly common in such situations farther north where summer precipitation is more dependable.

North of Waterton Park an extensive road system leads about 350 miles through intermountain valleys of the Alberta Rockies, between the Great Divide and the Front ranges. This route starts at Coleman, west of Lethbridge, and travels via the Forestry Trunk Road to the Bow River Valley, where it joins the Trans-Canada Highway to Banff and Jasper. Most of the route threads through lodgepole pine forests, but it also climbs to upper timberline at three major passes. Additionally, side roads, tramways, and numerous hiking trails afford excellent opportunities to observe upper timberline communities.

About 52 miles north of Coleman, at Wilkinson Summit, a dirt road climbs eastward to the broad, 8200-foot alpine mesa known as Plateau Mountain. This Front Range mountain is windswept and semi-arid as a result of its rain-shadow location and perhaps a dry substrate. The broad summit is covered with tundra formations and stone polygons, or rock nets, that result from sorting by repeated freezing and thawing. Small krummholz trees are sometimes found adjacent to the stone polygons, but the severe frost action probably damages conifer roots. Stands of small alpine larch occupy some of the less wind-exposed sites between 7000 and 7800 feet on Plateau Mountain, and a few whitebark pine are present; but most of the timberline is made up of Engelmann spruce with lesser amounts of stunted subalpine fir. These timberline communities are underlain by a low carpet of grouse whortleberry, with few other undergrowth plants. Near the 8000-foot mark the tundra is interrupted by Engelmann spruce krummholz that form bushy, hedgelike stringers and grow vegetatively 20 to 30 feet downwind. Bright orange growing tips often stand out like florescent paint on the krummholz, marking the results of desiccation during the previous winter.

Fifty miles north of Plateau Mountain, the Forestry Trunk Road climbs 7250-foot Highwood Pass at the headwaters of the Highwood River. The pass lies at forest line immediately east of the Great Divide. In contrast to Plateau Mountain, the timberline communities consist of well-developed alpine larch, Engelmann spruce, and subalpine fir trees with a luxuriant undergrowth of red and white mountain-heaths, smooth woodrush, and moist meadow herbs. Small amounts of white azalea, an inland-maritime species, are also present in the Highwood Pass stands. Annual precipitation is a modest 36 inches at the pass, based upon several years of record, but at this northerly latitude there is little or no summer drought, so effective moisture is greater than at timberline sites in the Northern Rockies of the United States.

Moist alpine larch timberline communities seem to reach their fullest development along the Great Divide Range in the southern part of Banff

*Alpine larch, Engelmann spruce, and subalpine fir at Sunburst Lake,
Mount Assiniboine Provincial Park*

National Park (Baig 1972). Wildlife biologists have discovered that grizzly
bears very often choose these larch communities as sites for winter dens
(Vroom and others 1980).

Alpine larch timberlines can be readily visited at the Sunshine
Plateau Ski Area west of Banff townsite, at Lake Louise Ski Area, at
Fortress Mountain Ski Area, and via a short, steep hike to Larch Valley
above Moraine Lake. Tree limit for alpine larch is near 7900 feet, higher
than that of subalpine fir and spruce. In these areas, a lush timberline
parkland develops, dominated by larch, which after a few centuries attains relatively large size—up to 30 inches in d.b.h. and 70 feet in height.
The larch parkland extends even across the more moderate south-facing
slopes, evidently because of the moist summer conditions. July and August each have mean monthly precipitation of about three inches in this
area. Alpine larch also forms denser, pure stands stretching from 6800 to
7500 feet on the broad northern slopes of the Great Divide Range, such as
above Kicking Horse Pass and near Lake Louise.

For no presently known reason, alpine larch reaches its northern
range limits abruptly near 51°35′N on Mount Hector, north of Lake

Louise, and at this latitude eastward all through the Front ranges. Extensive mountain icefields begin at this point on the Great Divide Range and extend northward. It is possible that the large glaciers and very heavy precipitation virtually exclude (or have hampered the spread of) alpine larch here, as is the case on the western slope of Washington's North Cascades. However, this possible explanation can not apply to the species' restriction northward in the Front ranges, because the climate there is much drier.

A few miles north of Mount Hector, the Banff-Jasper Highway ascends 6785-foot Bow Pass at the head of the Bow and North Saskatchewan rivers. A short side-road leads from Bow Pass to the Peyto Lake overlook amidst stunted Engelmann spruce and subalpine fir at about 6900 feet. However, tree line generally reaches 7500 feet on favorable sites. From this point northward, the broad glacial valley heads at upper timberline are occupied by large expanses of dwarf willows and bog birch (*Betula glandulosa*), and these areas have an appearance strikingly similar to that of timberlines in the Boreal Rockies.

Fifty-three miles north of Bow Pass, the Banff-Jasper Highway traverses the even more frigid glacial terrain at 6675-foot Sunwapta Pass, at the head of the Athabasca River. Sunwapta Pass lies directly below (and east of) glaciers flowing down from the Columbia Icefield. A side-road visits the fresh moraines at the snout of the Athabasca Glacier, where a stand of colorful tundra plants, including alpine fireweed (*Epilobium alpinum*) and dryads (*Dryas* spp.), has developed in the decade or two since glacial retreat; conifers are much slower to colonize the moraines.

Timberline parkland atop the Great Divide near Sunshine Ski Area, Banff National Park

Stunted subalpine fir, Jasper National Park

Another side-road climbs to an overlook above the Athabasca Glacier's snout and, in the process, passes through meadows and a band of krummholz Engelmann spruce and subalpine fir formed in response to biting winds that constantly blow down off the icecap. The less-exposed, northern slope a few miles southward has erect spruce and fir ascending several hundred feet higher. This latter, moist timberline is traversed by the short hiking trail that climbs atop a ridge overlooking the Saskatchewan Glacier, another outflowing lobe of the Columbia Icefield. Even the steep southern slope above the Saskatchewan Glacier has a meadowy timberline, reflecting not only the moist climate, but also the summer cloudcap that frequently envelops the major icefields even during clear weather.

About 60 miles north of Sunwapta Pass, along the highway to Jasper, a side-road ascends to the timberline zone at the foot of the Angel Glacier on Mount Edith Cavell (11,033 feet). Engelmann spruce, subalpine fir, and whitebark pine here are colonizing the moraine beneath the glacier's snout at about 6500 feet, while erect trees ascend above 7000 feet on more-distant slopes.

Overall, dominant vegetation of the upper timberline in Jasper National Park is considered to be subalpine fir and red mountain heath (La Roi and others 1980). This transition zone occurs primarily between 6500 and 7000 feet and is bordered above by diverse alpine tundra and glacial plant communities. Below lies the dense and extensive lodgepole pine-spruce-fir forest.

BOREAL ROCKIES

The mountainous "boreal" (far-northern) forest province encompasses the northern inland portion of British Columbia, the Yukon Territory and the adjacent Mackenzie District of the Northwest Territories, and central Alaska. This province stretches 1500 miles northwest from central British Columbia, at 55°N, to the southern slope of Alaska's Brooks Range, above the Arctic Circle, at 68°. Thus, it includes nearly half the length of the entire Rocky Mountain system. The inland slopes of the Alaska Range (Denali or Mount McKinley area) and of the northern coastal mountains in the Yukon and northern British Columbia have similar boreal timberlines and are also covered in this discussion.

Even the broad lowland valleys in this province have a subarctic continental climate in which winter is the prolonged season. The taiga, or northern boreal forest, blankets the lowlands, and there is comparatively little compositional change in the forest as one moves upward on the mountain slopes, except that the taiga does give way to alpine tundra at modest elevations.

Tree line varies from about 5000 feet in the northern interior of British Columbia and in the southeastern Yukon to between 2000 and 3000 feet in the Brooks Range of north-central Alaska. Throughout most of this province the highest mountain peaks rise to between 7000 and

Even the foothills of Alaska's Wrangell Mountains rise high above the boreal forest.

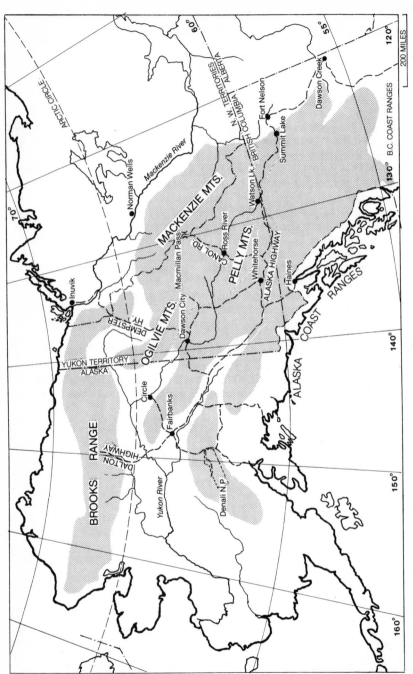

Boreal Rockies

10,000 feet and are covered with rock, persistent snowfields, small glaciers, and large expanses of alpine tundra. In the mountains of the Yukon, the Mackenzie District, and central Alaska this alpine tundra is quite similar in composition and general character to the upland arctic tundra on hills far north of the limit of trees. Consequently, these northern mountain tundras and timberlines are termed "subarctic" alpine communities. In contrast, however, the comparably low-elevation timberlines in the coastal mountains of southern Alaska are not "subarctic" in character, because they are dominated by maritime species from temperate-zone latitudes.

The climate in the boreal forest is dominated by cold, dry, stable air masses during the long winter; thus, mean temperatures for January are very cold (5 to −15°F) and extremes of −40°F or lower occur most years. *Average* daily temperatures are below freezing from late September until mid-May. In contrast, summer temperatures are quite warm, with extreme highs reaching 90°F in the lowlands and near 80°F at tree line. The mean temperature for July is about 60°F in lowland valleys and 50°F at tree line.

Annual precipitation is light, ranging from 6 to 15 inches in the taiga and perhaps 12 to 25 inches at alpine tree lines. More than half of this comes as rain and wet snow in the summer and early fall—June through September. Snowfall is modest (probably 100 to 250 inches annually) at these mountain timberlines, but it remains on the ground until June in most sites, when the nearly continuous daylight and solar heating become transforming features of the weather.

Permafrost, permanently frozen ground, occurs at scattered locations in the southern portions of the Boreal Rockies and becomes nearly continuous in the northern sections, where its presence close to the land's surface profoundly limits the distribution of trees. Though the amount of annual precipitation is relatively small, evaporation is low and permafrost forms an impervious layer; the result is that bogs and other wet sites cover much of the mountain terrain. Nevertheless, steep, rocky south- and west-facing slopes are often rather dry because of excess drainage and severe exposure to the sun (evaporative demand on vegetation) caused by the prolonged daily heating in summer.

Wildfires are an important factor in the taiga, and they even spread into timberline stands and tundra, superimposing a fire mosaic upon the pattern of different site conditions. Fires are most common in early summer in unusually dry years, and they sometimes spread through tens of thousands of acres of the subarctic vegetation. Vast fields of showy pink fireweed (*Epilobium angustifolium*) brighten the snagfields of fire-killed spruce on the landscape of the Boreal Rockies. These displays of fireweed are visible along many of the major roads and they attest to the prevalence of fire.

After a decade or two, quaking aspen, willow, paper birch (*Betula papyrifera*), and deciduous shrubs dominate the burned areas and provide abundant forage for moose. In some of the drier sites and areas of the

White spruce timberline at Camp Denali in the Alaska Range

southern Yukon and northern British Columbia, dense forests of lodgepole pine arise after fire. In most areas of the taiga, conifers re-establish dominance several decades or perhaps a century after conflagration. The conifers here are readily killed by fire but, in addition to lodgepole pine, black spruce is fire-adapted in that it retains closed cones in its treetops. These cones persist for several years in the upper crown, storing viable seeds which are released into the ashes after a forest fire, initiating a new stand.

Although the Boreal Rockies cover a very large region, the forests and upper timberlines here have only a modest variety of species compared with more southerly sections of the Rocky Mountain chain. White spruce is a major component of most timberlines. Subalpine fir becomes a major species southward from the central Yukon. Black spruce is locally common near timberline on boggy sites. Balsam poplar (*Populus balsamifera*) occasionally grows at or above the white spruce tree-limit, and tamarack (the eastern larch, *Larix laricina*) sometimes occupies wet areas in the timberline zone. All of these species are also elements of the lowland taiga, along with quaking aspen, paper birch, and lodgepole pine. The latter species usually do not ascend to upper timberline. Stands of the broad-leaved species and lodgepole pine generally develop following wildfire but give way to white spruce (and often subalpine fir) after a century or two without disturbance. On boggy sites, black spruce often dominates through all stages of succession.

Interestingly, similar boreal forest communities stretch eastward across Canada to the North Atlantic Coast and spread into the northern-most portions and the highest mountains of the northeastern and Great

Lakes states. However, east of the Boreal Rockies, lodgepole pine is replaced by the ecologically similar jack pine (*Pinus banksiana*) and subalpine fir is replaced by balsam fir (*Abies balsamea*), which is confined to the southern half of the boreal zone. White spruce and black spruce remain the characteristic boreal conifers from west-central Alaska to Newfoundland, a distance of 3600 miles.

Few detailed studies have been conducted on timberlines of the Boreal Rockies. Most of the available information is from areas reached by the sparse, but expanding network of roads, all of which are tributaries of the Alaska Highway. Current information on the status of the various routes can be obtained through the annually updated editions of *The Milepost* (Alaska Northwest Publishing Company, Anchorage).

Canadian Mountains

The Alaska Highway climbs through the higher ranges of the Rockies in northern British Columbia only in the vicinity of Summit and Muncho lakes, west of Fort Nelson. The 4250-foot pass at Summit Lake (58½°N, 125°W) is the highest point on the Alaska Highway. It lies at forest line, with tree limit occurring near 4800 feet. White spruce and occasional patches of black spruce are the only prominent conifers in this area, while shrubby willows occupy the stony mountain slopes a few hundred feet above the highest spruce. Muncho Lake lies within the boreal forest at 2800 feet but is surrounded by rugged 7000-foot peaks.

In the extreme northwestern corner of British Columbia, the Haines Highway climbs through a white spruce timberline on the inland slope of the coast range, tops out at 3500 feet in lush alpine tundra, and then descends into the maritime timberline and forests previously described for coastal Alaska.

Timberline communities are reached along a few roads in the southern Yukon Territory. The southern section of the Canol Road (between Johnson's Crossing and Ross River) climbs into a scenic forest-line environment, particularly at the headwaters of the Lapie River (61½°N, 133°W) in the Pelly Mountains. The Nahanni Range Road, to the mining town of Tungsten (62°N, 128°W), reaches timberline atop the Mackenzie Mountains on the border of the Northwest Territories.

The northern section of the Canol Road (northeast of Ross River) has recently been re-opened over 5900-foot Macmillan Pass (63°N, 130°W) in a spectacular alpine tundra setting atop the Mackenzie divide. This area of the Mackenzie Mountains has extensive rolling uplands of subarctic tundra high above tree line, which ranges from only 4000 feet at the Mackenzie divide to 5500 feet on southern exposures of mountains west and east of the divide. The Canol Road traverses alpine uplands for dozens of miles in the Macmillan Pass area and eastward. White spruce and subalpine fir form timberline atop the Mackenzie divide, with contiguous stands reaching 3900 feet and the highest groves attaining 4600 feet in sheltered locations along streams at the headwaters of the Keele River (Porsild 1945).

The highest spruce stands are very open, with fully crowned trees standing apart, generally above an undergrowth of willow shrubs. Many of the trees are old and gnarled, but young trees are seen also, suggesting that the tree line is not receding (Porsild 1945). Individual stunted, sometimes prostrate, white spruce are occasionally found far above the nearest groves.

Spruce is confined to protected draws and ravines, presumably because of favorable moisture conditions (Larsen 1980). The trees grow most vigorously on east-facing slopes, where they are exposed to direct sunlight only during the morning hours when evaporation rates are low. They grow less vigorously, if present at all, on colder north-facing slopes and on drier south- and west-facing slopes. The abundance of dry limestone substrates on the eastern slope of the Mackenzie Mountains no doubt is responsible for many of the drought effects observed in this otherwise moist region.

Scattered small groves of stunted subalpine fir also occur at tree limit in the Macmillan Pass area. In the highest mountains all along the Canol Road, west of Macmillan Pass, subalpine fir is primarily a tree of the timberline on moist northern and eastern exposures. It often forms a band of almost impenetrable scrub on steep slopes where snowslides are frequent (Porsild 1951). In addition to such thickets, subalpine fir develops layered tree islands with a mother tree at the center of each. This species reaches krummholz limit as high as 6000 feet.

Balsam poplar grows with white spruce along creeks and rivers at timberline in the Mackenzie Mountains, and at somewhat lower elevations patches of tamarack can be found near the watercourses. Black spruce generally dominates boggy muskegs below forest line; however, it forms pure stands at timberline on poorly drained glacial boulder clay west of Macmillan Pass. Permafrost remains within two feet of the surface in this area, and the soggy conditions presented a difficult problem for road construction. Here, the stunted black spruce often form "drunken forests" of tipped trees.

The tree line communities in this part of the Mackenzie Mountains are characterized by dense growths of 3- to 5-foot-high willow and bog birch with the lower-growing mountain cranberry (*Vaccinium vitis-idaea*), bog blueberry (*V. uliginosum*), Alaska spirea (*Spiraea beauverdiana*), and several wet-site grasses and forbs (Porsild 1945). Gravelly stream terraces and glacial deposits called eskers are common along the Mackenzie timberlines. These sites support open thickets of willow and bog birch along with a fluffy ground-layer carpet of caribou lichen (*Cladonia sylvatica*), an arctic fescue grass (*Festuca*), and a small arctic sagebrush (*Artemisia*). Most of these species are circumpolar in distribution, being abundant also in the boreal mountains and arctic timberlines of northern Europe, Siberia, and Greenland.

A. E. Porsild (1945) was one of the first botanists to travel the 513-mile-long Canol Road, which was built and originally used only during World War II to reach oil fields at Norman Wells on the Mackenzie River. Porsild provides a colorful description of the timberline country of the

Mackenzie Mountains, where forested river valleys give way to an immense high-country crowned with rugged 8000-foot snow-capped peaks:

> The scenery, which at any time would be remarkable for its grandeur, in September was particularly striking due to the riot of autumnal colours. The dark green spruce forest predominates in the valley bottoms, but on alluvial flood plains the solid green is broken by splashes of flame-coloured balsam poplars, and paper birches.
>
> The ordinarily sombre, black spruce covered transition from flood plain to the lower slopes is here enlivened by pale greenish yellow stands of tamarack. Farther up the sides of the valleys, a zone of about 1,000 feet is tinted purple or wine-red by the tiny leaves of the ground birch and blueberry bushes. Down through this warp descend wefts of purplish brown or yellow where willow or alder follow the downward course of a mountain brook. The steep upper slopes are white, not due to an early snow cover, but because they are formed of barren screes of huge, angular blocks of limestone torn from the towering rock walls above. Here and there rock slides, like small glaciers, or avalanches, have descended to the very floor of the valley.

Farther west in the Yukon Territory lie the sprawling Ogilvie Mountains, whose timberlines are reached via two roads. One of these climbs to the 5500-foot level in alpine tundra on Keno Mountain (6200 feet) in the Klondike mining region (64°N, 135°W) near Mayo Lake. Stunted white spruce and subalpine fir form tree line somewhat above 4000 feet on the mountain, but as is the case at most subarctic timberlines, there is very little krummholz.

North of Dawson City, the Dempster Highway climbs across the broad, unglaciated crest of the Ogilvie Mountains, ascending to the 4000-foot level in luxuriant subarctic tundra. Fields of cottongrass (*Eriophorum* spp.)—tufts of cottony down atop a foot-high stalk—highlight the wet meadows. Small spire-shaped white spruce are the principal timberline trees along this route. Subalpine fir apparently reaches its northern limits in this area, at the head of Fifteen Mile River at 65°N (Porsild 1951). Another widespread Rocky Mountain tree, lodgepole pine, also reaches its northern limits in this area, in the lowlands near Dawson (Viereck and Little 1972). At the highest elevations in the Ogilvie Mountains north of Dawson, spruce trees grow primarily along gravelly watercourses. On these microsites, the flowing water melts away the surface permafrost, giving white spruce sufficient soil depth to establish root systems above the frozen zone.

Alaskan Mountains

Alpine timberlines are conspicuous in central Alaska along the Alaska Range—which includes Denali (restored name of the former Mount McKinley) National Park—and along the southern slope of the

Willow on gravelly flood plain, in the alpine tundra on the north side of Mount McKinley

Brooks Range as well as on several less-prominent mountain uplands. The Denali Highway from Paxon to Cantwell and the road to Wonder Lake in Denali National Park travel for dozens of miles through a lush subarctic timberline. Also, the Steese Highway from Fairbanks to Circle wanders across somewhat drier timberline and tundra terrain on the Tanana-Yukon Uplands.

White spruce is usually the only conifer at tree line in these areas, although small, isolated groves of balsam poplar can be found several hundred feet above the spruce tree limit (Viereck and Little 1972). Balsam poplar inhabits recent moraines and other gravelly sites and in autumn becomes conspicuous at a distance when its leaves turn yellow. Small isolated patches of balsam poplar are the only trees in the great tundra landscape on the northern slope of the Brooks Range. Subalpine fir and lodgepole pine are absent from central Alaska.

Tree limit averages about 3500 feet in this area, but the timberline is often indistinct, with the highest stands consisting of widely scattered patches on the vast landscape. Although permafrost limits forest development on the lowlands at polar timberline, on the steeper mountain slopes of central Alaska its main effect may be more indirect. The seasonal thaw of perennially frozen ground contributes to a superabundance of soil moisture, which causes many upland slopes to creep. This movement, called solifluction, prevents establishment of trees (R. Haugen, footnote, page 45). The gentle upland terrain in valleys of Denali National Park and elsewhere in mountains of the Far North often exhibits an erratic distribution of forest that may be related to the depth to permafrost.

In the somewhat drier Tanana-Yukon Uplands, research findings suggest that temperature is by far the most important factor determining the position of timberline (R. Haugen). Moisture is of minor consequence since the soil is nearly always saturated, except on steep southern and western slopes. Wind and snow are not considered critical. Thus, in terms of these major factors, the situation resembles timberlines on the subtropical volcanoes of Mexico! However, the extreme contrast between summer and winter in central Alaska is, of course, totally unlike the subtropical mountains.

Much of the 90-mile-long road to Wonder Lake in Denali National Park traverses a very open, patchy, and indistinct subarctic timberline at 2500 to 3500 feet. More than half of the park lies above tree limit, and the coastal storm systems deliver heavy snowfalls, especially on the seaward slopes of the towering Alaska Range. This results in large glaciers, a feature not found in the drier and less-lofty mountains of the Boreal Rockies proper, including the Brooks Range. Although white spruce is the only common conifer at timberline in the Denali Park area, the timberline and tundra communities are replete with willows. More than 20 species of willows (*Salix*) grow in the park, and they range from brushy growths 20 feet tall to alpine mats projecting only two inches above the ground. Bog birch and dwarf alder are medium-sized shrubs common in the timberline zone, and shorter bog blueberry, crowberry (*Empetrum nigrum*), mountain cranberry, buffaloberry (*Shepherdia canadensis*), and alpine bearberry (*Arctostaphylos alpina*) are well distributed (Murie 1962). The annual berry crop from these shrubs is an important food for the great assortment of birds and mammals dwelling in the timberline zone of Denali National Park.

Unlike most of northern Canada and Eurasia, Alaska and the Yukon Territory have no true polar timberline where forest gives way to tundra on the arctic lowlands. Instead, a massive alpine mountain chain, the Brooks Range, cuts across the northern portion of Alaska and the Yukon, and the northernmost forests reach an alpine timberline at the modest elevation of 2000 to 3000 feet on its southern slope. The northern or arctic slope of the Brooks Range is essentially treeless, except for farflung and rare patches of balsam poplar. An exception is the occurrence of groves of white spruce with balsam poplar and tall bushes of feltleaf willow (*Salix alaxensis*) on the arctic slope in the vicinity of the Alaska-Yukon border in the upper Firth River drainage (Viereck and Little 1972). The lack of a lowland arctic timberline in Alaska and the Yukon is evidently the reason why white spruce is the northernmost forest tree; in the boggy arctic lowlands to the east, black spruce is predominant.

The white spruce timberlines on the southern slope of the Brooks Range are accessible via the Dalton Highway, which parallels the North Slope oil pipeline between Livengood and Prudhoe Bay. The farthest-north spruce trees along this route are reported at milepost 236 (from the south end of the highway). This point lies at 68°N and is 10 miles down the Dietrich River Valley from the Brooks Range divide, which the highway crosses at 4800-foot Atigun Pass. The last trees are straight and 20 to 30 feet tall.

8
The Arctic

The arctic, "polar," or "northern" timberline is a broad transitional zone separating the expansive lowland boreal forest from the frigid arctic tundra. This is probably the widest ecotone on earth. Its vastness can only be judged during a high-altitude flight on a clear day. Arctic timberline lies adjacent to the northernmost alpine timberlines in the Boreal Rockies, and these ecotones support generally similar vegetation.

As shown on the facing map, arctic timberline can be divided into two parts (Löve 1970, Hare and Ritchie 1972). The northern of these is the "forest-tundra zone" consisting of scattered patches of krummholz or stunted trees (or larger trees along rivers and sheltered sites) set in a matrix of tundra. The forest-tundra zone extends south from the arctic tree line (or krummholz line if that occurs) to the "open boreal forest" or "lichen woodland." The latter consists of open groves of erect trees underlain by a rich lichen carpet (mostly of caribou lichens, *Cladonia* spp.) sprinkled with herbs and low shrubs characteristic of the boreal forest (Löve 1970). The proportion of trees to lichen mat gradually increases southward toward "forest line," where trees cover 50 percent or more of the landscape (Black and Bliss 1978).

Although this zonation is comparable in some ways to that of alpine timberlines, it differs dramatically in spanning a belt 100 or more miles wide across the lowlands. Alpine timberlines are generally telescoped into a quarter- or half-mile on a mountain slope. The respective distances reflect the sharpness of the climatic gradients across arctic and alpine timberlines.

The broadness of the arctic timberline is biologically significant because it hampers tree regeneration from seeds. In contrast, alpine timberlines are occasionally showered with viable seeds from the stands near forest line. Partly because of its great breadth, arctic timberline is an ecotone that has been recognized as a distinct vegetative and climatic zone and is termed the "subarctic zone" by Ilmari Hustich (1966) and R. A. Black and L. C. Bliss (1980). Several prominent undergrowth species become most abundant in the arctic timberline zone, including crowberry, narrow-leaf Labrador tea (*Ledum decumbens*), cloudberry (*Rubus chamaemorus*), bog blueberry, and cranberry (*V. vitis-idaea*) (Larsen 1974).

The arctic timberline stretches at high latitudes all across North America, Europe, and Siberia (see map, page 240). But in western Alaska

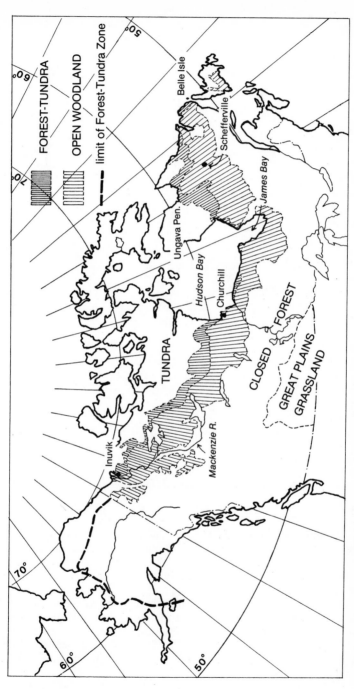

North American arctic timberline (after Hare & Ritchie 1972)

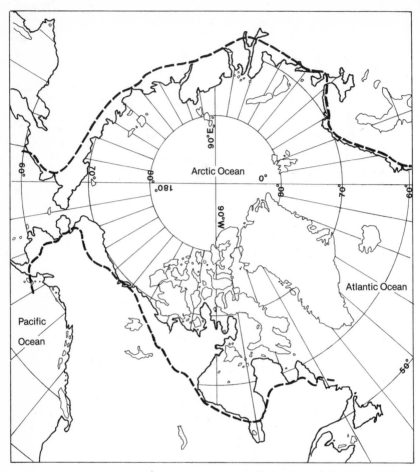

The arctic limits of tree growth —dashed line (after Hare & Ritchie 1972)

and adjacent eastern Siberia, this ecotone makes a 90 degree turn and parallels the Bering Sea, where a cold maritime climate prevents trees from colonizing the coastal lowlands. The northern limits of trees in Alaska and the Yukon are essentially an alpine timberline along the southern slope of the Brooks Range.

East of the Yukon Territory, the northern limit of trees reaches the shores of the Arctic Ocean (69°N) at the mouth of the huge Mackenzie River. Farther east, the forest frontier gradually retreats southward and skirts the southern edge of Hudson Bay. Timberline lies between 56 and 58°N in eastern Canada in response to a cold summer climate in this region.

Greenland and Iceland have no native forest other than localized groves of small birch; however, a number of boreal conifers have been grown successfully on Iceland. In northern Eurasia the arctic timberline develops at high latitudes (67 to 72°N) and is ecologically similar to its North American counterpart. Many species of undergrowth shrubs and herbs are found in both North America and Eurasia; but no tree species have circumpolar distributions. Nevertheless, species of spruce (*Picea*), larch (*Larix*), poplar (*Populus*), and birch (*Betula*) dominate the arctic timberline on both continents (Larsen 1980). The shrubby common juniper (*Juniperus communis*) does reach the arctic tree line in essentially all areas, as well as inhabiting Iceland and southern Greenland (Hustich 1966).

White spruce and black spruce are by far the most common trees at arctic timberline across North America; but these species differ ecologically. Black spruce grows primarily on poorly drained (boggy) sites, which are prevalent in the permafrost-underlain lowlands. This species regenerates vegetatively through layering and readily assumes a stunted or krummholz form on exposed sites. In contrast, white spruce generally forms an erect single trunk at tree line, and it reproduces mostly from seed. White spruce grows in well-drained soils, especially along streams where permafrost has been melted back by the flowing water. Other tree species associated with these spruces vary from western Alaska to Labrador, and are mentioned in the regional discussions.

The climate at arctic timberline is similar to that of the northern Boreal Rockies. Despite the fact that at the northernmost timberline areas the sun does not set during June and most of July, there is a great difference in the sun-angle (and in radiant heating) between early morning and midday. Thus, at Inuvik (68½°N, 133½°W) in the open boreal forest near the mouth of the Mackenzie River, the average daily maximum temperature during July is 67°F, while the average daily minimum is 45°F.

Mean temperatures for May and September are close to freezing and January averages a brisk −20°F at Inuvik and other timberline sites with inland climates. Annual precipitation at Inuvik averages only 10 inches, which is typical for an inland site. Annual snowfall is just 70 inches, and a similar amount is recorded at Churchill (59°N, 94°W) on the western coast of Hudson Bay. At Churchill annual precipitation is somewhat higher (about 16 inches), as is characteristic of a more maritime location.

Thus, snowfall at the arctic timberline is a small fraction of that received at most alpine timberlines in the temperate zone. Annual precipitation is also much less at arctic timberline, but because of permafrost and poor drainage there is a much higher proportion of wet sites than on the steep mountainsides at alpine timberline.

The Labrador-Ungava Peninsula east of Hudson Bay has a humid climate with very cloudy and rainy summers. For example, Schefferville, Quebec (55°N, 67°W) is an upland site within the arctic timberline. Here, the mean cloudiness for June, July, and August is 80 percent and annual precipitation is 28 inches (Vowinckel and others 1975).

Alaska and Yukon Territory

The western timberline approaching the Bering Sea is made up of groves of white spruce, paper birch, and balsam poplar (Viereck 1979). This maritime timberline differs from the arctic timberlines of Canada in that black spruce does not approach it; but the reason for the absence of that species has not been explained. The western timberline stretches from the vicinity of Kotzebue Sound (at the Arctic Circle—66½°N) to Katmai National Monument at the base of the Alaska Peninsula (58°N). Well-developed forests extend westward along the floodplains of the major rivers, such as the Yukon and Kuskokwim, in areas where the adjacent uplands are treeless (Viereck 1979). The active floodplain provides a permafrost-free site where trees grow rapidly and reach commercial size; on the nearby upland sites tree growth is severely restricted by permafrost near the ground surface.

Another factor besides permafrost may be responsible for the position of timberline in southwestern Alaska. As was discussed in the case of Sitka spruce on the southern Alaskan Coast, there may not have been adequate time for the forest to advance in response to a warming climate. Fast-growing white spruce in dense stands, producing viable seeds, grow close to the forest limit at the edge of the maritime tundra. This evidence, and weather records suggest that in some areas the forest has not yet been able to migrate to its current climatic limits. Seed years for white spruce are infrequent even in the warmest parts of interior Alaska. Balsam poplar, which has minute seeds borne in cottony down suitable for long-distance wind transport, grows far to the west of the limit of white spruce and paper birch in some areas.

At the maritime timberlines in northwestern Alaska the primary forest community is white spruce-bog birch (*Betula glandulosa*)-feathermoss (*Pleurozium schreberi* and *Hylocomium splendens*) (Viereck 1979). In southwestern Alaska the corresponding timberline type is white spruce-bog birch-sphagnum moss. Several species of *Sphagnum* replace feathermoss in the wetter maritime climate of southwestern Alaska. Tamarack (*Larix laricina*) approaches tree line in the Norton Sound-lower Kuskokwim River area but apparently not elsewhere in Alaska. Farther east, however, in the Richardson Mountains of the northern Yukon Territory, tamarack occasionally forms open timberline woodlands with an understory of prostrate white spruce. These are reminiscent of the alpine larch timberlines of the inland Pacific Northwest except that the tamarack stands apparently grow on limestone slopes (R. A. Black, personal communication).

Near the northern tip of the Yukon Territory, a lobe of white spruce extends down the Firth River Valley to within eight miles of the Arctic Ocean. This is the only appendage of inland forest spilling north across the crest of the Brooks Range in Alaska or the Yukon and thus forming a local arctic timberline. This remote stringer of white spruce forest is restricted to sites with calcareous (limestone) soils that thaw deeply but still retain an adequate moisture-holding capacity (Drew and Shanks 1965). Most of the surrounding terrain, away from the Firth Valley, is unsuitable for tree growth because permafrost lies near the ground surface. In addition, some of the well-drained sites become *too* dry for spruce seedlings to survive.

The oldest trees in the Firth Valley exceed 250 years, and there is no indication of advance or retreat of this arctic slope woodland. Reasons for the existence of this woodland may include the prevailing southerly winds that allow warmer summer temperatures from the interior of Alaska and Canada to spread down the Firth River Valley. Also, the calcareous substrate evidently results in a thicker thaw zone above the permafrost. Soil thawing in the flood plain is hastened by movement of water through the subsurface gravels.

Mackenzie District

North America's northernmost forest is found where the Mackenzie River empties into the Arctic Ocean (Larsen 1980). White spruce groves on the massive Mackenzie Delta extend many miles north of the edge of the forest on surrounding uplands. Tree line reaches slightly beyond 69°N in this region, whereas to the east, across Canada's immense Northwest Territories, this leading edge of the forest-tundra zone retreats gradually southward. Thus, tree line is formed near 59°N at Churchill, Manitoba, on the west coast of Hudson Bay. Along this entire length—1400 miles from the mouth of the Mackenzie to Churchill—arctic tree line projects north in many places along river valleys and, conversely, is pushed back southward by incursions of tundra along uplands.

It appears that in both North America and Eurasia the northern timberline coincides approximately with the average southern boundary of cold polar air masses in summer. This "average frontal position" would be expected to shift north or south in response to changes in the earth's weather circulation pattern, and the position of the northern timberline would follow suit. Several studies on the dynamics of tree line in northern Canada have concluded that this limit of tree growth is a relict from times of prior warmth and that the northernmost trees are only able to regenerate through vegetative means—that is, layering (Nichols 1976, Elliot 1979).

The hypothesis that the northern tree line is out of phase with today's climate is supported by the lack of viable seed and of seedlings at tree line. Also, where wildfires have destroyed the patchy conifer growth at tree line, the trees show little ability to regenerate (Payette 1980). In areas where black spruce forms tree line, that species may be able to maintain itself for centuries, or almost indefinitely, despite a deteriorating climate; but when a wind-driven wildfire kills the trees, the site reverts to tundra. This situation is at sharp contrast with the ecology of stands near forest line, where black spruce is well adapted to wildfire and regenerates from seed stored throughout the fire in closed (semi-serotinous) cones (Black and Bliss 1978 and 1980).

The Dempster Highway is a gravel road that leads 450 miles north from the vicinity of Dawson City, Yukon Territory, to the northern forest line at Inuvik on the eastern edge of the Mackenzie Delta in the Northwest Territories. Inuvik (68½°N, 134°W) lies within a floristically rich arctic

White spruce trees with birch and willow shrubs on the Mackenzie Delta

timberline. The predominantly boggy sites within the open boreal forest are occupied by black spruce-bog blueberry communities consisting of dense patches of spindly, stunted trees with a luxuriant low-shrub under-growth. The terrain is very hummocky (because of permafrost activity), which influences tree regeneration. Hummock tops tend to be droughty in summer while troughs between hummocks may be waterlogged (Black and Bliss 1980). Thus, regeneration is most successful on the sides of the hummocks.

Heading north toward tree line, a few miles past Inuvik, white spruce becomes most common along the shorelines and islands of the Mackenzie Delta, where depth to the permafrost is greater (Larsen 1980). Black spruce occupies sites that lie several feet above the river channel and that burn occasionally and are not prone to flood damage. Gravel terraces of intermediate elevation support apparent hybrid spruces (*Picea glauca* x, *P. mariana*) (R. A. Black, personal communication). Small amounts of tamarack are associated with the black spruce in the southern part of the forest-tundra zone, although tamarack reaches considerably larger size. Stands of white spruce also inhabit rock outcrops and eskers (narrow ridges of gravel and sand) in the Inuvik area. The ground cover is an assortment of low shrubs, mostly from the heath family, together with bog birch and willows among a carpet of lichens and mosses. Northward from the open boreal forest lies a zone of dwarf willow and bog birch with widely scattered spruce, then tundra with dwarf willow and bog birch, and finally tundra without the shrubs (Larsen 1980).

North-central and Northeastern Canada

The Canadian Shield forms a huge horseshoe of rocky terrain surrounding Hudson Bay and covering most of central and eastern Canada. This very ancient (Precambrian) rock mass has been heavily glaciated, resulting in a mosaic of different geologic surfaces, including glacially scoured bedrock of several rock types, moraines, eskers, and large areas of sandy glacial outwash.

In the area around Ennadai and Yathkyed lakes (approximately 62°N, 100°W) west of Hudson Bay, krummholz line is represented by clumps of white spruce and black spruce in sheltered valleys and along lakeshores (Larsen 1980). Spruce reproduction is primarily through layering, suggesting that the tree clumps are relicts of a warmer climatic period. The open boreal forest south of this area is characterized by well-spaced stands of white spruce, black spruce, and tamarack, with a thick mat of lichens and a layer of low shrubs—cranberry, crowberry, bog birch, and willows.

From Hudson Bay westward to Alaska, barren-ground caribou feed heavily on the lichen mat of *Cladonia* spp. East of Hudson Bay, barren-ground caribou are absent and the ground lichens often make up the most conspicuous understory vegetation near forest line. The open stands are termed "lichen woodland." The lichens are most abundant on sites where competition from other plants is low because of unfavorable moisture or temperature conditions (Larsen 1980). But little is known regarding the ecological requirements of lichens or competitive relationships of lichens to other vegetation at the arctic timberline. In general, dense stands of conifers and shrubs occupy lowlands while the open lichen woodlands occur on well-drained upland areas.

At the arctic timberline in the vicinity of Churchill on the west side of Hudson Bay, black spruce is restricted to peat deposits and mineral soils derived from acidic bedrock (Ritchie 1957). White spruce occurs on eskers and on certain alluvial soils, especially those of limestone origin. White spruce consistently grows more vigorously than black spruce. A chronological sequence of vegetation types (seral stages) has developed on mineral soils along the Churchill River. This sequence indicates that succession progresses from a meadow phase on freshly exposed flats to a shrub phase of dwarf willows and bog birch that in turn gives way to a seral forest of white spruce and tamarack, followed eventually by black spruce on a hummock-and-hollow topography. The latter formation is caused by permafrost, which becomes increasingly prevalent as distance from the river becomes greater.

The black spruce on the edge of permafrost mounds generally tilt away from the center, due to disturbance and instability in the shallow rooting zone (Ritchie 1957). On top of the oldest forested mounds, black spruce trees develop a "candelabrum" habit in which the oldest and tallest tree, in the center, is surrounded by a cluster of smaller trunks produced through layering.

East of Hudson and James bays lies the Labrador-Ungava Peninsula which has an exceptionally broad arctic timberline (Hare 1950). This results from the regional tilt of the land surface, which slopes up from a low elevation at tree line (near 58°N) to a general level of nearly 3000 feet some 400 miles to the south (at 52°N). This southward rise of elevation has the effect of offsetting, to some extent, the normal southward rise of temperature. Black spruce is the most abundant tree in the forest-tundra zone, although tamarack forms the northern limit of erect trees on much of the Ungava Peninsula (Payette and Gagnon 1979). White spruce is most common along Hudson and Ungava bays, where it seems better adapted to maritime moisture and fog.

In the inland portions of Ungava (Leaf River drainage), tamarack forms the northernmost stands of erect trees and relies on seed-produced regeneration (Payette and Gagnon 1979). Black spruce is its constant associate and is able to persist considerably farther north in a krummholz form, utilizing only vegetative reproduction. The northern black spruce krummholz zone is evidently a relict from centuries past when a more favorable summer climate prevailed.

The forest-tundra zone extends across northern Ungava-Labrador from the Hudson Bay coast to the Atlantic, where it is largely cut off by a coastal tundra, with a narrow scrub belt adjoining the open boreal forest (Hare 1950, Hustich 1966). The strip of coastal tundra extends southward all along the severely cold and windy Labrador Coast to the Strait of Belle Isle (52°N), opposite the northern tip of Newfoundland. However, occasional patches of white spruce forest do occur on sheltered sites as far north as 58°N, at the inner end of Napaktok (Black Duck) Bay on the Atlantic Coast (Elliott and Short 1979).

The open boreal forest, or lichen woodland, is a very extensive zone east of Hudson and James bays. At its northern extremity, long stringers of lichen woodland stretch north along the major rivers, while intervening uplands are entirely without trees (Hare 1950). Farther south, in the main lichen woodland, tall black and white spruce and a scattering of tamarack and balsam fir stand several yards apart in a sea of lichens (*Cladonia*). A muskeg of stunted black spruce, Labrador tea, and sphagnum covers the intervening wet sites. The lichen woodland presents an extensive and colorful landscape. Its *Cladonia* floor retains the imprints of footsteps for years, and its pastel hues defy duplication by color film.

9
Northern Appalachian Mountains

The Appalachians, stretching from northern Georgia to Quebec's Gaspé Peninsula, are the principal mountain range of eastern North America. This 1500-mile-long mountain system is entirely forested, up to the alpine timberline, and rises from humid, forested lowlands; thus, it has no lower or dry timberline. The Appalachians are very ancient, worn-down mountains, now of modest elevation, and only in the cool northern latitudes (beyond 44°N) in northern New York, New England, and adjacent Canada do some of the highest peaks support an alpine timberline.

The Appalachians are virtually contiguous with the uplands of eastern Quebec and Labrador. Thus, the Appalachian system is linked to the Arctic of eastern Canada in the same sense that timberlines in the Pacific Coast Mountains and the Rockies have a connection with the arctic vegetation of western Canada and Alaska. Arctic timberline and tundra plants from northeastern Canada extend southward along the highest summits of the northern Appalachians. Black spruce, the principal tree at arctic timberline, spreads south as a diminishing component of the Appalachian alpine timberlines. Conversely, balsam fir forms the principal tree at alpine timberlines in the Appalachians, and diminishes as it reaches northward into the southern portion of the arctic timberline. The third species at Appalachian timberlines in the northeastern United States is paper birch, which occurs northward also throughout the open boreal forest.

Paper birch and black spruce are boreal species that grow all across northern Canada but do not spread very far south as subalpine species in the Rockies. (They become confined to lower elevations near their southern range limits in western North America.) Balsam fir (*Abies balsamea*) seems to be the ecological equivalent of western North America's subalpine fir (*Abies lasiocarpa*). Each of these firs becomes the principal climax tree in humid subalpine forests on its half of the continent, but neither reaches north into the arctic forest-tundra zone.

White spruce and tamarack, companions of black spruce in the forest-tundra of eastern Canada, do not become components of the subalpine forest in the Appalachians south of Canada. Instead, they are confined to lower elevations in the northern part of this mountain system— the same limited way in which they spread southward in the Rockies. The black spruce of the Appalachians, and to a lesser extent the paper birch,

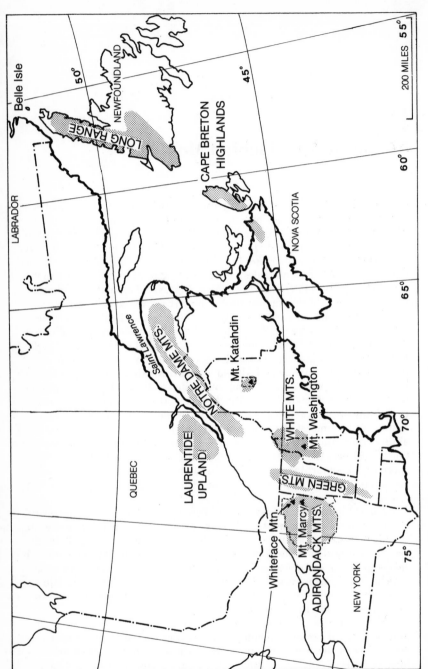

Northern Appalachian Mountains

represents the only case in North America of a tree from the arctic timber-line stretching southward to alpine timberlines at mid-latitudes.

Arctic and alpine timberline and tundra communities of eastern North America are more similar in composition to each other than those of western North America, and this may be due to more comparable climates. That is, in eastern North America arctic and alpine timberlines have super-humid weather in summer and, essentially, year-round. Southward in western North America, however, summer drought becomes a promi-nent environmental factor. Arctic timberline species seem poorly adapted to the western drought. Additionally, southward in western North America timberlines extend to high elevations, where a rarified atmo-sphere magnifies the effects of drought and excessive radiation. Eastern North American timberlines reach a maximum elevation of only about 5000 feet, because high (alpine) mountains do not occur south of New England.

The highest portion of the Appalachians occurs near 36°N in North Carolina and Tennessee. The loftiest peaks reach 6000 to 6684 feet and are capped with relict stands of subalpine forest vegetation, but they would have to rise substantially higher, or have a colder regional climate, to exhibit an alpine timberline. (Montane balds, or grass and shrub lands, that develop on dry upper slopes of these southern Appalachian peaks are discussed on page 48.)

Canadian Mountains

Immediately north of the Appalachian region an alpine timberline occurs at about 3000 feet in the highlands of southern Labrador and eastern Quebec (at 52 to 53°N). This lies upslope from an "open boreal forest," which is itself part of the broad arctic timberline zone of eastern Canada (Hare 1950). This northern alpine timberline is composed of the arctic tree-line dwellers, white spruce and black spruce, along with the subalpine and boreal conifer balsam fir. Northwest of the Appalachian region, across the Saint Lawrence Valley in southeastern Quebec, stands the Laurentide Upland which has some 3000-foot peaks supporting tim-berline communities of the above species.

The Long Range Mountains of Newfoundland and the Cape Breton Highlands on the nearby northern tip of Nova Scotia actually represent the northern end of the Appalachian system. Black spruce, white spruce, and balsam fir form a dense krummholz called "tuckamoor" at about 2000 feet on the highest of the Newfoundland peaks (Pruitt 1970). The highest summit on the sea-windswept Cape Breton Highlands is only 1750 feet; but several of the ridgetops are covered with caribou lichen (*Cladonia*) barrens, below which lies a timberline of the same three conifers (Roland and Smith 1969, Baig 1972).

The Notre Dame Mountains extend along the Gaspé Peninsula, northeast from the northern tip of Maine. About a dozen peaks exceed 3000 feet, the highest being Mount Jacques Cartier (4160 feet). Timber-line occurs near 3000 feet, where extensive krummholz of white spruce, black spruce, and balsam fir develops, along with a species-poor alpine tundra (Scoggan 1950, Baig 1972, Larsen 1980).

New England Mountains

In the northeastern United States alpine timberlines are found on Mount Katadin at 46°N in Maine and just north of 44°N on the summits of the White Mountains of New Hampshire, the Green Mountains of Vermont, and the Adirondacks of New York. The same general forest zonation occurs on all of these northeastern mountains. Lowland forest is primarily of beech (*Fagus grandifolia*), yellow birch (*Betula alleghaniensis*), and sugar maple (*Acer saccharum*) (Küchler 1964, Leak and Graber 1974a). Ascending the mountainsides, these northern hardwoods give way at about 2500 feet to subalpine forest, which is a red spruce (*Picea rubens*)-balsam fir-paper birch potential climax type (Oosting and Billings 1951).

At about the 4000-foot level red spruce becomes scarce and balsam fir becomes the principal tree species. Fir forms dense forests with sparse undergrowth that clothe the fog-shrouded mountainsides, and it becomes progressively shorter with increasing elevation. Near 5000 feet only wind-sheared krummholz, along with the lower fringes of alpine tundra vegetation, can be found. Black spruce becomes common only in the krummholz and stunted-tree belts, where it dwells with the ubiquitous

Stunted balsam fir at 3800 feet elevation along the Appalachian Trail near Avery Peak in southern Maine

balsam fir and scattered patches of paper birch.

This zonation occurs somewhat lower on 5267-foot Mount Katahdin because of its more northerly latitude, and alpine tundra with scattered krummholz cushions covers the broad summit block. Katahdin is a large, solitary mountain rising near the head of the Penobscot River in north-central Maine. Situated in the 200,000-acre Baxter State Park, this is the most geographically isolated and remote of the New England timberline areas, although the mountain's base is reached by a road from the town of Millinocket. Naturalist-philosopher Henry David Thoreau was one of the first people in history (in September 1846) to reach the harsh alpine environment atop Katahdin. After an arduous journey, squeezing his way through the dense fir and birch forest and pulling himself up cliffs via tree roots, Thoreau found himself deep within the cloud-cap on the thousand-acre alpine-tundra tableland that makes up the summit. Walter Harding (1967) described the philosopher's experience:

All he could see was a vast and fearful aggregation of loose rocks and clouds. For once he felt that "vast, Titanic, inhuman Nature" had got him at a disadvantage and seemed to say to him, "Why came ye here before your time. This ground is not prepared for you." This was not the gentle kindly Nature he knew on the banks of Walden Pond and he did not like it. Remembering conveniently that his companions were anxious to return, he turned back without reaching the highest point of the tableland and quickly and happily descended to friendlier regions.

Even in the mid-1800s Mount Katahdin's remoteness contrasted with the accessibility of New Hampshire's 6288-foot Mount Washington. This peak is the highest point in the northern Appalachians. It forms the center of New England's largest timberline and alpine area — the Presidential Range of the White Mountains. Mount Washington was already well known when Thoreau first climbed it in 1839, and by the time he returned on a botanical collecting trip in 1858 there were two inns (Tiptop and Summit House) established on the alpine tundra at the summit. In 1869 a cog railway began operation, taking visitors up the western slope of the mountain to the wind-lashed summit. The cog railway, still in operation, is a unique and picturesque contraption that ascends grades averaging 25 percent. Each car has its own locomotive.

A toll road climbs to the summit of Mount Washington via the eastern slope, and a network of popular hiking trails, complete with inns or hostels maintained by the Appalachian Mountain Club, threads through the White Mountains (Douglas 1961). The timberline peaks of the White Mountains arise in a 30-mile stretch between Franconia Notch to the west and the town of Gorham to the east.

The dense balsam fir forest becomes noticeably stunted (mature trees are about 40 feet tall) near the 4200-foot level, and upslope this conifer cloak is gradually reduced to an elfinwood that is impenetrable except where trails have been hacked through. Krummholz line averages about 5000 feet, but patches of cushion krummholz (balsam fir, black spruce, and

Cog railway on Mount Washington, New Hampshire

paper birch) reach a few hundred feet higher in depressions and in the lee of rock outcrops where there is less exposure to relentless blizzards (Bliss 1963). Stems of krummholz seldom exceed 100 years of age, but these plants are actually much older because all species spread through layering. In 1858 Thoreau examined the half-inch-thick stem of a dwarf conifer atop Mount Lafayette and was astounded that it showed 70 annual growth rings (Harding 1967).

Above krummholz line on Mount Washington and a handful of other lofty peaks lies an alpine tundra zone that covers a total of seven and a half square miles, by far the largest alpine area in the eastern United States (Bliss 1963). This well-developed alpine tundra is dominated by species from the Canadian Arctic as well as from the alpine communities of Scandinavia and central Europe. The most widespread tundra plants on Mount Washington include the mat-forming sedge *Carex bigelowii,* the rush *Juncus trifidus,* bog blueberry (*Vaccinium uliginosum*), and mountain-cranberry (*V. vitis-idaea*). There is scant similarity to alpine communities of the western United States. This difference is a result of the humid, foggy climate of northeastern alpine areas, which contrasts to the drier, sunnier summers of the High Sierra, Cascades, and Rocky Mountains.

Another factor in the close relationship of the timberline and alpine flora of the White Mountains to that of eastern Canada is the geographic continuity of subalpine areas northward to the Canadian Arctic. (There is a vast barrier of lowland environments between New England and the Rockies.) Evidently the arctic and alpine flora migrated south along the uplands of eastern North America during the Pleistocene ice ages and became confined to the highest New England peaks after the continental ice retreated. During the height of the most recent ice age (Wisconsin Glaciation), the ice sheet from Canada overrode the entire Presidential Range (Bliss 1963). This didn't happen in the Rockies and Pacific Coast mountains.

The White Mountains are composed primarily of mica schists and gneisses that weather to form a soil and substrate similar to those of much of the Canadian Shield and western North American mountains. The climate, however, is a more unusual aspect of the New England alpine habitat. This is illustrated by the year-round weather records from the summit of Mount Washington, which were begun in 1870. (A major U.S. Weather Bureau observatory was established here in 1932.) Low temperatures, heavy fog, and rather frequent hurricane-force winds characterize the alpine and timberline climate. On the alpine summit, winds in excess of 100 mph have been recorded in every month, with an absolute maximum of 231 mph—the strongest surface wind yet recorded on earth. The average year-round wind speed is 36 mph on the summit and apparently in excess of 20 mph at tree line (Reiners and Lang 1979). Atop Mount Washington, the average July temperature is 48°F and January's mean is only 6°F.

The climate is superhumid, with fog, high humidity, sleet, and rain characteristic of the summer season. Annual precipitation averages 74 inches and is evenly distributed throughout the year (Bliss 1963). Daytime cloud cover averages 75 percent and average relative humidity exceeds 85 percent for every month of the year. However, snowfall is modest (195 inches annually) compared with that in the mountains of western North America. Snow depth reaches only a few feet in the krummholz zone and rarely exceeds a few inches above timberline.

Because of the humid conditions, little winter desiccation of foliage occurs at timberline (Marchand and Chabot 1978). Evidently scrub line develops where the snowpack becomes too thin to protect foliage from mechanical wind damage. Marginally adequate warmth during the growing season is probably also a limiting factor for tree species. The cold, humid, windy conditions produce an extraordinary gradient of size reduction in the dense subalpine forest and krummholz belt, as described by Robert Griggs (1942):

> The trees become shorter and denser with ascent until, still retaining the erect arborescent form, they form a compact level-topped elfin forest over the top of which you may sometimes walk

but which you can penetrate only by chopping your way. Above this scrub, the trees, still further dwarfed, form in places extensive carpets close-clipped by wind and snow blast. These appear from a little distance like well-kept lawns.

The early ecologist C. H. Shaw (1909b) wrote the following description of timberlines on the White Mountains and the Adirondacks:

Timber lines caused by wind...are recognized by a gradual and ultimately great reduction in height of trees by their massing together in dense level topped societies, thus affording each other mutual protection, and by the occurrence of the upper outposts of the forest as clumps of dwarfs in local depressions and sheltered spots.

Robert Griggs (1942) concluded that tree-line and krummholz stands on Mount Washington had become established during a warmer climatic period several centuries ago. This accounts for the lack of seed-produced regeneration of tree species and their reliance on vegetative reproduction. Recent studies found that vegetative reproduction has thus far been adequate to keep tree line from retreating downslope (Leak and Graber 1974b).

The weather conditions atop the Presidential Range also result in the formation of luxuriant tundra communities on the broad, gentle slopes of Mount Washington and nearby peaks. The best-developed tundra includes the Alpine Garden, Bigelow Lawn, and Monticello Lawn (Bliss 1963).

The dense subalpine balsam fir forests have no "forest line" represented by a zone where subalpine meadows and other large openings occur. Instead, "forest line" is estimated based upon the elevation where mature trees become noticeably stunted—attaining heights of only about 40 feet. Despite the density of the subalpine and timberline stands, wave-like bands of dead trees can be seen covering some of the broad slopes near forest line. These "fir waves" have repeated the pattern of growth, senescence, and death in the rather short-lived balsam fir (Reiners and Lang 1979), which is somewhat comparable to the gap-phase regeneration in old-growth northern hardwood forests. Other broken patches observable in the contiguous stands near forest line are caused by occasional hurricane damage and avalanches. Small "snow glades" filled with herbaceous vegetation are present in the lee of some of the exposed ridges; this formation is much more common in the snowier mountains of western North America. Wildfire is evidently rare in these perpetually humid timberline stands.

Adirondack Mountains

West of the White Mountains, the highest peaks (4000 to 4392 feet) in the Green Mountains of Vermont have a few acres of timberline vegetation (krummholz balsam fir, *Vaccinium* heath, and sedge barrens) on their summits (Siccama 1974). Still farther west—about 100 miles from the

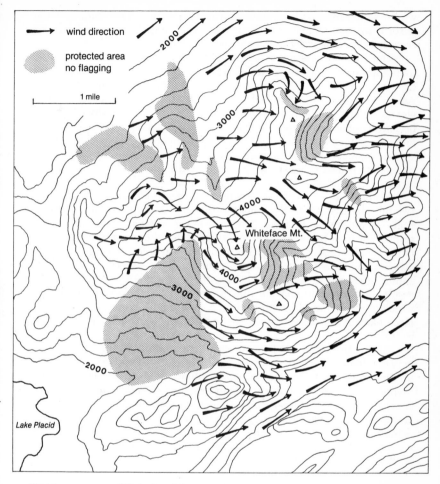

Wind patterns on Whiteface Mountain as indicated by flagged trees (after Holroyd 1970)

White Mountains—rise the Adirondacks of upper New York state. The loftiest peak here, 5344-foot Mount Marcy, supports a small area of alpine tundra, and several of the high peaks (4500+ feet) are capped with krummholz.

Whiteface Mountain (4867 feet), immediately north of Lake Placid, New York, has a large ski area on its slopes and was the site of the 1980 Winter Olympic Games. A climatologist was able to construct a detailed map of the direction of prevailing winds on the slopes of Whiteface and neighboring mountains by recording the shape and growth patterns of wind-trained trees and krummholz (Holroyd 1970). A very complex wind pattern was found, and wind instruments placed at numerous locations recorded the same wind directions indicated by the trees.

The Adirondacks are a nearly circular geologic dome, or uplifted plateau, about 100 miles in width. The core, or central area, is composed of Precambrian rocks similar to those found in the Canadian Shield. The Adirondacks were heavily glaciated and contain hundreds of lakes. Lower elevations are clothed in a beech-birch-maple forest, with red spruce becoming a dominant species at middle elevations. The upper subalpine forest is primarily balsam fir, with lesser amounts of paper birch. Black spruce is present only in krummholz form atop Mount Marcy and a few other high peaks. (This spruce is, however, also present in low-elevation bogs.)

Mount Marcy lies within a wild area (south of Lake Placid) in the two-million-acre Adirondack Forest Preserve that was set aside by the State of New York in 1892. This mountain—named Tahawas (cloud-splitter) by local Indians—is a cone with a domelike summit that remains in the clouds much of the time. The dense balsam fir forest forms scrub line at about 5000 feet, but krummholz communities extend nearly to the summit in ravines (Adams and others 1920). Presumably this effect is the result of snow accumulation that protects krummholz from damaging winds. A few krummholz cushions of balsam fir, black spruce, and paper birch eke out an existence on the summit itself, in the lee of sheltering rocks.

Alpine tundra plants form a sizeable community in the Adirondacks only on Mount Marcy, above the 4900 foot level. Still, their relationship to arctic and to White Mountains alpine tundra is clear. Principal species include bog birch, crowberry, Lapland rosebay (*Rhododendron lapponicum*), diapensia (*Diapensia lapponica*), bog blueberry, mountain-cranberry, and dwarf blueberry (*Vaccinium caespitosum*). Caribou lichen (*Cladonia rangiferina*) is common in the tree-line stands. This is the southern outpost of arctic-alpine and timberline vegetation in eastern North America.

10
Mexican Mountains

Mexico has some of the most diverse and interesting, but least-known, vegetation in North America. Stretching from the temperate zone to the tropics, the country includes extensive lowland, high plateau, and rugged mountain environments. Annual precipitation varies from only 5 inches in some of the northern deserts to more than 120 inches in the tropical rain forests. The vegetation of Mexico reflects a wide spectrum of climatic, geologic, and soil conditions.

Unlike most subtropical and tropical regions, Mexico supports mountain forests composed largely of pines and other conifers related to northern species. In northwestern Mexico the mountain forests are generally similar to those described for the mountains in the southernmost portions of California, Arizona, and New Mexico. The Mexican mountains harbor several additional tree species (especially pines and oaks), but drought-caused lower timberlines are formed above deserts and grasslands in a manner comparable to lower timberline formation in southern Arizona (page 178).

However, because of Mexico's southern latitude (16 to 32°N) only the highest peaks, above 12,000 or perhaps 13,000 feet, are cold enough to support alpine timberlines. These cold timberlines are mostly confined to the large volcanoes that project from the high plateau, or meseta, around Mexico City at 19°N. Mexico's seven highest peaks, 14,000 to 18,700 feet, arise from this central meseta. These islands of alpine habitat lie 1250 miles south of the closest tundra areas in the Rocky Mountains — near Sante Fe, New Mexico. Only one small area of upper timberline is known in all of northern Mexico. It is on the summit of Cerro Potosi near Monterrey. A few small communities of alpine timberline and tundra are also perched atop the 13,000-foot volcanoes that jut out above the tropical rain forests and cloud forests along the Pacific Coast of neighboring Guatemala (15°N), 550 miles southeast of Mexico City.

All of the Mexican alpine timberlines, and those in Guatemala, are similar in having only two closely related erect tree species, the Mexican mountain pines, *Pinus rudis* and *P. hartwegii*. Although the latter pine is the dominant species at upper timberline in central Mexico and Guatemala, it is essentially confined to this region and to the highest mountains in it (Critchfield and Little 1966). *Pinus rudis* occurs on Cerro Potosi and other high mountains in the region near Monterrey. The dwarf

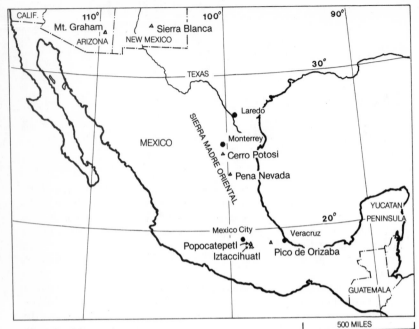

Mexican Mountains

trees, shrubs, and herbs of Mexican timberlines also include many species found only in this southern region. The Mexican timberline flora contrasts strongly with that of the Southern Rockies and southern California mountains. It also differs greatly from timberlines farther south, in the Andes of northern South America, where needle-leaf conifers are scarce and tree ferns, giant groundsels, and other forms of tall tropical plants dominate.

Despite their location four degrees south of the tropic of Cancer, the vegetation zones at high altitudes on the central Mexican meseta are not strictly tropical. Instead, the vegetation is augmented considerably by species from, or related to those of, the North American temperate zone. The climate of this area has been described as "rim tropical" because it lies at the edge of the tropics where temperate-zone air masses have a notable influence (Lauer 1973).

The vegetation zones in central Mexico illustrate the interplay between the north temperate and tropical climates. Along the coastal lowlands near Veracruz (19°N) on Mexico's eastern coast lies the *tierra caliente,* or "hot land," which is covered with evergreen rain forests and deciduous forests made up of tropical species (Lauer 1973). Above about 2600 feet lies the *tierra templada,* or "temperate land," which is covered with mountain forests containing both tropical and northern temperate species. The latter include several oaks, sweetgum (*Liquidambar*

Iztaccihuatl (17,343 feet) from Popocatepetl

styraciflua), beech, alder, hickory, basswood (*Tilia*), ash, and others. A few Mexican-Central American pines appear on dry sites.

Climbing west toward the central plateau, one encounters the *tierra fria,* or "cold land," lying between 6000 and 10,500 feet, where occasional frosts and light snowfalls occur during the winter. Along the coastal slope above Veracruz, this elevation zone supports a cloud forest where maritime winds cause thick fog banks to form. These cool, superhumid forests are made up of tropical mountain trees, including some from the Southern Hemisphere (*Podocarpus* and *Weinmannia*), some Mexican pines, evergreen oaks, and the true fir *Abies religiosa.*

Inland on the central plateau, the *tierra fria* supports semi-arid vegetation types comparable to the montane zone in southern Arizona and New Mexico (Lauer 1973). This vegetation ranges from plateau grasslands to woodlands of deciduous oaks, juniper, pinyon pine, and yucca to pine forest. With the help of irrigation, most of the arable land in the central plateau has been put into crop and hay production. Northern elements in the *tierra fria* include alligator juniper (*Juniperus deppeana*), Mexican pinyon (*Pinus cembroides*), and Chihuahua pine (*Pinus leiophylla*), which have closely related counterparts in the southwestern United States. Tropical species reach their upper limits in the *tierra fria* and do not extend into the subalpine forest belt, which is above 10,500 feet.

Mexican mountain pine at 13,000 feet on Popocatepetl

The major portion of the subalpine forest belt (about 11,000 to 13,100 feet) is composed entirely of Mexican mountain pine (*P. hartwegii*). This species is one of many Mexican yellow pines, which are somewhat similar to the ponderosa and Jeffrey pines of the western United States. Mexican mountain pine grows in open stands of erect, symmetrical trees with an undergrowth of coarse bunchgrasses (*Festuca tolucensis, Calamagrostis tolucensis,* and *Muhlenbergia tridentata*) (Lauer 1978). Above forest line these species form tussock grasslands called *Zacationales* that extend upslope into the loose volcanic rock rubble to become the patchy alpine vegetation belt, reaching to about 15,750 feet. Above this level, attained only on Mexico's three highest volcanoes, lies a zone of persistent firn snow, small glaciers, and largely barren rock. (The highest peaks are 17,883-foot Popocatépetl and 17,343-foot Iztaccihuatl, 40 miles southeast of Mexico City, and 18,700-foot Pico de Orizaba, 90 miles farther east.)

Forest line averages about 13,100 feet and tree line, representing the highest individuals of mountain pine, occurs at nearly 13,800 feet (Lauer 1978). Popocatépetl (which means smoking mountain in the local Indian language) erupted most recently in 1920-21, and ash and lava flows associated with volcanic activity seem to be responsible for depressing the level of timberline nearly 400 feet in elevation compared to that found on nearby, inactive Iztaccihuatl (Beaman 1962). The latter is an elongated mountain whose snowy profile suggests a sleeping, white-blanketed woman—hence the Indian name Iztaccihuatl, meaning white woman.

The summits of these two mountains and that of Pico de Orizaba project more than 10,000 feet above the surrounding highland valleys. A road from the village of Amecameca near Mexico City leads to the Paso de Cortes (12,070 feet) in the mountain pine forest, which is the low point in the saddle between Popocatépetl and Iztaccihuatl.

Upper timberlines on Iztaccihuatl and the inactive volcano Pico de Orizaba are characterized by mountain pine thinning out to form individual small trees, but there is no appreciable development of krummholz (Beaman 1962). In some areas a dwarf juniper (*J. monticola*) forms dense, low patches of scrub on rocky slopes above tree line. At tree line (13,776 feet) on Pico de Orizaba the annual temperature averages about 41°F (Lauer 1978). This is much warmer than the alpine timberlines in the temperate or boreal latitudes and results from the lack of a well-developed winter season. The coldest month (January) has a mean temperature of about 37°F—about the same as Richmond, Virginia, or Seattle, Washington. The warmest month at tree line, however, has a mean temperature of only 44°F, which is well below the 50°F warmest-month value for temperate and boreal zone tree lines of the Northern Hemisphere.

The Mexican mountain pine has become adapted to a much longer but cooler growing season than its northern relatives (Lauer 1978). At timberline spring growth of the mountain pine begins in early April and evidently continues through September. During this summer half of the year, frost is light and occurs on 35 to 40 percent of the days, for a few hours at a time. During the winter half of the year (October-March), frost occurs on 70 to 75 percent of the days and is more severe. Mexican mountain pine has

Highest village (10,000 feet) on Pico de Orizaba

a winter dormancy period, and its spring growth activity is evidently triggered by decreasing persistence of frost. This response differs from that of most northern trees, whose growth activity is related to increasing day-length or photoperiod. In the latitude of central Mexico, day-length changes are small.

By late morning each day, cloud banks develop around the high peaks, and this retards summer heating at the Mexican timberlines. Solar heating causes crackling thunderstorms on most summer days, with high winds and hail or cold, driving rain. Thus, the summer growing season at timberline is a time of adequate moisture. Conversely, the winter half of the year is relatively dry and sunny, and the above-freezing average temperatures prevent the accumulation of any significant snowpack, although snow from individual storms may linger for a few days. As an apparent result of the lack of snowpack there is little protection from winter drought and, therefore, scarcely any Mexican mountain pine develops into krummholz.

Dry lightning storms sometimes start fires in the mountain pine forests and timberline communities, especially in early summer (Lauer 1978), and these sweep through the tussock grassland killing many of the pine seedlings and saplings. However, such fires are infrequent and light enough to have little overall effect on the mountain pine-tufted grass vegetation.

Fires deliberately set by man have different effects. Their purpose is to improve mountain pastures and they are set annually during late winter when the grass, pine-needle litter, and the weather are dry. These fires are lit in the lower part of the subalpine forest and often crown out as they sweep upslope fanned by gusty winds. (Natural fires generally originate near the upper timberline and have a hard time spreading downslope against the winds.)

Fires, especially those set by herders, have the potential to depress timberline. An additional reason for the dearth of pine krummholz may be that such low growth forms are highly susceptible even to light natural fires. On favorably located sites with stony soils and little surface fuel, individual mountain pine trees grow as high up as 13,940 feet. Perhaps this represents the potential tree line without fire (Lauer 1978).

The mountain pines at these timberlines are comparatively fast-growing, short-lived trees (Beaman 1962). In a small sample taken on Iztaccihuatl and Popocatépetl, the oldest tree had only 66 annual rings at 4½ feet above the ground. Large trees of mountain pine at forest line are typically 20 inches in diameter and 50 feet tall. Mountain pines near the summit of Cerro Potosi in northeastern Mexico were found to be slower growing and older but still only somewhat over 100 years old (Beaman and Andresen 1966). The young age of mountain pines thus far investigated contrasts with the frequently ancient trees at alpine timberlines in the western United States. The comparative youth of the Mexican mountain pines also confounds interpretation of the causes of timberline formation and possible fluctuations in its position. The comparatively vigorous tree growth might suggest that regeneration difficulties limit the ascent of forest.

The scattered, small pine and bunchgrass growth at tree line seems to reflect a dry, cold environment and, in fact, the tree lines receive only about 31 to 35 inches of precipitation each year (Lauer 1978). The potential position of the mountain pine tree line may be limited by dry or chilled soils in the early part of the growing season. Cold temperatures in the surface soil during early morning would retard the uptake of moisture by roots of tree seedlings. This "physiological drought" would in turn limit photosynthesis (carbon assimilation) and growth during the high-radiation period of the day, before the cloud cap forms.

The following observations of regeneration at tree line on Pico de Orizaba seem consistent with the above hypothesis of a dry-cold limiting factor. Above tree line lies a narrow strip in which young mountain pines grow as small cushions among the tussock grasses (Lauer 1978). Shoots that grow beyond the wind shelter of the tufted grass continually die, while branchlets and buds close to the ground survive and continue to develop laterally. Only after a series of favorable growing seasons, or perhaps after an extensive root system has formed, can these saplings succeed in growing erect, out of the grass-shelter. The well-developed root system would reduce the danger of moisture deficiency. Moisture stress is intensified by strong solar heating of the foliage in late winter and early summer, at a time when moisture must be supplied through chilled surface roots. The phenomenon hypothesized here is comparable to that of alpine larch at tree line in Alberta, except that in Mexico, grass tussocks instead of snowpack create the sheltering micro-environment necessary for tree establishment.

Although the central Mexican volcanoes experience a tropical pattern of rainy weather in the summer, the winter weather differs from that of high mountains deep within the tropics. True tropical mountains have no cold season—only wet and dry seasons. In central Mexico, however, at the rim of the tropics, winter brings occasional influxes of cold air from the North American temperate zone. These invasions, called *nortes,* dump snow, sleet, and hail on the mountain pine forests. Also, temperatures often drop 9°F or more in a few hours with the passage of the cold front.

The boreal aspect of the Mexican mountain climate is clearly reflected in the high-mountain vegetation. Southward, in the inner tropics of northern South America, there are no temperate or boreal mountain trees, and timberline is formed at a modest elevation. Above these tropical timberlines lies a zone (called the Páramo and the Puna) without tree growth that in Mexico is replaced by boreal trees and grasses (Lauer 1973).

The lack of a consistent relationship between latitude and the elevation of timberlines in the tropics and subtropics contrasts with the linear relationship at latitudes above 30 degrees in both hemispheres (Daubenmire 1954). In fact, the altitude of timberline tends to dip slightly near the equator. This may result from a lack of cold-hardy species as well as the absence of a warmer-than-average season of the year to facilitate growth.

Outside of the central plateau—and excluding the few tropical alpine peaks near and across the Guatemala border—only one or two mountains in northern Mexico rise high enough to produce a small area of upper timberline. The best-known of these areas is Cerro Potosi, which is perhaps the highest peak in the northern Sierra Madre Oriental, about 50 miles south of Monterrey or 175 miles south of Laredo, Texas. The elevation of Cerro Potosi's summit is not known with certainty but appears to be somewhat over 12,000 feet (Rand McNally Atlas 1977). Pena Nevada is a similarly tall peak about 90 miles farther south in the Sierra Madre Oriental, but its summit is a bare rock dome. Beneath the dome lies a forest of the northern Mexican mountain pine, *Pinus rudis* (Beaman and Andresen 1966; D. K. Bailey, personal communication).

Unlike the high mountains of Mexico's central plateau, Cerro Potosi is not volcanic; its summit block is made up of limestone and calcareous shale. This vastly different geology and Cerro Potosi's isolated location (400 miles north of the alpine areas of central Mexico and 850 miles south of those in northern New Mexico) may account for the very distinctive, tundralike vegetation it supports. This community, covering about 40 acres, is a diverse assemblage of low-growing perennial herbs, including the genera *Potentilla, Arenaria, Astragalus, Thlaspi, Draba, Senecio, Phacelia, Castilleja,* and *Lupinus,* which are very common in the Rocky Mountain alpine tundra. Many of the individual species found on Cerro Potosi are endemics, however (Beaman and Andresen 1966). The tussock grasses of the central Mexican volcanoes are absent from this mountain, although a colony of scrubby dwarf juniper, like that on the volcanoes, was identified here.

In addition to the mountain pine forest, there is a dense stand of a dwarf pinyon pine called Potosi pinyon (*Pinus culminicola*). This species is the only high-elevation pinyon and is known only from Cerro Potosi and a few other peaks to the northwest (Riskind and Patterson 1975). The dense, almost-impenetrable pinyon scrub community nearly encircles the tundralike patch on the summit (Beaman and Andresen 1966). The scrub averages only 2 to 3 feet in height on the summit but becomes denser and taller several hundred feet below, growing about 15 feet tall near the edge of the Mexican mountain pine forest but never losing its bushy form. The transition from Potosi pinyon scrub to mountain pine forest occurs at roughly 11,500 feet. Below this level, Potosi pinyon becomes smaller and less common until it disappears near the 10,000-foot elevation. The shrubby growth habit of Potosi pinyon appears to be genetically controlled because this form is retained even in well-protected situations within the mountain pine forest (Beaman and Andresen 1966). Dwarf pine species are found at alpine timberlines in Europe (Swiss mountain pine, *P. mugo*) and Asia (Japanese stone pine, *P. pumila*) but evidently not anywhere in North America except Cerro Potosi and nearby peaks.

The tiny tundralike community atop Cerro Potosi is probably a result of extreme wind exposure on the rounded summit coupled with the excessively drained limestone soils (Beaman and Andresen 1966). Downslope subsurface drainage seems to deplete water at the summit and add it to the moisture budget on the slopes below, a common drainage pattern on limestone mountains. The climate at the top of Cerro Potosi is evidently similar to that on the central Mexican volcanoes, except that at this latitude (25°N) there is more contrast in temperatures between summer and winter. Still, summer is cool, moist, and cloudy, while winter is colder and dry.

The well-developed subalpine forest is entirely dominated by the northern Mexican mountain pine, but southwestern white pine (*P. strobiformis*), a Mexican fir (*Abies vejari*), and inland Douglas-fir (*Pseudotsuga menziesii* var. *glauca*) are present at lower elevations. In this area Douglas-fir is near its southern distributional limits, but it dominates the mountain canyons between about 7000 and 10,000 feet. On nearby Sierra de la Marta (11,000+ feet), a southern population of Engelmann spruce is present and growing with Potosi pinyon along the ridge crest (Riskind and Patterson 1975).

From the village of Diez y Ocho de Marzo, a road leads up the east side of Cerro Potosi past a microwave radio relay station to the summit. Evidently there has been much disturbance to this unique timberline in recent years.

11
Timberlines Worldwide

Although North American timberlines encompass great differences in species composition and environmental settings, timberlines throughout the world are still much more diverse! Because of this complexity, only a brief summary of the world's cold timberlines is made here for comparison with North America.

Cold timberlines can be found on mountains and polar lowlands on all continents except Antarctica (where no trees or shrubs exist), and they also occur on some oceanic islands. The outstanding differences among the world's cold timberlines are related to contrasting climates and regional vegetation coupled with geographic isolation of landmasses and high mountain areas. Contrasting geological substrates are also important.

North America's cold timberlines are (or *were* during some of the Pleistocene climates) more-or-less continuous along the high cordillera, or western mountain systems, that extends from the Arctic to Mexico. Appalachian timberlines were similarly connected to the North American Arctic. Except for a tropical influence in Mexico, North American cold timberlines are located in the temperate and boreal latitudes.

Outside of the Western Hemisphere, however, major mountain ranges often have an east-west-trending axis (for example, the Alps and Himalaya) and mountain areas are discontinuous between the polar and tropical latitudes. Some cold timberline areas, such as those in southern and eastern Africa, New Zealand, Australia, and tropical islands, are isolated by more than 2000 miles from any of the world's major mountain systems. Discontinuous high-mountain areas are scattered across the tropical latitudes, where few northern, cold-region plants exist. As a result, diverse tropical tree species form cold timberlines that are not comparable to those of the northern temperate zone.

Even if tropical timberlines were closely connected to those of the northern temperate zone, it is questionable whether they would be populated by northern trees: there is no truly warm or frost-free "growing season" on high mountains of the inner tropics. Thus, unique and unfamiliar (to northerners) kinds of tall plants form timberline in the tropics.

Most of the area in the temperate latitudes, and nearly all of it in higher latitudes, of the Southern Hemisphere is covered by ocean. As a result, there are only a few fragments of antarctic timberline on small islands, and the southern temperate zone timberlines are extensive only in southern South America and New Zealand. These very oceanic southern timberlines have vegetation more similar to that of the tropical highlands than to timberlines in the Northern Hemisphere (Troll 1973).

Still another factor distinguishing cold timberlines in North America from those in the rest of the world is the effect of human impact. In North America human activities have not appreciably altered vegetation at most of the cold timberline areas; whereas in most other continents heavy grazing and extensive tree felling (for fuel or to expand mountain pastures) have taken place for centuries. The result of this exploitation is often so widespread that it is difficult to deduce what climatic timberlines would have been like in terms of vegetation and elevational limits.

A small mountain of scientific literature in several languages deals with timberlines in various parts of the world. The following is a brief glimpse of cold timberlines in different regions. Readers interested in a more-detailed discussion of worldwide vegetation as a whole can find it in *Vegetation of the Earth, and Ecological Systems of the Geo-Biosphere,* an English-language paperback edition by the German ecologist Heinrich Walter (1979).

Arctic Timberline in Eurasia

The arctic timberline forms a wavy band, often 100 miles wide, stretching almost 6000 miles across northern Norway, Finland, European Russia, and Siberia. The forest-tundra belt in the Soviet Union alone is estimated to cover nearly 200,000 square miles, an area considerably larger than California (Tseplyaev 1961). The western portion of this band, in Fennoscandia, is primarily a strip of white birch woodland (*Betula pubescens* var. *tortuosa*) adjoining the tundra on the northern coast lowlands at 69 or 70°N. Only slightly southward, Scotch (Scots) pine (*Pinus sylvestris*) reaches its arctic limits (Hustich 1966). This species is distributed throughout the mountains and boreal regions of Europe and much of Asia. Like white birch, it regenerates readily following fires, and in the far north the mature pines often survive repeated surface fires. In northern Sweden numerous craggy old Scotch pines that date from the Viking era (over 700 years ago) bear pitch-filled scars from several ancient fires (Zackrisson 1977). The only other conifer at arctic timberline in Fennoscandia is the European spruce (*Picea abies*), whose northern limits are formed south of Scotch pine, perhaps due in part to its greater susceptibility to fire. Also, spruce is a climax species less vigorous in re-establishing itself on the severely exposed burned sites than white birch, European aspen (*Populus tremula*), and Scotch pine. Stands at the arctic tree line in Fennoscandia have been cut for centuries for fuel and have been effected by reindeer grazing.

East of Finland the climate at arctic timberline becomes increasingly continental, with severe winter temperatures and with permafrost underlying the surface soils. In response to these conditions, white birch and Scotch pine give way to Siberian spruce (*Picea obovata*) at the northern tree line eastward across European Russia. East of the Ural Mountains, in

Siberia, the climate becomes extremely continental, with the harshest winters outside of Antarctica. Siberian larch (*Larix sibirica*) becomes the dominant species at timberline in northwestern Siberia, and Dahurian larch (*L. dahurica*) forms extensive pure forests beyond the limits of other trees in central and eastern Siberia. The shady spruce, pine, and fir forests in European Russia and western Siberia are known as the "dark taiga," while the open, parklike larch forests of northern and eastern Siberia are called the "light taiga." The pure larch forests cover about 1.75 million square miles, an area half the size of the 50 United States (Küchler 1960, Tseplyaev 1961)! Dahurian larch forests extend almost 1000 miles northeastward in Siberia beyond the limit of other erect conifers. Japanese stone pine (*Pinus pumila*) is a dwarf species that often forms an understory beneath the larch.

Northeastern Siberia is evidently the only region in the Northern Hemisphere where evergreen conifers do not form timberline nearly coincident with the mapped line, or isotherm, where the July mean temperature equals 50°F (10°C). Lack of sufficient warmth in the growing season is the general factor in establishing alpine and arctic timberlines. However, in northeastern Siberia it is apparently the extremely long, frigid, and arid winters coupled with continuous permafrost near the earth's surface that prevent growth of erect evergreens despite a favorable growing season.

An example of the extreme continental timberline climate of northeastern Siberia is represented by weather data from Verkhoyansk (68°N, 134°E) on the Yana River. This location has mean monthly temperatures of −58°F for January, 4°F for April, and 56°F for July; the record low is −90°F (Critchfield 1966). Annual precipitation is a scant 5¼ inches and most of this falls in the summer as rain. The ground is underlain by continuous permafrost, but Dahurian larch has developed a shallow root system utilizing only the surface foot or two of muskeg soil that thaws in summer (Eyre 1963). Despite the limited precipitation, soil drought is not a widespread problem because the shallow permafrost releases water slowly as it thaws.

Dahurian larch grows northward to 72½°N on the Taimyr Peninsula of central Siberia (Tseplyaev 1961); this is 80 miles farther north than Point Barrow, the northern tip of Alaska. Both Dahurian and Siberian larch grow in diverse habitats where either severe climate or rocky or boggy sites prevent more shade-tolerant spruce, fir, or pine trees from out-competing them. S. P. Suslov (1961) explains that because Dahurian larch

> ...can form auxiliary roots on any part of the trunk above the root neck, it can grow on sphagnum bogs without being choked by the rapid growth of moss cover. In these bogs the larch may reach an age of 300 years, whereas under similar conditions the pine [*P. sibirica*] usually dies before it is 50 years old.

This larch forms krummholz communities near the cold, foggy coastal districts of far-eastern Siberia where no other conifers except the dwarf

Japanese stone pine and common juniper can survive.

Undergrowth throughout Eurasian arctic timberlines is similar in many respects to that of timberlines in Alaska and Canada, with bog blueberry (*Vaccinium uliginosum*), mountain-cranberry (*V. vitis-idaea*), alpine bearberry (*Arctostaphylos alpina*), and Labrador-tea (*Ledum palustre*) among the principal species forming a luxuriant carpet of heath (Walter 1979). In the driest forest communities lichens make up the principal groundcover.

Northern Mountain Timberlines

In the mountains of Scandinavia, the northern Urals, and the ranges of eastern Siberia, alpine timberlines are formed at low elevations and are similar to the arctic timberlines. Thus, in central Norway and Sweden the white birch woodland is found between about 3500 and 4000 feet. Below this lies the Scotch pine-European spruce timberline.

In the British Isles and on Iceland extensive clearing, heavy grazing, and burning of the heath (which has taken over ancient forest land as a result of disturbance) for over a thousand years has resulted in the loss of any semblance of a natural timberline (Wardle 1974). In the Cairngorm Mountains of Scotland the natural limit of Scotch pine lies between about 2000 and 2300 feet, but it has generally been lowered by human activities to about 1650 feet.

Remnant of subalpine forest in Scotland

Timberlines in the European Alps are quite varied and interesting, but they have been lowered substantially through centuries of pasturing and tree felling. In a north-to-south cross-section through the Swiss Alps, tree line rises from an elevation of about 5250 feet on the northern border to 7500 feet in the central area of the mountain mass (where the climate is most continental), and it descends to about 6500 feet in the southern area (Troll 1973).

Trees making up timberlines change considerably along such a transection. In the north, and eastward in continental areas of central Europe, European spruce dominates at upper timberline, along with the scrub species Swiss mountain pine (*Pinus mugo*). In the central Alps the spruce forest belt is superseded by a European larch (*Larix decidua*)-stone pine (*Pinus cembra*) timberline. These latter communities and their physical environment are reminiscent of alpine larch-whitebark pine timberlines in the North Cascades and Northern Rocky Mountains.

The spruce belt is absent in the maritime Alps of western and southern Europe, and a prominent member of the hardwood forest, European beech (*Fagus silvatica*), marks the upper timberline (Troll 1973, Walter 1979). Beech is often accompanied by white fir (*Abies alba*); both are trees of the temperate mountain forests. These beech timberlines can be seen in the Appennines Mountains of northern Italy, the Auvergne of southern France, and the western Pyrenees on the Franco-Spanish border. These non-boreal communities are the northern representation of a Mediterranean mountain flora.

In more southerly mountain ranges bordering the Mediterranean Sea, upper timberlines are dominated by an assortment of trees characteristic of this subtropical region (Troll 1973). For instance: in the Sierra Nevada and other mountains of southern Spain, a deciduous oak (*Quercus tozza*) forms the upper timberline at about 6500 feet; on Mount Olympus in Greece (at 7200 to 8200 feet) and in the mountains of Albania and southern Yugoslavia it is Bosnian pine (*Pinus heldreichii*); and in the western part of the Great Atlas of Morocco timberline is formed by evergreen holly oak (*Quercus ilex*) at 9200 to 9500 feet.

The climate becomes markedly continental and drier eastward in the Great Atlas and in other ranges south and east of the Mediterranean, including mountains of the Biblical Holy Land and ranges eastward as far as Afghanistan. In these semi-desert ranges the oceanic Mediterranean species are confined to northern slopes and moist cove sites. Here true cedars (*Cedrus*) — including the cedar of Lebanon (*C. libani*) — sometimes with mountain pines and firs, form the humid high-elevation forest. However, these moist forests are replaced at about 10,000 feet by a dry timberline woodland of treelike junipers. For instance, Spanish juniper (*Juniperus thurifera*) makes up timberline in the continental portions of the Great Atlas Range at 10,000 to 10,500 feet, and it develops a giant, although short form with a trunk 12 or occasionally even 16 feet in diameter (Troll 1973)! At these juniper tree lines, winter snow is sparse, so there is no krummholz belt. The plant communities above timberline represent a frigid desert and consist of widely spaced, low-growing, thorny

Mugo pine in Poland's Tatra Mountains, part of the Carpathian Range, south of the city of Krakow

cushion shrubs. This austere vegetation covers the loftiest peaks, above a juniper timberline, from the southern Mediterranean region to Afghanistan and the Pamirs of Russia.

Southward, in Africa, about 750 miles from the Mediterranean, two mountain ranges jut up in the center of the enormous Sahara Desert. These are the Ahaggar (23°N) and Tibesti (20°N) massifs, and they support an extremely drought-restricted forest. The upper timberlines are not formed where cold temperatures are the limiting factor; instead they are primarily related to a lack of moisture on the higher ridges (Messerli 1973). An arid-zone woodland of thorny acacias reaches about 7500 feet on these mountains, accompanied on moist sites by fig trees and palms. All these trees are frost-sensitive tropical species.

Mediterranean tree species are confined to small relict populations on these Sahara massifs (Messerli 1973). The endemic olive tree (*Olea laperrini*) grows scattered across the top of the Ahaggar, whose maximum elevation is 9850 feet. A tropical tree-heath (*Erica arborea*) ascends to 9500 feet in the Tibesti, whose highest summit is 11,204 feet. Snowfall happens only once in several years on top of these mountains, and summer rainfall is scant. Extreme radiation intensity and persistent arid winds cause severe evaporation despite the moderately low temperatures. These climatic features prevent development of the Mediterranean-Middle East forest or subalpine woodland species.

Another striking desert situation that pre-empts formation of upper timberlines and alpine communities occurs eastward, in Tibet, between 28 and 36°N. The high desert plateau (12,000 to 16,000 feet) immediately north of the Himalayas covers an area about the size of Alaska. Yet annual precipitation seldom exceeds four inches and there is no continuous snow cover. The small quantities of snow evaporate in the strong radiation and dry wind (Walter 1979). Although mean temperatures for July are well above 50°F in many areas, there are few nights without frost, and in the shade (of which there is very little), the daily temperature range can be as much as 67°F. A desert flora remains dominant as high as the upper limits of vegetation because even alpine steppe vegetation cannot survive. The few trees found on the Tibetan Plateau are mostly cultivated and watered (Swan 1967).

West and north of the gigantic Tibetan and Mongolian desert plateaus lie several major mountain ranges, forested primarily with boreal species. In western Mongolia the Altai Mountains have forests consisting mostly of Siberian larch (Suslov 1961). Larch often forms upper timberline near 6600 feet alone or with Siberian stone pine (*Pinus sibirica*), which is closely related to Swiss stone pine and whitebark pine. Siberian larch also constitutes the lower timberline, descending into the dry mountain steppes along the stream courses.

Southwest of the Altai Mountains lies the Tien Shan Range, east of the Soviet city of Tashkent. The Tien Shan and the Pamirs, immediately to the south, are awesome massifs that include numerous 20,000-foot peaks. They have a dry continental climate. The Tien Shan Range supports a subalpine forest of the central Asian spruce (*Picea schrenkiana*) that forms tree line at about 10,000 feet (Zimina 1973). A belt of subalpine shrubbery called "archa" is common in much of the northern and eastern Tien Shan and the landscape harbors a complex of meadows, dry grass-lands, archa, and groves of spruce. (Archa is made up of a bushy juniper, willow, honeysuckle, and the pea-shrub *Caragana*). The drier, southern Tien Shan Range and much of the Pamirs have a complete absence of trees and tall shrubs. Conversely, richer archa and subalpine forest belts occur westward in the Caucasus and Carpathian mountains of southern Russia and Romania.

The Himalayan chain forms a gargantuan barrier separating the lofty Tibetan Plateau from the tropical rain forests of India and Nepal. The southernmost of the multiple Himalayan ranges have luxuriant forest vegetation developed under the influence of tropical monsoon air masses that sweep northward from the Indian Ocean. Thus, in the Punjab area of the western Himalayas the humid forest zone reaches from about 2000 feet to over 11,000 feet; whereas, in heading north across the Himalayan ranges, a traveler will find that the humid forest shrinks, finally being reduced to a narrow subalpine belt at about 13,000 feet on the Karakoram Range (Troll 1973).

In the especially humid eastern Himalayas on the slopes north of Darjeeling, India, tropical rain and cloud forests dominate to about 6500 feet (Walter 1979). Above this level tree-rhododendrons and tall, reedlike plants (*Arundinaria*) dominate in a dense woodland, which is replaced at still higher elevations by conifers — including Himalayan fir (*Abies spectabilis*), juniper, and hemlock. This fir forest belt at 10,000 to 12,800 feet is then superseded upslope by a subalpine woodland of handsome evergreen rhododendrons, which gradually diminish in size in the alpine belt.

Northward, in the drier ranges along the Tibetan border, the humid conifer forests are confined to shadowy northern slopes; the southern slopes have mountain grasslands with juniper trees, while tree line on both slopes is at about 15,100 feet (Walter 1979). These marked ecological contrasts are probably related to the extreme intensities of solar radiation experienced in summer at such high altitudes. In contrast, shady slopes receive very little diffuse or indirect radiation at such altitudes; thus, the shadows (shady slopes) are especially dark.

Westward in the drier regions of the Himalayas, birch (*Betula utilis*) forms a tree-line woodland at 12,500 to 13,000 feet, above a boreal conifer forest of European spruce, west-Himalayan spruce (*Picea smithiana*), and Himalayan fir. This is comparable to the tree-line birchwoods of Scandinavia. Eastward, as the Himalayas come under increasing influence from tropical monsoon moisture, the birch zone is replaced by a dense rhododendron woodland.

The eastern Himalayas have spruce and fir forest, with tree rhododendrons above; however, two species of larch locally become the highest ascending conifers in this remote region. The forest, composed of *Larix potanini,* spruce, and fir, reaches its upper limits at 15,000 feet in the Konkaling Mountains (28½°N, 100°E) of southwestern China, giving way to 25- to 30-foot rhododendrons that form tree limit at 15,500 feet (Rock 1931). C. H. Ostenfeld and C. Larsen (1930) describe the Sikkim larch (*Larix griffithii*) as being

> ...indigenous to the highest tree-clad regions of the eastern Himalayas in the neighbourhood of the forest line, and only in the heart of vallies leading from north and south to the mighty peaks, the final and only mantle of which is the eternal snow. [Sir Joseph] Hooker found it growing over ancient moraines at a height of 3600 m. [12,000 feet] above sea-level, where it attained its best development.

The two Himalayan larches are the southernmost representatives of that boreal genus, reaching 27°N. Moreover, the southeastern Himalayas, including the mountains of southwestern China, mark the southern limits of most Eurasian boreal species. The mountains of southeastern Asia are too low to support the northern boreal vegetation, and the nearest high peak (at 6°N on Borneo) is engulfed in tropical vegetation.

Along the Pacific Coast of Asia an oceanic climate prevails and results in moist mountain forests comparable to those in the eastern Himalayas and the Appalachians and Cascade Mountains of North America (Franklin and others 1979). Mountains on the island of Taiwan support the southern extension of this rich temperate-zone conifer forest. The highest Taiwan peaks are clothed with stands of fir, spruce, hemlock, and pine, often with understories of dwarf bamboo (*Pleioblastus*). The dense forests are replaced above 10,000 feet by a dense scrub of juniper, rhododendron, and mahonia (*Berberis*), which ascends to the summits, maximum elevation being 13,113 feet (Wardle 1974).

To the northeast, on the mountains of central and northern Japan, timberlines are well developed and remarkably rich and varied. A monsoon climate pervades the Japanese mountains during much of the summer but is replaced in winter by frigid northwesterly winds that dump large quantities of snow on slopes facing the Sea of Japan. This weather pattern produces snow-deluged timberlines on the westernmost mountains and a drier, rain-shadow zone on the mountains facing the Pacific. Peter Wardle (1977) has described two contrasting patterns of subalpine vegetation in these mountains, one on old igneous and metamorphic rock, the other occupying recently active volcanoes.

On the older geologic types, the well-established subalpine forest consists of fir, spruce, and birch, generally superseded by a belt of the dwarf species Japanese stone pine (Wardle 1977). On the snowy western side of Honshu's Northern Alps, fir (*Abies mariesii*) becomes stunted and badly deformed at the 6500-foot level, evidently as a result of excessive snowpack that lingers well into summer. The average maximum snow depth at tree line is about 13 feet (Yoshino 1978). Dwarf pine, alder, rhododendron, mountain-ash (*Sorbus*), other broadleaved shrubs, birch groves, and dwarf bamboo (*Sasa* and *Sasamorpha*) all occur intermixed with herbaceous meadows above the conifer tree line.

A few miles farther inland (eastward), snowfall is no longer extreme. Here, fir ascends higher and exhibits flags and other symptoms of wind deformation (Wardle 1977). On the more inland peaks in Japan's Northern Alps the conifer tree line reaches about 7900 feet. Spruce, hemlock, and two species of fir attain this level, along with the more abundant tree birch (*Betula ermani*). On the northern island, Hokkaido, comparable timberlines develop about 2000 feet lower, in response to the colder overall climate.

On Mount Fuji and Honshu's other volcanic highlands, Japanese larch (*Larix leptolepis*) becomes a prominent species at tree line, along with fir (*Abies mariesii*) and alder shrubs. Most of the ground between the trees is bare or lichen-covered volcanic rubble (Wardle 1977). Japanese larch is a pioneer species that is confined to a small area of Japan's subalpine zone and extends in stunted forms to above 9000 feet.

Overall, the Japanese subalpine and timberline zones are extraordinarily rich. With their complement of moist-site conifers, birch, mountain-ash, and rhododendron, they resemble, but are richer floristically than, the Appalachian mountain forests (Franklin and others 1979). Wavelike patterns of mortality and regeneration in high-elevation fir (*Abies*) forests are another feature shared by the Japanese and Appalachian mountains. The subalpine growth of rhododendrons mixed with other broadleaved shrubs and dense stands of dwarf bamboo are reminiscent of the eastern Himalayas, while the prevalent mountain heaths (*Vaccinium vitis-idaea, V. uliginosum,* and *Empetrum nigrum*) are clearly arctic-alpine species (Wardle 1977).

Tropical Timberlines

The fundamental difference between cold timberlines on mountains in the humid equatorial regions compared with those in the temperate latitudes is that the tropics lack cold and warm seasons. Instead, their cold altitudinal belts are controlled by the year-round presence of nightly frost or near-freezing temperatures. There may be a rainy season that brings a thin covering of snow, but only high above timberline (Troll 1973). Tropical timberlines are usually formed by a dense evergreen forest consisting of numerous species of broadleaved trees. Their crowns are very often dome shaped, and they are described as "spherical umbrella trees." This growth form is found in dozens of different families. Trunks and branches within this "cloud forest" formation are draped with mosses, beard-lichens, ferns, orchids, and other plants — a result of the regular daytime cloudiness and mist.

Single species of more frost-hardy trees often form a fringe of woodland above the cloud forest; but determining the position of tree line is often complicated by the presence of "megaphytes" above the highest woodlands (Troll 1973). These are tall and old woody plants, each with a stout unbranched stem and thick overlapping woolly leaves on top. The great leaf clusters close around the growing tips at night, protecting the developing leaves from severe frost, and the thick pith may provide a store of water when uptake from the chilled soil is difficult (Wardle 1974). The large, stiff leaves seem to warm to well above air temperature in sunshine. The "tree" yuccas, such as the Joshua-tree, of the American Southwest are visually similar to the tropical megaphytes.

On Mount Kenya and Mount Kilimanjaro in equatorial East Africa, tropical mountain forests composed of broadleaved evergreens are replaced upslope by a woodland of distinctive tree heaths (*Erica arborea* and *Philippia* spp.) that have no equivalent elsewhere in the world (Hora 1981). The tree heath timberline reaches as high as 13,450 feet on the southeastern slope of Kilimanjaro (Plesnik 1980). This is superseded upslope by an "Afro-alpine" vegetation zone dominated by megaphytes called giant groundsels (*Senecio* and *Dendrosenecio*) (Coe 1967). One of these groundsels (*Senecio keniodendron*) reaches a maximum height of 20 feet and grows among the tussock grasses at elevations as high as 14,800 feet. Erect groundsels of smaller stature extend to 15,700 feet on one of Kilimanjaro's peaks (Salt 1954).

The island of New Guinea, at about 5°S, is capped with a rugged backbone containing several peaks between 13,000 and 16,500 feet. Even the uppermost forest on Mount Wilhelm is floristically rich. Peter Wardle (1974) listed 13 species of trees and tall shrubs at tree line (13,100 feet), including the Southern Hemisphere conifer genus *Podocarpus* (yellow woods), along with rhododendron, huckleberry (*Vaccinium*), and tree ferns (*Cyathea*).

A few oceanic subtropical islands (the Azores, Canary Islands, and Hawaii) are high enough to support cold timberlines, but the elevations of these ecotones are comparatively low for their latitudes (Wardle 1974). One reason for this is the extreme maritime climate; another is that hardier species, capable of ascending to higher elevations, may have failed to reach such isolated high-mountain sites, most of which are recent volcanoes. For example, tree limit on the Hawaiian volcano Mauna Kea (13,796 feet) is formed at 10,000 feet by a tropical broadleaf, "mamani" or pagoda tree (*Sophora chrysophylla*). This genus is distributed throughout much of the Pacific, and since its pods can float on sea water and retain viable seed for up to three years, it was probably dispersed by the ocean currents (Hora 1981).

A striking example of comparatively low cold timberlines has been reported on the mountains near Rio de Janeiro, Brazil, at 22°S (Clausen 1963). Tree line occurs near 6400 feet, which coincides with the level where an occasional light frost occurs in winter. Evidently no cold-tolerant tree species are present in this area.

The Andes of western South America form a wall of high mountains stretching 5000 miles, from 10°N to 55°S. This broad, rugged, and lofty mountain chain supports the world's most extensive tropical and southern temperate zone timberlines. Only in the Andes does a continuous chain of timberline environments extend from the tropics through the southern temperate zone, barely reaching the southern polar (antarctic) limit of trees. Despite this continuity of timberline habitat, distinctly different types of trees dominate in the various regions of the Andes.

At the northern end of the Andes, in Venezuela, a tropical cloud forest reaches 10,500 feet and then often gives way on rocky mountainsides to a subalpine woodland of small, spreading *Polylepis* (rose family) trees that sometimes attain an elevation of over 14,000 feet (W. D. Billings, personal communication). In other areas of Venezuela, the cloud forest is superseded by a shrub zone; but both subalpine shrub and polylepis communities give way above to the extensive high mountain grassland known as the Páramo. Giant, old woody plants (megaphytes) called *frailejones* (*Espeletia* spp.), grow in the Páramo, which stretches from Venezuela to Ecuador between about 11,500 and 14,500 feet. The large mass of dead leaves that covers the thick stem evidently protects the *frailejones* from nightly frost.

Small stands of polylepis trees (*P. sericea*) are occasionally found in the middle of the Páramo (at about 13,800 feet) but only on steep east- or west-facing talus slopes exposed to the morning or afternoon sun (Walter 1979). These trees are thought to be able to survive high above the normal timberline because their roots are deeply anchored in the sun-warmed rocks, and nightly cold air slips past these sites, collecting in the valleys below.

Espeletia *in the Paramo at about 13,800 feet in the Colombian Andes*

Southward in Peru, Bolivia, Chile, and Argentina, the Andes become increasingly arid. The barren Loma and Atacama deserts stretch along the Pacific lowlands and lower slopes of the Andes in Peru and northern Chile between 3 and 30°S. However, in a few areas striking examples of perpetual cloud belts and accompanying cloud forests are perched high above the huge gorgelike valleys leading into the Andes. The cloud forest marks the zone of daily condensation caused by upslope winds.

In the gorge of the La Paz River in Bolivia a woodland of small polylepis trees constitutes the upper fringe of cloud forest (Troll 1973). Polylepis forms a drought-caused upper tree line at 11,800 feet, giving way above to the great Puna, an arid grassland that is the prevalent "alpine" type of vegetation in the central Andes. Much of the polylepis woodland has been cut for firewood and replaced by the Puna (Hora 1981), and in drier areas of the central Andes there are no trees at all between the parched sea-level deserts and the snow-clad summits that rise above 20,000 feet. Locally on sites where a foggy condensation zone occurs a narrow band of polylepis woodland makes up the vestiges of a cloud forest.

Farther inland, along the Andean divide in Chile and Bolivia, an unusual species of polylepis (*P. tomentella*), adapted to especially dry and cold conditions, grows in a second condensation or cloud belt above the

Puna plateaus (Troll 1973). This small tree grows at a maximum elevation of 15,750 feet or perhaps somewhat higher, evidently making it the highest-growing erect tree in the world.

Southern Temperate and Antarctic Timberlines

Whereas a large proportion of the northern temperate and boreal latitudes is occupied by land masses, only a tiny fraction of the Southern Hemisphere's temperate and cold latitudes is land covered. The southern temperate zone's land area is essentially confined to southern Chile and Argentina in South America, the southern end of Africa, New Zealand, Tasmania, and the southeastern tip of Australia. Land masses supporting subantarctic vegetation are restricted to the southern tip of South America and a few small oceanic islands.

Because of the preponderance of ocean in the southern latitudes, southern temperate zone climates are strongly maritime, in contrast with the marked continental climates in the northern latitudes. The mountain vegetation of the southern cold and temperate latitudes is related more closely to that of the tropics than to vegetation of northern latitudes (Troll 1973). This evidently happens because the climates of the northern and southern temperate zones differ and because the small southern temperate zone is isolated by the broad band of tropical vegetation.

The strongly oceanic timberlines of the southern temperate zone are ecologically rather similar to timberlines in the humid tropical highlands. A long list of genera, species, and life forms is shared between the antarctic, southern temperate, and tropical cold timberlines; relatively few of these are common to northern alpine and arctic timberlines (Troll 1973). Prevailing life forms in both the tropical and southern-latitude cold timberlines include evergreen broadleaved trees with partly dome-shaped crowns, tree ferns, tussock grasses, woolly herbs, hard cushion plants, and dwarfed carpet shrubs. The most common and widespread trees at Southern Hemisphere timberlines include the needle-leaf conifer yellow woods (*Podocarpus*), consisting of about 100 species, and especially the broad-leaved southern beech (*Nothofagus*), with about 36 species of evergreen and deciduous trees.

On the Andes south of 36°S, southern beech is the primary forest tree under the moist, temperate climate (Wardle 1974). At lower elevations both deciduous and evergreen species of this genus occur, but timberline is formed exclusively by deciduous species (*N. pumilio* and *N. antarctica*). These species and one other (*N. betuloides*) form the southern limit of tree growth (Antarctic timberline) at 56°S. Some evergreen beeches also reach the southern limits of tree growth on the islands southwest of Tierra del Fuego, near Cape Horn (Wardle 1973).

The deciduous timberline beeches of the southern Andes have an undergrowth of herbs and shrubs that are more comparable to northern boreal species than to those of the antarctic timberlines (Wardle 1974). This contrasts with the "moorland" of tussocks and cushion plants of subantarctic species that covers the hills and exposed slopes along the cold, storm-battered coast of Chile beyond 48°S. Here the windy oceanic climate and rocky granite substrate restrict southern beech forest to sheltered sites. The situation has an obvious parallel along the western coasts of the British Isles, Norway, and southwestern Alaska as well as the coast of Labrador, where moorland is also common.

The northern tip of Antarctica—the Palmer Peninsula at 63°S—lies immediately south of Cape Horn and is separated from South America by less than 600 miles of ocean. However, even this northern projection of the antarctic continent has a full polar climate, and the icy rock landscape is occupied by only two small seed-bearing plants, along with mosses and lichens. Fossils of yellow woods and several other Southern Hemisphere trees indicate that forests grew on the Palmer Peninsula as recently as the Jurassic Period, roughly 160 million years ago (Florin 1963). It has been demonstrated that the southern continents, including Australia, were joined together prior to the Jurassic as the super-continent Gondwanaland (Dietz and Holden 1970), which accounts for many of the floristic similarities among today's widely separated Southern Hemisphere land masses.

New Zealand, especially the mountainous southern island, has abundant timberline terrain within the southern temperate zone. Peter Wardle (1973) classified two major types of cold timberlines here. The most widespread of these is a dense growth of small-leaved, evergreen southern beech woodland, which often develops an abrupt boundary that gives way to a luxuriant tussock grassland. In areas where beech is scarce (perhaps because of past glaciation and vulcanism) a mixed forest composed of several tree species grades upward into a subalpine scrub, which in turn becomes lower and scattered as it merges into tussock grassland. The scrub is made up of many diverse species, nearly all of which are evergreens.

At tree line, beeches are rather large; silver beech (*Nothofagus menziesii*) may attain 40 feet, with a trunk over 6 feet in diameter (Wardle 1973). The reason for the abrupt forest line is that beech seedlings cannot survive in the open, exposed sites at higher elevations. They are unable to harden off their foliage during the short growing season, and so they succumb to desiccation in early winter when the soil is chilled and water is not available to replace transpiration losses. In experimental plantings, artificially shaded beech seedlings have become established 600 feet above the present timberline. Also, North American lodgepole pine has been successfully established at the beech timberlines in New Zealand, and lodgepole is regenerating and spreading naturally above the beech limits in some areas (Wardle 1965).

Additional evidence that southern beech and other timberline species in New Zealand are more sensitive to frost than North American timberline trees is apparent in the conspicuous absence of forest in the bottoms of glacial valleys, where cold air ponds up at night. Yet these valley floors, covered with tussock grasses, are surrounded by a dense southern beech forest that clothes the slopes above. At 41°S, in the central area of New

Zealand, tree limit on the coastal ranges occurs near 3900 feet (Wardle 1973). On the inland mountains, however, it rises to about 4900 feet, reflecting the warmer summers in the rain-shadow zone. It drops to about 3000 feet in the southern fiordland at 46°S. About 450 miles south of New Zealand, tiny Campbell Island (52½°S) has a tree limit of tall scrub (*Dracophyllum*) at only 650 feet, below a tussock grassland (Wardle 1974).

New Zealand has a very oceanic climate, so even at timberline, winter temperatures are relatively mild. Below timberline, snow usually persists for only a few days at a time, but above that ecotone there is a rapid increase in the development of winter snowpack (Wardle 1973). A permanent snowline occurs about 3300 feet above timberline, and numerous glaciers occupy the high peaks in the Southern Alps. At timberline midwinter (July) monthly temperatures average near or slightly above freez-

Snowgum in Australia's Snowy Mountains

ing, milder than winters at maritime timberlines in North America, although severe windstorms are rather common. Summer temperatures are evidently comparable to those at timberlines in North America and Europe.

Tree lines in New Zealand lie 1200 miles across the Pacific from those on the highest mountains of southeastern Australia and Tasmania. Despite this relatively close proximity (by Southern Hemisphere standards), Australian and Tasmanian timberlines are very different from those of New Zealand. The Australian Alps have a climate with pronounced dry seasons, and these mountains support only one species at timberline, the snow gum (*Eucalyptus pauciflora*). Snow gum often recovers from fire by sprouting from underground stems called lignotubers. This adaptation is well suited to the Australian fire-environment. New Zealand timberline species lack fire tolerance (Wardle 1973).

The Tasmanian timberline is made up primarily of Tasmanian snow gum (*Eucalyptus coccifera*) and Tasmanian cedar (*Athrotaxis cupressoides*), a member of the redwood family (*Taxodiaceae*), along with other endemic conifers and the shrubby, deciduous tanglefoot beech (*Nothofagus gunnii*) (Wardle 1974). Although 500 species of eucalypts are native to Australia and islands to the north, none are native in New Zealand.

In Tasmania and Australia only the few highest peaks rise slightly above timberline. Tree line occurs at 6000 to 6500 feet in the Australian Alps or Snowy Mountains (at 37°S) and at 4000 to 4200 feet in Tasmania (at 43°S) (Wardle 1974). In both Tasmania and Australia, forests open out more gradually toward timberline than do the New Zealand beech forests.

Common and Scientific Names of Trees and Tall Shrubs

acacias	*Acacia* spp.
Alaska-cedar	*Chamaecyparis nootkatensis*
alder	*Alnus* spp.
Arizona	*A. oblongifolia*
red	*A. rubra*
Sitka	*A. sinuata*
aspen	*Populus* spp.
European	*P. tremula*
quaking	*P. tremuloides*
basswood	*Tilia* spp.
beech	*Fagus* spp.
American	*F. grandifolia*
European	*F. silvatica*
birch	*Betula* spp.
Alaska paper	*B. papyrifera* var. *neoalaskana*
bog	*B. glandulosa*
paper	*B. papyrifera*
white	*B. pubescens*
yellow	*B. alleghaniensis*
cedar (true)	*Cedrus* spp.
Cedar-of-Lebanon	*C. libani*
chokecherry	*Prunus virginiana*
cottonwood	*Populus* spp.
black	*P. trichocarpa*
Fremont	*P. fremontii*
cypress, Arizona	*Cupressus arizonica*
dogwood, Pacific	*Cornus nuttallii*
Douglas-fir	*Pseudotsuga* spp.
bigcone	*P. macrocarpa*
coast	*P. menziesii* var. *menziesii*
Rocky Mt. or interior	*P. menziesii* var. *glauca*
fir (true)	*Abies* spp.
balsam	*A. balsamea*
California red	*A. magnifica* var. *magnifica*
California white	*A. concolor* var. *lowiana*
corkbark	*A. lasiocarpa* var. *arizonica*
grand	*A. grandis*
Himalayan	*A. spectabilis*
noble	*A. procera*
Pacific silver	*A. amabilis*
red	*A. magnifica*

Rocky Mt. white	*A. concolor* var. *concolor*
Shasta red	*A. magnifica* var. *shastensis*
subalpine	*A. lasiocarpa*
white	*A. concolor*
frailejones	*Espeletia* spp.
groundsels, giant or tree	*Senecio* spp.
hemlock	*Tsuga* spp.
mountain	*T. mertensiana*
western	*T. heterophylla*
hickory	*Carya* spp.
honeysuckle	*Lonicera* spp.
incense-cedar, California	*Calocedrus decurrens*
Joshua-tree	*Yucca brevifolia*
juniper	*Juniperus* spp.
alligator	*J. deppeana*
California	*J. californica*
one-seed	*J. monosperma*
Rocky Mt.	*J. scopulorum*
Sierra	*J. occidentalis* var. *australis*
Spanish	*J. thurifera*
Utah	*J. osteosperma*
western	*J. occidentalis* var. *occidentalis*
larch	*Larix* spp.
alpine	*L. lyallii*
Dahurian	*L. dahurica*
eastern (tamarack)	*L. laricina*
European	*L. decidua*
Japanese	*L. leptolepis*
Siberian	*L. sibirica*
Sikkim	*L. griffithii*
western	*L. occidentalis*
madrone, Pacific	*Arbutus menziesii*
maple	*Acer* spp.
bigleaf	*A. macrophyllum*
bigtooth	*A. grandidentatum*
sugar	*A. saccharum*
mountain-ash	*Sorbus* spp.
mountain-mahogany	*Cercocarpus* spp.
curl-leaf	*C. ledifolius*
oak	*Quercus* spp.
blue	*Q. douglasii*
California black	*Q. kelloggii*
canyon live	*Q. chrysolepis*
evergreen holly	*Q. ilex*
Gambel	*Q. gambelii*
Oregon white	*Q. garryana*

olive	*Olea* spp.
pine	*Pinus* spp.
Apache	*P. engelmannii*
Arizona	*P. ponderosa* var. *arizonica*
Bosnian	*P. leucodermis*
bristlecone, Colorado	*P. aristata*
bristlecone, Great Basin	*P. longaeva*
Chihuahua	*P. leiophylla* var. *chihuahuana*
Colorado pinyon	*P. edulis*
Coulter	*P. coulteri*
Digger	*P. sabiniana*
foxtail	*P. balfouriana*
jack	*P. banksiana*
Japanese stone	*P. pumila*
Jeffrey	*P. jeffreyi*
limber	*P. flexilis*
lodgepole, Rocky Mt.	*P. contorta* var. *latifolia*
lodgepole, Sierra	*P. contorta* var. *murrayana*
Mexican mountain pines	*P. hartwegii and P. rudis*
Mexican pinyon	*P. cembroides*
ponderosa, Pacific	*P. ponderosa* var. *ponderosa*
ponderosa, Rocky Mt.	*P. ponderosa* var. *scopulorum*
Potosi	*P. culminicola*
Scotch	*P. sylvestris*
shore	*P. contorta* var. *contorta*
Siberian stone	*P. sibirica*
singleleaf pinyon	*P. monophylla*
southwestern white	*P. strobiformis*
sugar	*P. lambertiana*
Swiss mountain	*P. mugo*
Swiss stone	*P. cembra*
western white	*P. monticola*
whitebark	*P. albicaulis*
polylepis (Rose family)	*Polylepis* spp.
poplar, balsam	*Populus balsamifera*
redcedar, western	*Thuja plicata*
redwood	*Sequoia sempervirens*
rhododendron	*Rhododendron* spp.
sequoia, giant	*Sequoiadendron giganteum*
serviceberry, western	*Amalanchier alnifolia*
snow gum, Australian	*Eucalyptus niphophila*
snow gum, Tasmanian	*Eucalyptus coccifera*
southern beech	*Nothofagus* spp.
spruce	*Picea* spp.
black	*P. mariana*
blue	*P. pungens*
Brewer	*P. brewerana*

Engelmann	*P. engelmannii*
European (Norway)	*P. abies*
red	*P. rubens*
Siberian	*P. obovata*
Sitka	*P. sitchensis*
white	*P. glauca*
sweetgum	*Liquidambar styraciflua*
tamarack	*Larix laricina*
tanoak	*Lithocarpus densiflorus*
Tasmanian cedar	*Athrotaxis cuppressoides*
tree-ferns	*Cyathea* spp. *and Dicksonia* spp.
tree heath	*Erica arborea and Philippia* spp.
willow	*Salix* spp.
feltleaf	*S. alaxensis*
yellow wood	*Podocarpus* spp.

References

Adams, C. C., G. Burns, T. Hankinson, B. Moore, and N. Taylor. 1920. Plants and animals of Mount Marcy, New York. *Ecology* 1:71–94, 204–233, and 274–288.

American Forestry Assn. 1982. National register of big trees. *American Forests* 88(4):17–48.

Arno, S. F. 1966. Interpreting the timberline: An aid to help park naturalists to acquaint visitors with the subalpine-alpine ecotone of western North America. Masters thesis, Univ. Montana, Missoula. 206 pp.

* _____. 1969. Glaciers in the American West. *Natural History* 78(2):84–89.

_____. 1970. Ecology of alpine larch (*Larix lyallii* Parl.) in the Pacific Northwest. Ph.D. dissertation, Univ. Montana, Missoula. 264 pp.

* _____ (Art by J. Gyer). 1973. *Discovering Sierra trees.* Yosemite and Sequoia Natural Hist. Assns., Yosemite National Park, California. 89 pp.

* _____ (Art by Ramona Hammerly). 1977. *Northwest trees.* The Mountaineers, Seattle. 222 pp.

_____. 1979. *Forest regions of Montana.* USDA Forest Service Res. Pap. INT-218. Intermt. For. & Range Exp. Sta., Ogden, Utah.

_____. 1980. Forest fire history in the Northern Rockies. *Jour. Forestry* 78:460–465.

*recommended reading for general audiences

Arno, S. F. and G. Gruell. 1983. Fire history at the forest-grassland ecotone in southwestern Montana. *Jour. Range Mgmt.* 36:332–336.

Arno, S. F. and J. R. Habeck. 1972. Ecology of alpine larch (*Larix lyallii* Parl.) in the Pacific Northwest. *Ecol. Monogr.* 42:417–450.

Arno, S. F. and R. Hoff. 1984 (in press). *Pinus albicaulis,* whitebark pine. In *Silvics of trees of the United States.* USDA Forest Service Gen. Tech. Rept., Washington, D.C.

Baig, M. N. 1972. Ecology of timberline vegetation in the Rocky Mountains of Alberta. Ph.D. dissertation, Univ. Calgary, Calgary, Alberta.

Baig, M. N. and W. Tranquillini. 1976. Studies on upper timberline: morphology and anatomy of Norway spruce (*Picea abies*) and stone pine (*Pinus cembra*) needles from various habitat conditions. *Canadian Jour. Botany* 54:1622–1632.

Bailey, D. K. 1970. Phytogeography and taxonomy of *Pinus* subsection *Balfourianae. Annals of the Missouri Botanical Gardens* 57:210–249.

Bailey, V. 1913. *Life zones and crop zones of New Mexico.* U.S. Dept. Interior, Biol. Survey, N. American Fauna, vol. 35. 100 pp.

Baker, F. S. 1944. Mountain climates of the western United States. *Ecol. Monogr.* 14:223–254.

Baker, W. H. 1951. Plants of Fairview Mountain, Calapooya Range, Oregon. *Amer. Midland Naturalist* 46:132–173.

Barrett, S. W. and S. Arno. 1982. Indian fires as an ecological influence in the Northern Rockies. *Jour. Forestry* 80:647–651.

Bates, C. G. 1924. *Forest types in the central Rocky Mountains as affected by climate and soil.* USDA Forest Service, Dept. Bull. 1233. 163 pp.

Beaman, J. H. 1962. The timberlines of Iztaccihuatl and Popocatepetl, Mexico. *Ecology* 43:377–385.

Beaman, J. H. and J. Andresen. 1966. The vegetation, floristics, and phytogeography of the summit of Cerro Potosi, Mexico. *Amer. Midland Naturalist* 75:1–33.

Beasley, R. S. and J. Klemmedson. 1980. Ecological relationships of bristlecone pine. *Amer. Midland Naturalist* 104:242–252.

Bega, R. V., tech. coordinator. 1978. Diseases of Pacific Coast conifers. USDA Forest Service, Agriculture Handbook 521. 206 pp.

Bell, K. L. and R. Johnson. 1980. Alpine flora of the Wassuk Range, Mineral County, Nevada. *Madrono* 27:25–35.

Billings, W. D. 1950. Vegetation and plant growth as affected by chemically altered rocks in the western Great Basin. *Ecology* 31:62–74.

_____ . 1951. Vegetational zonation in the Great Basin of western North America. *Compt. Rend. du Colloque sur les bases ecologiques de la regeneration de la vegetation des zones arides,* pp. 101–122. Union Internat. Soc. Biol., Paris.

_____ . 1966. *Plants and the ecosystem.* Wadsworth Publ. Co., Belmont, California. 154 pp.

_____ . 1969. Vegetational pattern near alpine timberline as affected by fire-snowdrift interactions. *Vegetatio* 19:192–207.

_____. 1978. Alpine phytogeography across the Great Basin. *Great Basin Naturalist Memoirs* 2:105–118. Brigham Young Univ., Provo, Utah.

Billings, W. D., E. Clebsch, and H. Mooney. 1961. Effect of low concentrations of carbon dioxide on photosynthesis rates of two races of Oxyria. *Science* 133:1834.

Billings, W. D. and A. Mark. 1957. Factors involved in the persistence of montane treeless balds. *Ecology* 38:140–142.

Billings, W. D. and J. Thompson. 1957. Composition of a stand of old bristlecone pines in the White Mountains of California. *Ecology* 38:158–160.

Black, R. A. and L. C. Bliss. 1978. Recovery sequence of *Picea mariana-Vaccinium uliginosum* forests after burning near Inuvik, Northwest Territories, Canada. *Canadian Jour. Botany* 56:2020–2030.

_____. 1980. Reproductive ecology of *Picea mariana* (Mill.) BSP., at tree line near Inuvik, Northwest Territories, Canada. *Ecol. Monogr.* 50:331–354.

Bliss, L. C. 1963. Alpine plant communities of the Presidential Range, New Hampshire. *Ecology* 44:678–696.

Brink, V. C. 1959. A directional change in the subalpine forest-heath ecotone in Garibaldi Park, British Columbia. *Ecology* 40:10–16.

Brooke, R. C., E. Peterson, and V. Krajina. 1970. The subalpine mountain hemlock zone. In *Ecology of western North America* 2(2):151–307. Univ. British Columbia, Dept. of Botany, Vancouver.

Brown, D. E. and C. Lowe. 1980. Biotic communities of the Southwest (map). USDA Forest Service Gen. Tech. Rep. RM-78. Rocky Mtn. For. & Range Exp. Sta., Fort Collins, Colorado.

Brown, R. W., R. Johnston, and D. Johnson. 1978a. Rehabilitation of alpine tundra disturbances. *Jour. Soil and Water Conserva.* 33:154–160.

Brown, R. W., R. Johnston, and K. Van Cleve. 1978b. Rehabilitation problems in alpine and arctic regions. In *Reclamation of drastically disturbed lands,* pp. 23–44. Amer. Soc. of Agronomy, Madison, Wisconsin.

Bryson, R. A., W. Irving, and J. Larsen. 1965. Radiocarbon and soil evidence of former forest in the southern Canadian tundra. *Science* 147:46–48.

Caldwell, M. M., R. Robberecht, and W. Billings. 1980. A steep latitudinal gradient of solar ultraviolet-B radiation in the arctic-alpine life zone. *Ecology* 61:600–611.

Caraher, D. L. 1977. The spread of western juniper in central Oregon. In *Proc. of the W. juniper ecology and mgmt. workshop,* pp. 3–8. USDA Forest Service, Pacific NW For. & Range Exp. Sta., Portland, Oregon.

Carrara, P. E. and R. McGimsey. 1981. The late-Neoglacial histories of the Agassiz and Jackson Glaciers, Glacier National Park, Montana. *Arctic & Alpine Res.* 13:183–196.

Cary, M. 1911. *A biological survey of Colorado.* U.S. Dept. Interior, Biol.

Survey, N. American Fauna, vol. 33.

Clausen, J. 1963. Tree lines and germ plasm—a study in evolutionary limitations. *Proc. National Academy of Sciences* 50:860–868.

——. 1965. Population studies of alpine and subalpine races of conifers and willows in the California High Sierra Nevada. *Evolution* 19:56–68.

Clokey, I. W. 1951. Flora of the Charleston Mountains, Clark County, Nevada. *Univ. Calif. Publ. in Botany* 24:1–274.

Coe, M. J. 1967. *The ecology of the alpine zone on Mount Kenya.* W. Junk Publ., The Hague. 136 pp.

Cole, D. N. 1982. *Vegetation of two drainages in the Eagle Cap Wilderness, Wallowa Mountains, Oregon.* USDA Forest Service Res. Pap. INT-288. Intermt. For. & Range Exp. Sta., Ogden, Utah.

Cole, D. N. and G. Schreiner, compilers. 1981. *Impacts of backcountry recreation: site management and rehabilitation—an annotated bibliography.* USDA Forest Service Gen. Tech. Rep. INT-121. Intermt. For. & Range Exp. Sta., Ogden, Utah.

Collaer, P. 1934, 1940. Le role de la lumiere dans l'establissement de la limite superieure des forets. *Ber. Schweiz. Bot. Ges.* 43:90–125 and 50:500–516.

Cooke, W. B. 1940. Flora of Mount Shasta. *Amer. Midland Naturalist* 23:497–572.

——. 1955. Fungi of Mount Shasta (1936–1951). *Sydowia, Annales Mycologici* 9:94–215.

Cooper, W. S. 1908. Alpine vegetation in the vicinity of Long's peak, Colorado. *Botanical Gazette* 45:319–337.

——. 1923. The recent ecological history of Glacier Bay, Alaska. *Ecology* 4:93–128, 223–246, and 355–365.

Cowling, E. B. 1982. Acid precipitation in historical perspective. *Environmen. Sci. Technol.* 16(2):110A–123A.

Cox, C. F. 1933. Alpine plant succession on James Peak, Colorado. *Ecol. Monogr.* 3:299–372.

Critchfield, H. J. 1966. *General climatology.* Prentice-Hall, Inc., Englewood Cliffs, New Jersey.

Critchfield, W. B. and G. Allenbaugh. 1969. The distribution of Pinaceae in and near northern Nevada. *Madrono* 20:12–25.

Critchfield, W. B. and E. Little, Jr. 1966. *Geographic distribution of the pines of the world.* USDA Forest Service, Misc. Publ. 991. 97 pp.

Cronquist, A., A. Holmgren, N. Holmgren, and J. Reveal. 1972. *Intermountain flora: vascular plants of the Intermountain West, U.S.A.,* vol. 1. Hafner Publ. Co., New York.

Currey, D. R. 1965. An ancient bristlecone pine stand in eastern Nevada. *Ecology* 46:564–566.

Curry, R. R. 1962. Geobotanical correlations in the alpine and subalpine regions of the Tenmile Range, Summit County, Colorado. Masters thesis, Univ. Colorado, Boulder. 123 pp.

Daniel, T. W. 1980. The middle and southern Rocky Mountain region. In *Regional silviculture of the United States,* ed. J. W. Barrett, pp.

277–340. John Wiley & Sons, New York.

* Danner, W. R. 1955. *Geology of Olympic National Park*. Univ. Wash. Press, Seattle. 68 pp.

Daubenmire, R. 1954. Alpine timberlines in the Americas and their interpretation. *Butler Univ. Botanical Studies* 11:119–136.

_____. 1959. *Plants and environment: a textbook of plant autecology*. John Wiley & Sons, New York. 442 pp.

_____. 1981. Subalpine parks associated with snow transfer in the mountains of northern Idaho and eastern Washington. *NW Science* 55:124–135.

Davis, M. L. 1980. Variation in form and growth rate of Engelmann spruce at tree line. *Amer. Midland Naturalist* 104:383–386.

Despain, D. G. 1973. Vegetation of the Big Horn Mountains, Wyoming, in relation to substrate and climate. *Ecol. Monogr.* 43:329–355.

Dietz, R. S. and J. Holden. 1970. The breakup of Pangaea. *Scientific Amer.* 223(4):30–41.

* Douglas, W. O. 1961. The friendly huts of the White Mountains. *National Geographic* 119(8):205–239.

Douguedroit, A. 1978. Timberline reconstruction in Alpes de Haute Provence and Alpes Maritimes, southern French Alps. *Arctic & Alpine Res.* 10:505–517.

Drew, J. V. and R. Shanks. 1965. Landscape relationships of soils and vegetation in the forest-tundra ecotone, upper Firth River Valley, Alaska-Canada. *Ecol. Monogr.* 35:285–306.

Dunwiddie, P. W. 1977. Recent tree invasion of subalpine meadows in the Wind River Mountains, Wyoming. *Arctic & Alpine Res.* 9:393–399.

Dye, A. J. and W. Moir. 1977. Spruce-fir forest at its southern distribution in the Rocky Mountains, New Mexico. *Amer. Midland Naturalist* 97:133–146.

Eliot, W. A. 1938. *Forest trees of the Pacific Coast*. G. P. Putnam's Sons, New York. 565 pp.

Elliott, D. K. and S. Short. 1979. The northern limit of trees in Labrador: a discussion. *Arctic* 32:201–206.

Elliot, D. L. 1979. The current regenerative capacity of the northern Canadian trees, Keewatin, N.W.T., Canada: some preliminary observations. *Arctic & Alpine Res.* 11:243–251.

Eyre, S. R. 1963. *Vegetation and soils: a world picture*. Aldine Publ. Co., Chicago. 324 pp.

Fenneman, N. M. 1931. *Physiography of western United States*. McGraw-Hill Book Co., New York.

* Ferguson, C. W. 1968. Bristlecone pine: science and esthetics. *Science* 159:839–846.

Ferlatte, W. J. 1974. *A flora of the Trinity Alps of northern California*. Univ. Calif. Press, Berkeley. 206 pp.

Florin, R. 1963. The distribution of conifer and taxad genera in time and space. Uppsala. *Acta. Horti Bergiani*. Band 20. N:o 4. pp. 121–312.

Fonda, R. W. and L. Bliss. 1969. Forest vegetation of the montane and subalpine zones, Olympic Mountains, Washington. *Ecol. Monogr.* 39:271–301.

Forcella, F. and T. Weaver. 1977. Biomass and productivity of the subalpine *Pinus albicaulis-Vaccinium scoparium* association in Montana, U.S.A. *Vegetatio* 35:95–105.

Fowells, H., ed. 1965. *Silvics of forest trees of the United States.* USDA Forest Service, Agriculture Handbook 271. 762 pp.

* Franklin, J. F. and C. Dyrness. 1973. *Natural vegetation of Oregon and Washington.* USDA Forest Service Gen. Tech. Rep. PNW-8. 417 pp. Pac. NW For. & Range Exp. Sta., Portland, Oregon.

Franklin, J. F. and K. Krueger. 1968. Germination of true fir and mountain hemlock seed on snow. *Jour. Forestry* 66:416–417.

Franklin, J. F., T. Maeda, Y. Ohsumi, M. Matsui, H. Yagi, and G. Hawk. 1979. Subalpine coniferous forests of central Honshu, Japan. *Ecol. Monogr.* 49:311–334.

Franklin, J. F., W. Moir, G. Douglas, and C. Wiberg. 1971. Invasion of subalpine meadows by trees in the Cascade Range, Washington and Oregon. *Arctic & Alpine Res.* 3:215–224.

Geiger, R. 1957. *The climate near the ground.* Translation by M. N. Stewart and others of the second German edition of *Das Klima der bodennahen Luftschicht.* Harvard Univ. Press, Cambridge. 494 pp.

Gersmehl, P. 1973. Pseudo-timberline: the southern Appalachian grassy balds. *Arctic & Alpine Res.* 5:A137–A138.

Graham, E. H. 1937. Botanical studies in the Uinta Basin of Utah and Colorado. *Annals of the Carnegie Museum* 26:1–432.

Griffin, J. R. 1977. Oak woodland. In *Terrestrial vegetation of California,* eds. M. G. Barbour and J. Major, pp. 383–416. John Wiley & Sons, New York.

Griffin, J. R. and W. Critchfield. 1976. The distribution of forest trees in California. USDA Forest Service Res. Pap. PSW-82. Pacific SW For. & Range Exp. Sta., Berkeley, California.

Griggs, R. F. 1934. The edge of the forest in Alaska and the reason for its position. *Ecology* 15:80–96.

—————. 1936. The vegetation of the Katmai District. *Ecology* 17:380–417.

—————. 1937. Timberlines as indicators of climatic trends. *Science* 85:251–255.

—————. 1938. Timberlines in the northern Rocky Mountains. *Ecology* 19:548–564.

—————. 1942. Indications as to climatic changes from the timberline of Mount Washington. *Science* 95:515–519.

Grinnell, J. 1908. The biota of the San Bernardino Mountains. *Univ. Calif. Publ. in Zoology* 5(1):1–170.

Gruell, G. E. 1979. *Fire's influence on wildlife habitat on the Bridger-Teton National Forest, Wyoming,* vols. 1 and 2. USDA Forest Service Res. Pap. INT-235 and 252. Intermt. For. & Range Exp. Sta., Ogden, Utah.

_____. 1983. *Fire and vegetative trends in the Northern Rockies: Interpretations from 1871–1982 photographs.* USDA Forest Service Gen. Tech. Rep. INT-158. Intermt. For. & Range Exp. Sta., Ogden, Utah. 117 pp.

Habeck, J. R. 1961. The original vegetation of the mid-Willamette Valley, Oregon. *NW Science* 35:65–77.

_____. 1969. A gradient analysis of a timberline zone at Logan Pass, Glacier Park, Montana. *NW Science* 43:65–73.

Hadley, J. R. and W. Smith. 1983. Influence of wind exposure on needle desiccation and mortality for timberline conifers in Wyoming, U.S.A. *Arctic & Alpine Res.* 15:127–135.

Hall, H. M. 1902. A botanical survey of San Jacinto Mountain. *Univ. Calif. Publ. in Botany* 1:1–140.

Hanley, D. P. 1976. *Tree biomass and productivity estimated for three habitat types of northern Idaho.* Univ. Idaho Forest, Wildlife & Range Exp. Sta. Bull. 14.

* Harding, W. 1967. *The days of Henry Thoreau.* Alfred A. Knopf, New York. 472 pp.

Hare, F. K. 1950. Climate and zonal divisions of the boreal forest formation in eastern Canada. *Geographical Review* 40:615–635.

Hare, F. K. and J. Ritchie. 1972. The boreal bioclimates. *Geographical Review* 62:333–365.

* Hart, J. 1982. *Hiking the Great Basin.* Sierra Club, San Francisco.

Hayward, C. L. 1948. Biotic communities of the Wasatch chaparral, Utah. *Ecol. Monogr.* 18:473–506.

_____. 1952. Alpine biotic communities of the Uinta Mountains, Utah. *Ecol. Monogr.* 22:93–120.

Heusser, C. J. 1960. *Late-Pleistocene environments of north Pacific North America.* Amer. Geographical Soc. Spec. Publ. 35. 308 pp.

* Hitch, C. J. 1982. Dendrochronology and serendipity. *Amer. Scientist* 70:300–305.

Hoff, R. J., R. Bingham, and G. McDonald. 1980. Relative blister rust resistance of white pines. *European Jour. Forest Pathology* 10:307–316.

Hoffman, G. R. and R. Alexander. 1976. Forest vegetation of the Bighorn Mountains, Wyoming: a habitat type classification. USDA Forest Service Res. Pap. RM-170. 38 pp. Rocky Mt. For. & Range Exp. Sta., Fort Collins, Colorado.

_____. 1980. Forest vegetation of the Routt National Forest in northwestern Colorado: a habitat type classification. USDA Forest Service Res. Pap. RM-221. 41 pp. Rocky Mt. For. & Range Exp. Sta., Fort Collins, Colorado.

Holroyd, E. W., III. 1970. Prevailing winds on Whiteface Mountain as indicated by flag trees. *Forest Science* 16:222–229.

Holtmeier, F. 1973. Geoecological aspects of timberlines in northern and central Europe. *Arctic & Alpine Res.* 5(3):A45–A54.

* Hora, B., ed. 1981. *The Oxford encyclopedia of trees of the world.* Oxford Univ. Press, Oxford. 288 pp.

Houston, D. B. 1973. Wildfires in northern Yellowstone National Park. *Ecology* 54:1111–1117.

Hunt, C. B. 1967. *Physiography of the United States*. W. H. Freeman & Co., San Francisco. 480 pp.

Hustich, I. 1966. *On the forest-tundra and the northern treelines*. Rep. of Kevo Subarctic Sta. 3:7–47. Annales, Univ. Turkuensis.

Hutchinson, T. C. and M. Havas, eds. 1980. *Effects of acid precipitation on terrestrial ecosystems*. Plenum Press, New York. 654 pp.

Ittner, R., D. Potter, J. Agee, and S. Anschell, eds. 1979. *Recreational impact on wildlands. Conf. Proc., Oct. 27–29, Seattle*. USDA Forest Service Region 6, Publ. 1. Portland, Oregon. 333 pp.

Johannessen, C. L., W. Davenport, A. Millet, and S. McWilliams. 1971. The vegetation of the Willamette Valley. *Annals of the Assn. of Amer. Geogr.* 61:286–302.

Kay, P. A. 1978. Dendroecology in Canada's forest-tundra transition zone. *Arctic & Alpine Res.* 10:133–138.

Kearney, M. S. and B. H. Luckman. 1983. Holocene timberline fluctuations in Jasper National Park, Alberta. *Science* 221:261–263.

Keen, F. P. 1937. Climatic cycles in eastern Oregon as indicated by tree rings. *Monthly Weather Review* 65:175–188.

Kendall, K. C. 1981. Bear use of pine nuts. Masters thesis, Montana State Univ., Bozeman. 25 pp.

* Kirk, R. 1965. *Exploring Death Valley*. Stanford Univ. Press, Stanford, California. 88 pp.

Krajina, V. J. 1965. Biogeoclimatic zones and classification of British Columbia. *Ecol. of W. N. America* 1:1–17. Univ. of British Columbia, Botany Dept., Vancouver.

Kruckeberg, A. R. 1969. Soil diversity and the distribution of plants, with examples from western North America. *Madrono* 20:129–154.

Kryuchkov, V. V. 1968. Soils of the far north should be conserved. *Priroda* 12:72–74. Translation in *The effect of disturbance on permafrost terrain,* trs. J. Brown and others, pp. 11–13. U.S. Army Corps Engin. Spec. Rep. 138. Cold Regions Res. Lab., Hanover, New Hampshire.

Küchler, A. W. 1960. World natural vegetation (map). In *Goode's World Atlas*. Rand McNally, Chicago.

_____. 1964. Potential natural vegetation of the conterminous United States (map). Amer. Geographical Soc. Spec. Publ. 36.

LaMarche, V. C. and H. Mooney. 1967. Altithermal timberline advance in western United States. *Nature* 213:980–982.

_____. 1972. Recent climatic change and development of the bristlecone pine (*Pinus longaeva* Bailey) krummholz zone. Mount Washington, Nevada. *Arctic & Alpine Res.* 4:61–72.

LaMarche, V. C. and C. Stockton. 1974. Chronologies from temperature-sensitive bristlecone pines at upper treeline in the western United States. *Tree-Ring Bull.* 34:21–45.

Langenheim, J. H. 1962. Vegetation and environmental patterns in the

Crested Butte Area, Gunnison County, Colorado. *Ecol. Monogr.* 32:249–285.

* Lanner, R. M. 1981. *The Piñon Pine—A natural and cultural history.* Univ. Nevada Press, Reno. 208 pp.

* _____. 1984. *Trees of the Great Basin: A Natural History.* Univ. Nevada Press, Reno. 215 pp.

Lanner, R. M. and S. B. Vander Wall. 1980. Dispersal of limber pine seed by Clark's Nutcracker. *Jour. Forestry* 78:637–639.

LaRoi, G. H. and R. Hnatiuk. 1980. The *Pinus contorta* forests of Banff and Jasper national parks: A study in comparative synecology and syntaxonomy. *Ecol. Monogr.* 50:1–29.

Larsen, J. A. 1974. Ecology of the northern continental forest border. In *Arctic and alpine environments,* eds. J. D. Ives and R. Barry, pp. 341–369, Methuen Publ., London.

Larsen, J. A. 1980. *The boreal ecosystem.* Academic Press, New York. 500 pp.

Lauer, W. 1973. The altitudinal belts of the vegetation in the central Mexican highlands and their climatic conditions. *Arctic & Alpine Res.* 5(3)part 2:A99–A113.

_____. 1978. Timberline studies in central Mexico. *Arctic & Alpine Res.* 10:383–396.

Lawrence, D. B. 1939. Some features of the vegetation of the Columbia River Gorge. *Ecol. Monogr.* 9:217–257.

_____. 1958. Glaciers and vegetation in southeastern Alaska. *Amer. Scientist* 46:89–122.

Leak, W. B. and R. Graber. 1974a. *Forest vegetation related to elevation in the White Mountains of New Hampshire.* USDA Forest Service Res. Pap. NE-299. NE For. Exp. Sta., Upper Darby, Pennsylvania. 7 pp.

_____. 1974b. A method for detecting migration of forest vegetation. *Ecology* 55:1425–1427.

Ligon, J. D. 1974. Green cones of the piñon pine stimulate late summer breeding in the piñon Jay. *Nature* 250:80–82.

_____. 1978. Reproductive interdependence of piñon jays and piñon pines. *Ecol. Monogr.* 48:111–126.

Little, E. L. Jr. 1966. Eight pine species at Onion Valley, California. *Leaflets of W. Botany* 10:289–292.

_____. 1971. *Atlas of United States trees.* Conifers and important hardwoods, vol. 1. USDA Forest Service, Misc. Publ. 1146. 200 maps.

_____. 1979. *Checklist of United States trees (native and naturalized).* USDA Forest Service, Agriculture Handbook 541. 375 pp.

Loope, L. L. 1969. Subalpine and alpine vegetation of northeastern Nevada. Ph.D. dissertation, Duke Univ., Durham, North Carolina.

Löve, D. 1970. Subarctic and subalpine: where and what? *Arctic & Alpine Res.* 2:63–73.

* Lowdermilk, W. C. 1953. *Conquest of the land through 7,000 years.* USDA Soil Conservation Service, Agriculture Bull. 99. 30 pp.

* Lowe, C. H. 1964. *Arizona's natural environment: landscapes and habitats.* Univ. Ariz. Press, Tucson. 136 pp.

MacMahon, J. A. and D. Andersen. 1982. Subalpine forests: a world perspective with emphasis on western North America. *Progress in Physical Geogr.* 6:368–425.

Major, J. and D. Taylor. 1977. Alpine. In *Terrestrial vegetation of California,* eds. M. G. Barbour and J. Major, pp. 601–678. John Wiley & Sons, New York.

Marchand, P. J. and B. Chabot. 1978. Winter water relations of tree-line plant species on Mt. Washington, New Hampshire. *Arctic & Alpine Res.* 10:105–116.

Marr, J. W. 1948. Ecology of the forest-tundra ecotone on the east coast of Hudson Bay. *Ecol. Monogr.* 18:117–144.

_____. 1961. Ecosystems of the east slope of the Front Range in Colorado. *Univ. Colo. Studies in Biol.,* vol. 8. 134 pp.

_____. 1977a. A classification of tree island forms in the mountains of Colorado. *Colo.-Wyo. Academy of Sci.* 9:35.

_____. 1977b. The development and movement of tree islands near the upper limit of tree growth in the southern Rocky Mountains. *Ecology* 58:1159–1164.

Mastrogiuseppe, R. J. and J. Mastrogiuseppe. A study of *Pinus balfouriana* Grev. and Balf. (Pinaceae). *Systematic Botany* 5:86–104.

McAvoy, B. 1931. Ecological survey of the Bella Coola region. *Botanical Gazette* 92:141–171.

McLean, A. 1970. Plant communities of the Similkameen Valley, British Columbia, and their relationships to soils. *Ecol. Monogr.* 40:403–424.

Mehringer, P. J., Jr., S. Arno, and K. Petersen. 1977a. Postglacial history of Lost Trail Pass Bog, Bitterroot Mountains, Montana. *Arctic & Alpine Res.* 9:345–368.

Mehringer, P. J., Jr., E. Blinman, and K. Petersen. 1977b. Pollen influx and volcanic ash. *Science* 198:257–261.

Mehringer, P. J., Jr. and C. Ferguson. 1969. Pluvial occurrence of bristlecone pine (*Pinus aristata*) in a Mojave Desert mountain range. *Jour. Ariz. Academy Sci.* 5:284–291.

Merriam, C. H. 1899. *Results of a biological survey of Mount Shasta, northern California.* U.S. Dept. Interior, Biol. Survey, N. American Fauna, vol. 16. 179 pp.

Messerli, B. 1973. Problems of vertical and horizontal arrangement in the high mountains of the extreme arid zone (central Sahara). *Arctic & Alpine Res.* 5(3), part 2:A139–A147.

* Mills, E. 1920. Trees at timberline. Published in 1937 in *Essays of our day,* ed. B. E. Ward, pp. 258–267. D. Appleton-Century, New York.

Moir, W. H. and J. Ludwig. 1979. *A classification of spruce-fir and mixed conifer habitat types of Arizona and New Mexico.* USDA Forest Service Res. Pap. RM-207. Rocky Mt. For. & Range Exp. Sta., Fort Collins, Colorado. 47 pp.

Moir, W. H. and H. Smith. 1970. Occurrence of an American salamander, *Aneides hardyi* (Taylor), in tundra habitat. *Arctic & Alpine Res.* 2:155–156.

Moore, T. C. 1965. Origin and disjunction of the alpine tundra flora on San Francisco Mountain, Arizona. *Ecology* 46:860–864.

* Muench, D. and D. Lambert. 1972. *Timberline ancients.* Charles Belding, Portland, Oregon. 128 pp.

* Muir, J. 1894. *The mountains of California.* Reprinted in 1961 by Doubleday and Co., Garden City, New York.

* Murie, A. 1962. *Mammals of Mount McKinley National Park, Alaska.* Mount McKinley Natural History Assn., Pisani Printing Co., San Francisco. 56 pp.

* Mutel, C. F. 1976. *From grasslands to glacier: an ecology of Boulder County, Colorado.* Johnson Publ. Co., Boulder, Colorado.

Neal, D. L. 1980. Blue oak — Digger pine. In *Forest cover types of the United States and Canada,* ed. F. H. Eyre, pp. 126–127. Soc. Amer. Foresters, Washington, D.C.

Nichol, A. A. 1937. *The natural vegetation of Arizona.* Univ. Ariz. Agr. Exp. Sta. Tech. Bull. 68. 41 pp.

Nichols, H. 1976. Historical aspects of the northern Canadian tree-line. *Arctic* 29:38–47.

Oosting, H. J. and W. Billings. 1951. A comparison of virgin spruce-fir forest in the northern and southern Appalachian system. *Ecology* 32:84–103.

Ostenfeld, C. H. and C. Larsen. 1930. The species of the genus *Larix* and their geographic distribution. Det Kgl. Danske Videnskabernes Selskab. *Biologiske Meddelelser* 9(2). 106 pp.

Pace, N., D. Kiepert, and E. Nissen. 1968. *Climatological data summary for the Crooked Creek Laboratory and Barcroft Laboratory.* Univ. Calif. White Mt. Res. Sta.

Parsons, D. J. 1972. The southern extensions of *Tsuga mertensiana* (mountain hemlock) in the Sierra Nevada. *Madrono* 21:536–539.

Payette, S. 1980. Fire history at the treeline in northern Quebec: A paleoclimatic tool. In *Proc. of the Fire History Workshop, Tucson, Arizona,* pp. 126–131, USDA Forest Service Gen. Tech. Rep. RM-81. Rocky Mt. For. & Range Exp. Sta., Fort Collins, Colorado.

Payette, S. and R. Gagnon. 1979. Tree-line dynamics in Ungava Peninsula, northern Quebec. *Holarctic Ecology* 2:239–248.

Pearson, G. A. 1931. Forest types in the Southwest as determined by climate and soil. USDA Forest Service, Tech. Bull. 247. 144 pp.

_____. 1941. What forest trees tell about climate and soil. In *Conservation of Renewable Natural Resources* (Univ. Penna. Bicentennial Conf.), eds. R. Zon and others, pp. 19–32. Univ. Penna. Press, Philadelphia.

Peet, R. K. 1978. Latitudinal variation in southern Rocky Mountain forests. *Jour. Biogeography* 5:275–289.

Petersen, K. L. 1981. 10,000 years of climatic change reconstructed from fossil pollen, La Plata Mountains, southwestern Colorado. Ph.D.

dissertation, Washington State Univ., Pullman. 191 pp.

Petersen, K. L. and P. Mehringer, Jr. 1976. Postglacial timberline fluctuations, La Plata Mountains, southwestern Colorado. *Arctic & Alpine Res.* 8:275–288.

Pfister, R. D., B. Kovalchik, S. Arno, and R. Presby. 1977. Forest habitat types of Montana. USDA Forest Service Gen. Tech. Rep. INT-34. Intermt. For. & Range Exp. Sta., Ogden, Utah. 174 pp.

Phillips, F. J. 1910. The dissemination of juniper by birds. *Forestry Quarterly* 8:60–73.

Plesnik, D. 1980. (The vertical differentiation of vegetation and the upper timberline on Kilimanjaro)—in German. *Acta Facultatis, Rerum Naturalium Universitatis Comenianae, Geographica* 21:29–51.

Porsild, A. E. 1945. *The alpine flora of the eastern slope of Mackenzie Mountains, Northwest Territories.* Nat. Mus. Canada, Bull. 101. 35 pp.

Porsild, A. E. 1951. *Botany of southeastern Yukon adjacent to the Canol Road.* Nat. Mus. Canada, Bull. 121. 400 pp.

* Progulske, D. R. and R. Sowell. 1974. Yellow ore, yellow hair, yellow pine: A photographic study of a century of forest ecology. S. Dakota State Univ. Agr. Exp. Sta. Bull. 616. 169 pp.

Pruitt, W. O., Jr. 1970. The Newfoundland National Park potential. *Canadian Field Naturalist* 84:99–115.

Reiners, W. A. and G. Lang. 1979. Vegetational patterns and processes in the balsam fir zone, White Mountains, New Hampshire. *Ecology* 60:403–417.

Richards, J. H. 1981. Ecophysiology of a deciduous timberline tree, *Larix lyallii* Parl. Ph.D. dissertation, Univ. Alberta, Edmonton. 228 pp.

Richmond, G. M. 1962. *Quaternary Stratigraphy of the La Sal Mountains, Utah.* U.S. Geol. Survey, Prof. Pap. 324. 135 pp.

Riskind, D. H. and T. Patterson. 1975. Distributional and ecological notes on *Pinus culminicola. Madrono* 23:159–161.

Ritchie, J. C. 1957. The vegetation of northern Manitoba: II. A prisere on the Hudson Bay lowlands. *Ecology* 38:429–434.

Ritchie, J. C. and F. Hare. 1971. Late-Quaternary vegetation and climate near the arctic tree line of northwestern North America. *Quaternary Res.* 1:331–342.

* Roberts, L. 1983. Is acid deposition killing West German forests? *Bioscience* 33:302–305.

* Rock, J. F. 1931. Konka Risumgongba, holy mountain of the outlaws. *Nat. Geographic* 60:1–65.

* Rogers, G. F. 1982. *Then and now: A photographic history of vegetation change in the central Great Basin desert.* Univ. Utah Press, Salt Lake City. 152 pp.

Roland, A. E. and E. Smith. 1969. Flora of Nova Scotia. *Proc. Nova Scotia Institute Sci.* 26:274–743.

Ronco, F. 1970. Influence of high light intensity on survival of planted

Engelmann spruce. *Forest Sci.* 16:331–339.

Rundel, P. W., D. Parsons, and D. Gordon. 1977. Montane and subalpine vegetation of the Sierra Nevada and Cascade Ranges. In *Terrestrial vegetation of California,* eds. M. G. Barbour and J. Major, pp. 559–600. John Wiley & Sons, New York.

Rydberg, P. A. 1913. Phytogeographical notes on the Rocky Mountain region: I. Alpine region. *Bull. Torrey Botanical Club* 40:677–686.

St. Andre, G., H. Mooney, and R. Wright. 1965. The pinyon woodland zone in the White Mountains of California. *Amer. Midland Naturalist* 73:225–239.

Sakai, A. 1970. Mechanism of desiccation damage of conifers wintering in soil-frozen areas. *Ecology* 51:657–664.

Sakai, A. and C. Weiser. 1973. Freezing resistance of trees in North America with reference to tree regions. *Ecology* 54:118–126.

Salisbury, F. B. and C. Ross. 1978. *Plant physiology.* 4th ed. Wadsworth Publ. Co., Belmont, California. 422 pp.

Salt, G. 1954. A contribution to the ecology of upper Kilimanjaro. *Jour. of Ecology* 42:375–423.

Saville, D. B. O. 1963. Factors limiting the advance of spruce at Great Whale River, Quebec. *Canadian Field-Naturalist* 77:95–97.

Sawyer, J. O. and D. Thornburgh. 1977. Montane and subalpine vegetation of the Klamath Mountains. In *Terrestrial vegetation of California,* eds. M. G. Barbour and J. Major, pp. 699–732. John Wiley & Sons, New York.

* Schmid, R. and M. Schmid. 1975. Living links with the past. *Natural History* 84:38–45.

* Schulman, E. 1958. Bristlecone pine, oldest known living thing. *Nat. Geographic* 63:355–372.

Schulze, E. D., H. Mooney, and E. Dunn. 1967. Wintertime photosynthesis of bristlecone pine (*Pinus aristata*) in the White Mountains of California. *Ecology* 48:1044–1047.

Scoggan, H. J. 1950. *The flora of Bic and the Gaspé Peninsula.* Nat. Mus. Canada, Bull. 115.

Shaw, C. H. 1909a. Present problems in plant ecology: III. Vegetation and altitude. *Amer. Naturalist* 43:420–431.

_____. 1909b. The causes of timberline on mountains: the role of snow. *Plant World* 12:169–181.

Siccama, T. G. 1974. Vegetation, soil, and climate on the Green Mountains of Vermont. *Ecol. Monogr.* 44:325–349.

Smith, C. C. 1970. The coevolution of pine squirrels (*Tamiasciurus*) and conifers. *Ecol. Monogr.* 40:349–371.

Spaulding, W. G. and K. Petersen. 1980. The late Pleistocene and early Holocene paleoecology of Cowboy Cave. In *Cowboy Cave,* eds. J. D. Jennings and others. *Univ. Utah Anthropological Papers* 104:163–177.

Spurr, S. H. 1964. *Forest ecology.* Ronald Press, New York.

Spurr, S. H. and B. Barnes. 1980. *Forest ecology.* John Wiley & Sons, New York. 687 pp.

Steele, R., R. Pfister, R. Ryker, and J. Kittams. 1981. Forest habitat types of central Idaho. USDA Forest Service Gen. Tech. Rep. INT-114. Intermt. For. & Range Exp. Sta., Ogden, Utah. 138 pp.

Steele, R., S. Cooper, D. Ondov, D. Roberts, and R. Pfister. 1983. Forest habitat types of eastern Idaho and western Wyoming. USDA Forest Service Gen. Tech. Rep. INT-144. Intermt. For. & Range Exp. Sta., Ogden, Utah. 122 pp.

Stokes, M. A., L. Drew, and C. Stockton, eds. 1973. Tree-ring chronologies of western America, vol. 1. Lab. of Tree-ring Res., Univ. Ariz., Tucson.

Stokes, M. A. and T. Smiley. 1968. *Introduction to tree-ring dating.* Univ. Chicago Press, Chicago. 73 pp.

Strickler, G. S. 1961. Vegetation and soil condition changes on a subalpine grassland in eastern Oregon. USDA Forest Service Res. Pap. 40. Pac. NW For. & Range Exp. Sta., Portland, Oregon. 45 pp.

Suslov, S. P. 1961. *Physical geography of Asiatic Russia.* W. H. Freeman & Co., San Francisco. 594 pp.

Swan, L. W. 1967. Alpine and aeolian regions of the world. In *Arctic and alpine environments,* eds. H. E. Wright, Jr. and W. Osburn, pp. 29–54. Indiana Univ. Press, Bloomington.

Swedberg, K. C. 1973. A transition coniferous forest in the Cascade Mountains of northern Oregon. *Amer. Midland Naturalist* 89:1–25.

Tande, G. F. 1979. Fire history and vegetation pattern of coniferous forests in Jasper National Park, Alberta. *Canadian Jour. Botany* 57:1912–1931.

Taylor, W. P. 1922. A distributional and ecological study of Mount Rainier, Washington. *Ecology* 3:214–236.

Thilenius, J. F. 1968. The *Quercus garryana* forests of the Willamette Valley, Oregon. *Ecology* 49:1124–1133.

Thompson, R. S. and J. I. Meade. 1982. Late Quaternary environments and biogeography in the Great Basin. *Quaternary Res.* 17:39–55.

Thorne, R. F. 1977. Montane and subalpine forests of the transverse and peninsular ranges. In *Terrestrial vegetation of California,* eds. M. G. Barbour and J. Major, pp. 537–558. John Wiley & Sons, New York.

Tomback, D. F. 1978. Foraging strategies of Clark's nutcracker. *Living Bird* 16:123–160.

Tranquillini, W. 1979. *Physiological ecology of the alpine timberline: tree existence at high altitudes with special reference to the European Alps.* Springer-Verlag Publ., New York. 137 pp.

Trexler, K. A. 1965. Report of bristlecone pine investigations within the proposed Great Basin National Park during the summer of 1965. Office report, Lehman Caves Nat. Mon., Baker, Nevada. 3 pp.

Troll, C. 1973. The upper timberlines in different climatic zones. *Arctic & Alpine Res.* 5(3), part 2:A3–A18.

Tseplyaev, V. P. 1961. *The forests of the U.S.S.R.* Translation by Israel Program for Sci. Transla., Jerusalem. 1965. 521 pp.

Turcek, F. J. and L. Kelso. 1968. Ecological aspects of food transportation and storage in Corvidae. *Commun. Behavioral Biol.* Part A, I:277–297.

* USDA. 1941. *Climate and man.* U.S. Govt. Printing Off., Washington, D.C. 1248 pp.

Vale, T. R. 1977. Forest changes in the Warner Mountains, California. *Annals of Assn. Amer. Geographers* 67:28–45.

Vasek, F. C. and R. Thorne. 1977. Transmontane coniferous vegetation. In *Terrestrial vegetation of California,* eds. M. G. Barbour and J. Major, pp. 797–834. John Wiley & Sons, New York.

Viereck, L. A. 1979. Characteristics of treeline plant communities in Alaska. *Holarctic Ecology* 2:228–238.

* Viereck, L. A. and E. Little, Jr. 1972. *Alaska trees and shrubs.* USDA Forest Service, Agriculture Handbook 410. 265 pp.

* Vogelmann, H. W. 1982. Catastrophe on Camels Hump. *Natural History* 91(11):8–14.

Vowinckel, T., W. Oechel, and W. Boll. 1975. The effect of climate on the photosynthesis of *Picea mariana* at the subarctic tree line: 1. Field measurements. *Canadian Jour. Botany* 53:604–620.

Vroom, G. W., S. Herrero, and R. Ogilvie. 1980. The ecology of winter den sites of grizzly bears in Banff National Park, Alberta. In *Proc. Fourth International Conf. on Bear Res. and Mgmt.,* pp. 321–330. Bear Biol. Assoc., Kalispell, Montana.

Walter, H. 1979. *Vegetation of the Earth, and ecological systems of the geo-biosphere.* Springer-Verlag Publ., New York. 274 pp.

Wardle, P. 1965. A comparison of alpine timber lines in New Zealand and North America. *New Zeal. Jour. Botany* 3:113–135.

_____. 1968. Engelmann spruce (*Picea engelmannii* Engel.) at its upper limits on the Front Range, Colorado. *Ecology* 49:483–495.

_____. 1973. New Zealand timberlines. *Arctic & Alpine Res.* 5(3), part 2:A127–A135.

_____. 1974. Alpine timberlines. In *Arctic and alpine environments,* eds. J. D. Ives and R. Barry, pp. 371–402. Methuen Publ., London.

_____. 1977. Japanese timberlines and some geographical comparisons. *Arctic & Alpine Res.* 9:249–258.

* Watts, M. T. 1975. *Reading the landscape of America.* Collier Books, Macmillan Publ., New York. 354 pp.

Webster, B. 1982. World's mountains crumbling: Man and nature threatening the balance. N.Y. Times News Service account of Conf. on Mt. Resources, Mohonk Lake, N.Y. In *the Missoulian,* Dec. 24, p. 30. Missoula, Montana.

Wells, P. V. 1983. Paleobiogeography of montane islands in the Great Basin since the last Glaciopluvial. *Ecol. Monogr.* 53:341–382.

Wert, S. L., P. Miller, and R. Larsh. 1970. Color photos detect smog injury to forest trees. *Jour. Forestry* 68:536–539.

Whitfield, C. J. 1933. The vegetation of the Pike's Peak region. *Ecol. Monogr.* 3:75–105.

Whittaker, R. H. 1961. Vegetation history of the Pacific Coast states and the "central" significance of the Klamath region. *Madrono* 16:5–23.

Whittaker, R. H. and W. Niering. 1965. Vegetation of the Santa Catalina Mountains: II. A gradient analysis of the south slope. *Ecology* 46:429–452.

Wright, R. D. and H. Mooney. 1965. Substrate-oriented distribution of bristlecone pine in the White Mountains of California. *Amer. Midland Naturalist* 73:257–284.

Yoshino, M. M. 1978. Altitudinal vegetation belts of Japan with special reference to climatic conditions. *Arctic & Alpine Res.* 10:449–456.

Young, J. A. and R. Evans. 1981. Demography and fire history of a western juniper stand. *Jour. Range Mgmt.* 34:501–505.

Zackrisson, O. 1977. Influence of forest fires on the northern Swedish boreal forest. *Oikos* 29:22–32.

Zimina, R. P. 1973. Upper forest boundary and the subalpine belt in the mountains of the southern USSR and adjacent countries. *Arctic & Alpine Res.* 5(3), part 2:A29–A32.

* Zwinger, A. H. and B. E. Willard. 1972. *Land above the trees: a guide to American alpine tundra*. Harper & Row, New York. 489 pp.

Index

Page numbers in italics indicate captions.